This series of essays by one of today's most original and respected scholars on Nazi Germany concerns three central subjects: relations with 'the east', 'euthanasia' and extermination. They are linked closely by the sub-themes of professionals or 'experts' and an interest in competing systems of morality.

The collection includes important and wholly new contributions to the German–Soviet war and other national tragedies; to the controversial question of whether the Nazi analogy has any relevance to contemporary ethical discussions; and to the contemporary historiography, including works of fiction and literary criticism, of the Holocaust. The book will be essential reading for anyone interested in current scholarship on Nazi Germany, or indeed in how we might view the period in future decades.

Ethics and extermination

From reviews of Michael Burleigh's previous book *Death and Deliverance: 'Euthanasia' in Germany c. 1900–1945* (1994):

'Michael Burleigh's outstanding and chilling new book . . . He provides one of the most penetrating insights yet written into the individual mentalities – and the resulting collective mentalities – of Nazism.' Niall Ferguson, *The Sunday Telegraph*

'It is difficult to believe that this account could be improved upon.' Anthony Storr, *The Times*

'This is an impressive and harrowing book whose suppleness, fluency and accretion of histories and anecdotes particularise the horror.' Jonathan Meades, *The Mail on Sunday*

'Book of the Year 1995.' Jonathan Meades, *The Guardian*

'Well-thought through, highly informed and decently written.' Norman Stone, *The Sunday Times*

'Indictment is brilliantly combined with memorial . . . History writing is rarely this moving, or so admirably, effectively moralistic.' David Cesarani, *The Guardian*

'Here we have in raw, horrifying detail the whole history of the Nazi euthanasia project . . . Remarkable . . . The first thorough investigation of the whole issue, an exceptional achievement in itself.' Richard Overy, *The Observer*

'Burleigh has trawled the massive archive which records the rise of the euthanasia programme with meticulous scholarship . . . It is a gripping read.' *Journal of Medical Ethics*

'A totally absorbing and extremely important book.' *The Jewish Quarterly*

'The book succeeds as a definitive account of this hideous aspect of the Third Reich and provides a wider insight into moral dilemmas which continue to stalk through our era.' *History*

'Comprehensive and compelling.' *The Times Literary Supplement*

'This book is among the most important recently published about Germany and the Second World War . . . Michael Burleigh has tackled with the very highest standards of scholarship a subject so distasteful that, like the Holocaust, the mind is by turns bewildered and distressed . . . This book is a major contribution to historical knowledge.' Sir Martin Gilbert, *The Times Higher Education Supplement*

'Michael Burleigh warns his reader that he's writing on "a bleak subject" . . . but his approach is so intellectually lively that his polite forewarning need not be offputting.' *The Washington Times*

'This superb study.' *Holocaust and Genocide Studies*

'The story of Nazi "euthanasia" has been told before, but Michael Burleigh . . . has constructed the most artful and dispassionate account to date.' Robert Proctor, *The New York Times Book Review*

'A singularly powerful, disturbing, and incisive history . . . That it is also written with such power and insight, so resistant to cant and cover-up, only increases its value.' Dan Callahan, *Commonwealth*

'There is a wealth of original research in this volume, based both on original documents and publications of the time. It deserves the widest possible readership, not least by those who are interested in following current debates about "euthanasia" and "mercy killing" from a wider historical perspective.' John Solomos, *Ethnic and Racial Studies*

'Burleigh's book is solidly researched and very readable . . . This is certainly the direction in which the historiography on "euthanasia" should develop.' Stefan Kuhl, *Bulletin of the German Historical Institute*

'This book is to be very strongly recommended for its scholarship, clarity and contemporary relevance.' *Journal of Forensic Psychiatry*

'Early reviewers of the book have praised it widely and I can only add my voice to theirs . . . this is a formidable achievement. As Auden forecast, accurate scholarship may uncover what has driven a culture mad: here is a contribution to that process.' Bernard Ineichen (Charing Cross and Westminster Medical School), *Social History of Medicine*

'Brilliant . . . This is one of those books that no reader will ever forget.' Jonathan Steinberg, *History Today*

'Thanks in good part to Burleigh's work, the "racial paradigm" has become increasingly important to our understanding of Nazi rule.' *German History*

'The research is prodigious, grounded in rare archival materials, trial records, and interviews with an extensive list of survivors. [Burleigh] comes as close as the historian is likely to get to a ground-level history of the Nazi euthanasia program.' Karl Schleunes, *Journal of Modern History*

Ethics and extermination

Reflections on Nazi genocide

MICHAEL BURLEIGH

PUBLISHED BY THE PRESS SYNDICATE OF THE UNIVERSITY OF CAMBRIDGE
The Pitt Building, Trumpington Street, Cambridge CB2 1RP, United Kingdom

CAMBRIDGE UNIVERSITY PRESS
The Edinburgh Building, Cambridge, CB2 2RU, United Kingdom
40 West 20th Street, New York, NY 10011-4211, USA
10 Stamford Road, Oakleigh, Melbourne 3166, Australia

First published 1997

Printed in the United Kingdom at the University Press, Cambridge

Typeset in Galliard 10.5/13pt

A catalogue record for this book is available from the British Library

Library of Congress Cataloguing in Publication data

Burleigh, Michael, 1955–
Ethics and extermination: reflections on Nazi genocide /
Michael Burleigh.
p. cm.
Includes index.
ISBN 0 521 58211 3 – ISBN 0 521 58816 2 (pbk.).
1. World War, 1939–1945 – Atrocities. 2. National socialism – Germany. 3. Euthanasia – Germany – History. 4. Genocide – Soviet Union. 5. Genocide – Europe, Eastern. 6. Massacrest – Europe, Eastern. 7. Holocaust, Jewish (1939–1945) I. Title.
D804.G4B777 1997 940.54'05–dc21 96–47660 CIP

ISBN 0521 58211 3 hardback
ISBN 0521 58816 2 paperback

Contents

Acknowledgments *page* x

Introduction 1

Part I: The Germans and the east

1 The Knights, nationalists and the historians 9
2 Albert Brackmann, *Ostforscher*: the years of retirement 25
3 'See you again in Siberia': the German–Soviet war and other tragedies 37

Part II: 'Euthanasia'

4 Psychiatry, German society and the Nazi 'euthanasia' programme 113
5 The Churches, eugenics and the Nazi 'euthanasia' programme 130
6 The Nazi analogy and contemporary debates on euthanasia 142

Part III: Extermination

7 The racial state revisited 155
8 A 'political economy of the Final Solution'? Reflections on modernity, historians and the Holocaust 169
9 The realm of shadows: recent writing on the Holocaust 183

Notes 225
Index 256

Acknowledgments

I am grateful to Cambridge University Press, the *Jewish Chronicle*, Oxford University Press, Sage Publications and the *Times Literary Supplement* for permission to reproduce previously published material. The archival research on which many of these essays are based was made possible by the British Academy, Leverhulme Trust and Nuffield Foundations, without whom work abroad would be impossible.

Some of these essays developed from memorable contexts. Chapter 4 has been delivered in the form of a lecture to Professor Richard Evans's lively Nazi German Special Subject class at Birkbeck College, London, more times than I care to remember, as well as to the Human Values in Health Care Forum. I am especially indebted to Professor Charles Engel of the Medical Education Unit at University College Medical School for this invitation. Chapter 6 is a revised version of a talk to an American audience of leading ethicists, investment bankers, lawyers, philanthropists, physicians and psychiatrists in the Park Avenue apartment of Ronald and Ronay Menschel. My wife and I are very grateful to Dan Callahan, President of the Hastings Center for Bioethics in New York, for arranging our visit to New York, and to John and Pat Klingenstein for dinner in Manhattan. The concluding chapter below is a revised and expanded version of reviews which originally appeared in the *Jewish Chronicle*, *Journal of Modern History* and *Times Literary Supplement*. I would like to record my gratitude to those who commissioned the work which provided the initial impetus for this chapter.

I have benefited enormously over the years from discussions with

Omer Bartov, David Cesarani, Niall Ferguson, John Gillingham, Desmond King, Jonathan Osmond, Richard Overy, Amos Perlmutter, Antony Polonsky and John Röhl, none of whom are responsible for the views expressed in the final products. A collection of essays seems as good an occasion as any to acknowledge the historians who have directly or indirectly most influenced my approach to history, namely Robert Conquest, Saul Friedländer and Fritz Stern, although only two of them write about Germany. Linden has endeavoured to remove all traces of mediocrity and pretension, but despite her the influence of universities is still considerable.

Introduction

The nine essays assembled here for the first time are a representative selection of a larger corpus of work on National Socialist Germany produced over the last twelve years. Broadly speaking, these essays cover three interests: the German 'east', so-called 'euthanasia' and Nazi racial exterminism, with the activities of professionals forming one bridge between all three, the other being an interest in the history of morality within this period.

My earliest work was on medieval history, albeit late medieval Prussia.[1] Study of the medieval past necessarily entailed wider reading in the historiography of the subject over the last 200 years, reading which suggested the extent to which the history of the Middle Ages had been instrumentalised and manipulated for contemporary political uses. This was obviously not unique to either this subject or German historical writing in general. History has probably been used by politicians since the activity was first thought worthwhile, and continues in more or less subtle ways in the present. The opening chapter below, slightly altered to locate the Stasi state known as the German Democratic Republic in the past, follows the complex shifts in how over two centuries historians and others conceived of the history of an international military religious order, whose historical reality was usually strikingly at variance with what they made of it. Although the subject was a far frontier of western Christendom, it is gratifying to see that the article is still regarded as serviceable by writers concerned with the protean contemporary scene on the borderlands between eastern and western Europe.[2]

The approach in chapter 1 was still based on the history of ideas, liberally interpreted, an approach whose limitations were being highlighted in the early 1980s by such scholars as Geoff Eley and David Blackbourn. In subsequent work I began to investigate the manifold relations between historians and government, loosely defined, during the Weimar and Nazi periods. Working in German and Polish archives on historians and other so-called experts who studied the ethnic German presence in eastern Europe and Russia (*Ostforschung*), it became apparent that they had not simply produced propagandised versions of the past to legitimise current policy, but that alongside other professionals, had enthusiastically volunteered their expertise in the service of ethnic cleansing and racial annihilation.[3] Although these scholars included the usual quota of cranks, it was striking to see the similar commitment of major scholarly figures, including some such as Albert Brackmann, Werner Conze, Walter Kuhn or Theodor Schieder, who had become pillars of the post-war West German historical establishment. Not surprisingly, West German scholars, who were taught by, and advanced by these men, had not poked around very thoroughly in these closets, while East German historiography resembled a form of purposive character assassination, systematically overrating their importance. One of the most professionally powerful of these scholars was the medievalist Albert Brackmann, of whom the second chapter is a biographical portrait. His case illustrates how, given the 'right' political conditions of a totalitarian regime, a sort of unreflective professional amorality can be translated into the capacity to do other people serious harm. The chapter could be read as a description of an activist academic 'type', one moreover whose enveloping political rhetoric could nowadays just as easily be ethnic, feminist or socialist. There are morals in this for everyone.

Just as one wearies of newspapers consisting of endless articles about other journalists, so historiography has finite charms, tending as it does to professional narcissism or solipsism. Beyond these professionals was the larger complex of German relations with eastern Europe and Russia, where in the third and longest chapter below, the *Ostforscher* effectively dissolve into a footnote amidst the titanic struggle of the 1941–5 Russo-German war, although this designation begs several questions. Although generally agreeing with the Irish historian Roy Foster that military history is the academic equivalent of train-spotting, a view borne out if one surveys the weedy clientele who frequent specialist bookshops, the chapter begins with a broad outline of the military drama, before exploring the subjects of morale, occupation policies and the dilemmas and double disenchantment of many Soviet nationalities. This chapter grew out of a fascinating, if more limited, assignment from Niall Ferguson, namely to reflect on what might have happened had Hitler been victorious on the Eastern Front, a challenge which has triggered a fresh interest in Russian history, and a renewed appreciation of how things can be aleatory even within subjects with such a powerful in-built teleology as Nazi Germany. My approach was also strongly influenced by a powerful critique by Professor Norman Davies of Gerhard Weinberg's 'global' history of the Second World War, a global history which contrived to leave out the fate of eastern Europe and non-Russian Soviet nationalities, for whose peoples 1945 did not bring liberation.[4] In post-totalitarian Europe, we are all obliged to understand at least something of the complex histories of the Chechens, Cossacks, Ingush, Tatars, Ukrainians or Volga Germans rather than still construing the conflict through the eyes of the defunct imperial power.

Part II is devoted to the so-called 'euthanasia' programme. Having originally conceived of this in terms of a study of medical criminality, the project that became the book *Death and Deliverance: Euthanasia in Germany 1900–1945* developed into a much broader undertaking.[5] This was partly because it became apparent that this malign enterprise grew out of developments during the liberal Weimar Republic. This applied to both the intellectual rationalisations, notably the debate stimulated by the 1920 tract of Binding and Hoche, but also to the negative consequences of 'progressive' psychiatric reforms, namely the creation of a potentially eradicable chronic sub-class within the already marginalised psychiatric population.

But this was also no mere history of psychiatric institutions or a sub-Foucauldian critique of psychiatry, rationality and reform. Just as historians such as Robert Gellately were emphasising the societal sea of denunciation without which the Gestapo could not effectively swim, so a study of popular opinion towards the mentally and physcially handicapped revealed that some families or individuals were not ill disposed towards the state killing their sick relatives by proxy.[6] If this was the case, then it is not surprising that the Nazis could persecute unpopular minorities such as foreign forced workers, homosexuals, Jews or Sinti and Roma with relative impunity. The main findings of this research are reflected in chapter 4 below. It attempts to bring together the history of ideas, ethical attitudes and behaviour, health economics, the history of psychiatry, as well as the more familiar themes of Nazi eugenics and racial science.

The 'euthanasia' programme affected the religious in the sense that while Christians of both major denominations subscribe to the doctrine of the sanctity of human life, many of the victims of the 'euthanasia' programme came from ecclesiastically controlled institutions. Chapter 5 examines the extent to which responsible churchmen embraced essentially secular scientific ideologies (for a preoccupation with the worldly was not simply a product of the quasi-Marxist theologies of the 1960s), meeting the Nazis half-way on this slippery ground even as they, accurately enough, denounced Nazism as a form of latterday paganism, replete with its own ersatz sub-Nietzschean morality. Although due scope is given to the undeniable pressures which a totalitarian government of this kind could bring to bear upon individual religious communities – included threats to alter charitable tax status, expropriation or charges of sexual impropriety – the fact remains that with a few exceptions they generally endeavoured to refine Nazi policies rather than confront them. In the upper reaches of both hierarchies, bishops and cardinals used the time-honoured methods of all establishments to bring informal influence to bear on a government consisting mostly of gangsters or cowed conservatives. Below this level, individual asylum staff were confronted by horrible dilemmas, which I have tried to convey fairly and, I hope, sympathetically. In so far as anyone should be condemned for their actions, we should confine this to the purposive minority who actively brought about these policies rather than those who had to negotiate their grim consequences. Opposing Nazi policy was not akin to exposing some abuse in the National Health Service.

Having written about euthanasia as an historical problem, I have had the disconcerting experience of spectating as representatives of the US Hemlock Society (*sic*) and pro-life lobbyists battled it out without any reference to what I had just been talking about. Such lessons in the power of obsessions, and one's own irrelevance, are salutary. Chapter 6 below is an attempt to show why I think the Nazi analogy is pretty marginal to contemporary discussions about euthanasia – an issue where my personal sympathies are in favour of cautious liberalisation. Given that all contemporary advocates of euthanasia are ultimately motivated by respect for individual autonomy and compassion for suffering individuals, I fail to see what a regime which murdered the mentally and physically handicapped for reasons of racial purity and cost has to do with it. The issue of euthanasia is separable from attempts to engineer biological utopias, where the example of contemporary communist China is in any case as serviceable as Nazism. Opponents of euthanasia will have to come up with something rather better than the analogy with what happened in Germany fifty years ago. In this respect at least, the shadow cast by Nazism is shortening.

The concluding part of the book is concerned with the Holocaust. Chapter 7 reflects and develops themes I first explored together with the German historian Wolfgang Wippermann in our monograph *The Racial State: Germany 1933–1945*.[7] It differs from the book in the sense of giving greater prominence to international developments in eugenics, especially in the United States of America, and in the stress upon societal factors which gave added impetus to Nazi policies, and without which the organs of the state would not have been able to function so efficiently. Explicitly critical of the distortions introduced to this subject by various kinds of Marxism, the book tried to study the subject in the terms that evidently mattered to the Nazis, revealing the energy and implacability they brought to realising their overall vision.

The final chapters are essentially concerned with how one writes about the Holocaust. Chapter 8 deals with a fad enjoying current popularity in some German historical circles, namely the idea that the 'Final Solution' represented an attempt to implement rationally conceived objectives, i.e. the rationalisation of the backward, overpopulated economies of occupied eastern Europe and the Soviet Union. This is an extreme variant of modernisation theories, theories which seem to appeal to a cross-section of younger, mainly German, historians whose personal politics and political agendas are often diametrically opposite. Attempts to ascribe modernity to this or that aspect of Nazi policy run up against sources which speak of relapses into medieval barbarism, on the part of a movement which self-consciously strove to revive the primitive. Solipsistic in effect, the essay is not entirely cynical, since some of the trends it attacks – such as an ill-informed indictment of 'science' – are worryingly influential, at least in parts of western academia.

If this critique is trenchantly expressed, the final chapter is a paradoxical celebration of the rich varieties of recent writing on the Holocaust, an almost random cross-section of where we are now. It discusses not only some very fine examples of recent historical scholarship, particularly by Austrian and Israeli historians, but also survivor testimonies; works devoted to the responses of bystanders, including the Western Allies; an autobiography by the distinguished historian Raul Hilberg; and an outstanding example of literary criticism; as well as incorporating some oblique comments on cinematic representations of the subject, such as Lanzmann's *Shoah* or Spielberg's *Schindler's List*. The 'Historikerstreit' (historians' debate) of the 1980s conveyed the misleading impression that all the facts were known, leaving just the matter of interpretation and broader historical context. Given the recent appearance of important research monographs by younger historians such as Dieter Pöhl or Hans Safrian, this view seems with hindsight highly premature.

The essay from which chapter 9 developed was written amidst the celebrations to mark the end of the Second World War in the European theatre of operations, a context that illustrated the curious, super-nova like capacity of this subject to gain energy as the events themselves recede in time, a phenomenon for which I have seen no satisfactory explanation, and which is in such marked contrast to relative western (and apparently Russian) indifference to other recent examples of mass murder, notably in the former Soviet Union.[8] This obsession is potentially unhealthy, not simply in terms of the sourness it injects into contemporary relations with Germany, an ally, trading partner and exemplary liberal democracy more than ready to flagellate itself with its own history, but more generally in the sense that the world has moved on to a new set of problems, to which this episode evidently does not afford useful guidance, and where perhaps there are more apposite contemporary analogies.[9]

PART 1

The Germans and the east

CHAPTER ONE

The Knights, nationalists and the historians

For a long time the history of the German or Teutonic Order has caught the imaginations of historians, poets, painters, publicists, novelists and film-makers. A list would be long and would embrace obscure figures such as the early nineteenth-century narrative history painter Karl Wilhelm Kolbe as well as, to conjure with a few famous names, Eichendorff, Freytag, Treitschke, Sienkiewicz and Eisenstein. However, since 1945 in Germany, the circle of those interested in the history of the Order has narrowed to a small number of professional medievalists who, in the nature of things, are not household names. One major West German creative writer – Günter Grass – has touched on the subject, but then only to add some astute historical reference to his evocation of pre-war West Prussia: the Danzig of Mazerath and Jan Bronski, the Polish Post Office and the milieu of the Kashubian petite-bourgeoisie.[1]

In the German Democratic Republic interest in the Order was minimal despite recent 'differentiated' reassessments of the Prussian heritage. In contrast to the large East German literature on the Hanseatic League, the Order was the subject of one article in the main historical journal of the GDR.[2] There are a number of reasons, both pragmatic and ideological, for this apparent indifference. The territories once ruled by the Order were beyond the borders of the GDR and are now part of Poland and the Soviet Union. Most of the sources are housed in West Berlin. Secondly, there are ideological difficulties. Founded in 1949, the GDR possessed about one-third of the remaining territorial area of Germany and roughly one-quarter of its population. In a real sense the GDR was a country without a history. This meant that whereas in 1982 East Berlin hosted an exhibition entitled 'Thirteen Hundred Years of the Bulgarian State', or while for that matter Stalin could cast himself in the role of heir to the medieval military-patriotic leader Alexander Nevsky, the GDR could lay claim to a little over thirty years of history.[3] Moreover, the emphasis in those thirty years was on a radical break with centuries of almost apostolic continuity that stretched from the *Ostpolitik* of Otto the Great via the Order, Frederick the Great, Bismarck, the Eastern Marches Association of the Wilhelmine Empire and Hindenburg to Hitler, gathered like so many malignant ancestral spirits behind the heirs of reactionary *Preussentum* in the post-war Federal Republic.[4] The historiographical corollary of this negative, integrative teleology was to trace continuities between the nationalist historians of the nineteenth century, those historians who plied their trade under the Nazi regime and *Ostforscher* in the West today. This means that more attention was given in the *Zeitschrift für Geschichtswissenschaft* to denunciations of Treitschke, Brackmann or Erich Keyser than to a reassessment, along Marxist-Leninist lines if you will, of the subjects that these figures wrote about.[5]

In post-war Poland, the circle of interest is substantially wider than in either West or East Germany. For the state it is a chapter in Poland's history that is worth some investment. The celebrations held in 1960 to commemorate the Polish victory over the Order at Tannenberg in 1410 were attended by between 50,000 and 200,000 people, depending on whose crowd estimates one accepts. No expense was spared in this demonstration of the 'Unity, Strength and Readiness of the Polish people', including a fly-past by sixty-four fighters tracing red and white smoke trails across the sky.[6] That this was not investment in an emotional vacuum can be understood from the extraordinary popularity of the novels of Hendryk Sienkiewicz. Whereas nowadays few people in Germany bother with the copious quasi-historical works of Gustav Freytag, Sienkiewicz's virulently anti-German, by turns brutal and saccharine *The Teutonic Knights* (1897–1900), went through more than twenty editions between 1944 and 1960. Moreover, indirectly the reach of the book is even greater. Leaving aside translations into Russian or English, within nine months of its release in 1960–1, Alexander Ford's epic film of the book was seen by six and a half million Poles.[7]

These contemporary references are like the erratic beats of a once strong pulse, for at various times in the past the history of the Order –

or a transcendental, symbolic version of it – has been used to provide historical legitimisation for a variety of political objectives. More importantly for present purposes, contemporary political preoccupations and patterns of thought can be shown to have heavily influenced the ways in which historians and others have written about the Knights. These interactions are highly complex, so at the outset it should be stressed that only a few facets of the development of an ideology of the Order have been singled out for comment in this brief review of the subject from the Enlightenment to modern times.[8]

Although historical writing on the Order begins with the chroniclers of the Middle Ages, it seems appropriate to begin with the philosophic historians of the late eighteenth century: appropriate, because in contrast to virtually all subsequent German writing on the subject, the historians of the Enlightenment had an almost uniformly negative view of the Order. For example, Johann Gottfried Herder (1744–1803) thought that the crusades in general and military religious orders in particular were phenomena that European civilisation could have dispensed with. The military religious orders had been the recipients of lavish endowments to promote their work in Palestine. After the loss of the Latin states they were effectively without purpose. As for the German Knights, any positive aspects of their translation to Prussia (of which there were none) were far outweighed by the forcible conversion of the native Prussians to Christianity, involving the destruction of their identity and their division amongst German overlords like so many herds of stray sheep.[9] Dedicated to the peaceful arts of trade and agriculture, the Slavs had the unique misfortune of occupying rich lands coveted by the warlike Germans, Danes and nomadic peoples of the East. Their treatment at the hands of the Germans was comparable with the Spanish mishandling of the Peruvians in Latin America.[10]

It would be incorrect to ascribe these thoughts to generalised notions such as Enlightenment anti-clericalism or rationalist contempt for the Middle Ages. To begin with, Herder stands in a very uneasy relationship to French *dix-huitième* thought and was severely critical of the desiccated, categorising knowledge of the *philosophes*. Rather, his lack of sympathy for the crusades and military religious orders stemmed from both an intense detestation of anything that conquered and crushed other communities and an almost childlike impressionability and sensitivity to peoples very different from those of his own time.[11] While that might result in an over-compensatory hostility towards his own historical milieu, it also meant a remarkable sympathy for every manifestation of human diversity. As Herder wrote, the Cherokee and Huswana or Mongol is as much a letter in the great word of our family as the most educated Englishman or Frenchman.[12] Each historical stage was as valuable as the different ages through which each individual passed and every culture or epoch was an end in itself, with its own internal development towards its own goals. The Order had reached in from without, violently imposing a relentless uniformity where once there had been variety and at least the potentiality of freedom.[13]

Herder's cosmopolitan view of history and his relativistic notion of progress were not destined to last. A number of factors are involved in the transition from a negative to a positive evaluation of the Order in the early nineteenth century, including changing perceptions of Poland, the reduction of Herderian interest in nations as such to a growing belief in the unique mission of the German volk and, finally, the diffusion of a Romantic and paradoxically less anachronistic understanding of the Middle Ages.

First, an earlier image of Poland as a land of religious tolerance – an asylum for German Protestants from Bohemia or Silesia[14] – and of republican liberty with a mission to defend Europe against Asiatic barbarism was supplanted in the course of the eighteenth century by one whose salient features were a fanatical clergy, a uniquely chaotic constitution – 'Polonia confusione regitur' – and an over-large aristocracy whose *raffiné* members took as much delight in wielding the knout as in the more civilised aristocratic pursuits. Ever contemptuous of 'that imbecile crowd whose names end in -ki', Frederick the Great delivered the classic Prussian judgment on Poland and the Poles. In 1746 he wrote:

> That kingdom is caught in eternal anarchy. Conflicting interests separate all the magnate families. They put their own advantage above the public good and unite among themselves only to consider cruel and atrocious means of oppressing their serfs, whom they treat like cattle. The Poles are vain and haughty when favoured by fortune, abject in defeat, capable of the greatest baseness when money is to be gained . . . but after getting it, they throw it out of the window. Frivolous, they have neither judgement nor firm opinion . . . In this kingdom, reason has become the vassal of women, they intrigue and decide about everything, while their men worship the bottle.[15]

What might be called the governmental position on the medieval *Ostsiedlung* – a subject of more than academic interest in view of Prussian policy in partitioned Poland – can be seen in the work of Johann Friedrich Reitemeier. The transference of 'the surplus multitude' to the east was comparable with European migration to North America. Although the native Wends and Prussians had been expelled from their villages and forcibly 'Germanised', they had adopted the superior civilisation of the victors. The 'transformation of the Wends through the German nation, the destruction of their religion and their Asiatic customs by Christianity, the German cultivation of the wildernesses of that place and the advance of civilisation in these territories' were the medieval contribution to the growth of 'a European power under the Hohenzollern dynasty'.[16]

The contradiction between Enlightened sympathy for the native populations and belief in the value of the Order's civilising mission can be seen in the work of Johannes Voigt (1786–1863). The son of a Thuringian village barber surgeon, Voigt studied theology and history at Jena. In 1817 he was summoned to Königsberg where he combined the directorship of the Geheime Archiv with a post at the university. Accustomed to begin the working day at 5 a.m., Voigt published a succession of works on the Order that have both the merits and defects of daily contact with the archival sources. In the preface to the second volume of his monumental *Geschichte Preussens*, Voigt explained that he 'had tried to explain the phenomenon of the German Knights, as it entered the territories of Prussia with the cross and the sword, according to the spirit of the times'.[17] This meant that while he was devoid of Herderian sympathy for the vanquished Prussians, he had a more consistent, and hence un-Herderian ability to empathise with the victors. It would be anachronistic, he argued, to condemn the Order's treatment of the native Prussians on moral grounds since in the eyes of the medieval Church they were an 'outrageous blot' whose least trace it would be entirely praiseworthy to eradicate.[18] Although he could appreciate the pain resulting from loss of a people's identity, he argued that it was better that the Prussians had come under the civilising sway of the Germans rather than the swords of the Russians or Lithuanians who, in the nature of things, would have denied the Prussians the indubitable benefits of 'German spirit', 'German law', 'German customs', 'German manners' and 'German bourgeois life'.[19]

The political corollary of this belief in the superiority of German civilisation was the rejection of Polish demands for reconstituted statehood. During the Poland debate in the Frankfurt Parliament in July 1848, German liberals used a variety of arguments to combat Polish claims: fear of a Polish alliance with reactionary Russia, Polish intolerance of national and religious minorities, and the historically based superiority of Germans over Slavs. The left-wing liberal Wilhelm Jordan argued that 'the preponderance of the German race over most Slav races, possibly with the sole exception of the Russians, is a fact . . . and against history and nature decrees of political justice are of no avail'.[20] The two peoples were 'deadly enemies' and one could not disguise the fact that the Germans represented the higher civilisation. One should never forget, when dealing with 'these charming mazurka dancers', that Poland was an example of anarchy and that the partitions were nothing more than 'the burial of a long-decomposing corpse'.[21] The Order's conquest of Prussia was not merely conquest by the sword but the victory of a higher civilisation – conquest by the German plough.

In the hands of Heinrich von Treitschke (1834–96), whose essay *Das deutsche Ordensland Preussen* appeared in August 1862, these chauvinistic sentiments were developed to the point of caricature. In order to explain why this essay is important it is essential to understand something about the future career of the then twenty-eight-year-old author. Despite a number of personal handicaps, including virtually lifelong deafness, the death of his eleven-year-old son in 1881 and his wife's worsening mental illness, Treitschke enjoyed massive public esteem. He held a succession of academic posts in Leipzig, Freiburg, Kiel, Heidelberg and Berlin, where from 1873 he occupied a chair. He was also co-editor of the influential *Preussische Jahrbücher* and, late in life, enjoyed membership of the Prussian Academy of Sciences and the editorship of the *Historische Zeitschrift*.[22] However, this array of glittering prizes did not add up to academic respectability. Three of his academic posts were the result of either local or Prussian government intervention against the wishes of the faculties concerned;[23] his published work was often attacked on scholarly grounds and his lectures condemned for their anti-Semitic rhetoric.[24] However, the professional disdain of such distinguished guardians of 'the legacy of Lessing' as Theodor Mommsen did not check his ascent in the public sphere. Bismarck thought Treitschke sufficiently worth cultivating to go to the bother of committing 'fantastic madnesses' into the professor's deaf-aid over lunch, while among those who literally fought for the privilege of attending the crowded lectures of 'the deaf Demosthenes of Prussia' were the young naval officer Tirpitz and the future Pan-German leader Heinrich Class.[25] The monotonous roar of Treitschke's voice and the tears which came with each new climax – he had faulty tear-ducts – were apparently spell-binding.

The origins of the 1862 essay can be reconstructed from Treitschke's correspondence. In January 1856, when he was still wavering between a career as a scholar or poet, Treitschke informed his friend Wilhelm Nokk that he had found 'magnificent dramatic material' and that once he had mastered the unfamiliar historical setting he would set to work on a play.[26] In July he outlined the subject of an historical tragedy. Closely based upon a volume of Voigt's *Geschichte Preussens*, which Treitschke dismissed as a 'dry compilation of facts', the drama concerned the fate of Heinrich von Plauen who, having saved Marienburg from the Poles after Tannenberg, was deposed from the Grand Mastership of the Order by conspirators intent both upon thwarting his plans for reform and on a war of revenge against Poland. Brooding upon his lot in exile, Plauen decided to betray the Order to the Poles as a way of hitting back at the 'mean spirits' who had brought about his downfall. In a word, it was about the 'triumph of everyday ordinariness over brilliant energy'.[27]

Treitschke's letters reveal the difficulties that arose between the conception and the creation of the Plauen tragedy. The period was unfamiliar to him; the subject lacked material for characterisation in depth; he found the 'atmosphere' of power politics in a quasi-monastic state 'cold and piercing'.[28] In April 1857 he ruefully acknowledged that although he had been ruminating upon the plot for a year, 'in poetry inspiration is not enough'. The intractable material, fear of being accused of dilettantism, concurrent work on his *Habilitationsschrift* and a dramatic sense that derived more from philosophic works on aesthetics than from any real engagement with the stage consipired to close off this particular avenue to success.[29] With his mind more focused by failure, Treitschke returned to the subject – in essay form – early in 1862. His letters reveal some of the problems that the work involved. Moving in academic circles in Leipzig, he had been amazed that 'no one other than myself had hitherto heard of the Marienburg'. In order to make his celebration of medieval Prussia more telling, he had deliberately stressed his own Saxon origins.[30] Once again he commented upon the difficulties of the subject. Only a few important characters seemed tangible amidst 'the grey fog'. However, the Order as a collectivity had character: specifically, 'aggressive strength and haughty, pitiless hardness'.[31]

The object of the essay was to provide historical credentials for the parvenu Prussian state and to instil 'a vigorous sense of security in our hearts' by showing 'how the work which has so suddenly ripened had the way prepared for it by many centuries of arduous toil'. It also had the equally pragmatic purpose of conveying 'to the mind of a South German boy an intimation of the most stupendous and fruitful occurrence of the later Middle Ages – the northward and eastward rush of the German spirit and the formidable activities of our people as conqueror, teacher, discipliner of its neighbours'.[32]

The result is a grotesque piece of attitudinising, dressed up with a brassy sort of patriotism and sinister-sounding Social-Darwinian biological determinism. Any minor difficulties in the search for continuities between the *Ordensstaat* and the Hohenzollern monarchy were removed by the assertion of the spirit over the evidence. For example, Frederick the Great's utter indifference to the Order – the castle at Marienburg remained a dilapidated ruin throughout his reign – was explained away by 'how little understanding there was in those days of Enlightenment for the romantic greatness of the Ordensland'.[33] Treitschke preferred notions like 'the innermost nature of the Prussian people' or, more mystically, 'spells' rising from the blood-drenched ground, to support his case for continuity. Metaphors that were to be common coin for the Pan-German and Eastern Marches Association publicists abound.[34] The Ordensland was a 'breakwater' or 'protective wall' in the 'wave-tossed sea of the eastern peoples'.[35] The Slavs were 'a deadly menace' to the Germans.[36] However, there is no menace so deadly that ridicule cannot defuse it. The word 'anarchy' or a derivative becomes an habitual mutter whenever Treitschke mentioned the Poles or Slavs: 'Polish anarchy'; 'stateless anarchy of the Poles'[37]; 'aristocratic Polish anarchy';[38] 'anarchic crudity of the Slavs';[39] '[for] Polish freedom, read despotic rule of the nobles'[40] and 'the lamentable political incapability of the Poles'.[41] The latter are 'heedlessly frivolous',[42] 'practised and over-refined seducers of women',[43] or more simply 'liars'.[44] German–Slav conflict is in the nature of things;[45] Slav rule over Germans is 'unnatural'.[46] The Germans are 'masters',[47] 'teachers' and 'discipliners' bearing the gifts of a higher civilisation to their primitive neighbours.[48] 'Our side' occasionally produces men who are 'hard of heart'[49] or 'harsh and unamiable' with sufficiently 'tenacious will'[50] to halt the flood of drift and disorder. In one of his numerous asides concerning the treatment of the subject population, the thoroughly sedentary Treitschke observed that 'in the unhappy clash between races, inspired by fierce mutual enmity, the blood-stained savagery of a quick war of annihilation [die blutige Wildheit eines raschen Vernichtungskrieges] is more humane, less revolting, than the specious clemency of sloth which keeps the vanquished in a state of brute beasts'.[51] What was considered deviant and irrational by the historians of the Enlightenment had become axiomatic and, so to speak, in the nature of things.

Although there were respectable scholarly alternatives to this view of things, not least among provincial Prussian historians like Max Toeppen (1822–93), whose great contributions to scholarship were made from a headmastership in Elbing, among Prussia's ruling elite Treitschke's crude and easily digested fare was preferred. Chancellor Bülow, responsible for bolstering the position of the Poznanian German estate owners and for passing a series of exceptional expropriatory laws designed to weaken 'the Slavic flood', in other words Prussia's own Polish subjects, claimed that a copy of Treitschke's 'splendid study of the Order lay for many years on my desk'.[52] His master, Wilhelm II, was also keen to establish connections between himself and this by now heavily propagandised chapter in German history. Keenly conscious of the value of 'national history' as a means of 'combating the spread of socialistic and communistic [*sic*] ideas' among the young, Wilhelm took part in a bombastic costume festival in 1902 to celebrate the restoration of Marienburg.[53] In the course of the festivities he telegraphed his relative the King of England to remind the latter that his 'forefather' Henry IV, as earl of Derby, had 'fought side by side with the Knights of the Order' in the closing years of the fourteenth century. In eastern Europe reactions to this affair were mixed. One workers' newspaper in Prague published mock police 'Wanted' notices in which a fugitive mental patient called Wilhelm Kaiser, last seen making deranged speeches in Marienburg, was sought; while in Poland, offprints of Sienkiewicz's virulently Germanophobe historical novel on the Knights were distributed to the congregation attending a thanksgiving ceremony to celebrate the Polish victory of 1410.[54]

Nor was the German high command immune from this sort of identification. Before 1914 several regiments were renamed – for example Field Artillery Regiment 71 'Great Commander' – while in the course of the war opportunities were not missed to construe present victory as revenge for past defeat.[55] In late August 1914 a battle took place 'in the vicinity of Ortelsburg-Gilgenburg' which was rapidly renamed Tannenberg. Claiming credit for this discovery, Ludendorff later noted:

> At my suggestion, the battle was named the Battle of Tannenberg, in memory of that other battle long ago in which the German Knights succumbed to united Lithuanian and Polish hosts. Will the German permit it now, as then, that the Lithuanian and more especially the Pole derive profit from our impotence and violate us? Shall centuries of ancient German culture be lost?[56]

Although the suggestion was a trifle immodest, it was none the less an accurate and laconic statement of the views of many German historians since it assumed both the inevitability of German–Slav conflict and the superiority of German civilisation.

During the Weimar period, the Order served as an increasingly historical symbol for nationalist demands for a new order in the east. The tone of much 'professional' writing did little to discourage lesser lights. Most of the leading scholars of the Order contributed to a book entitled *Deutsche Staatenbildung und deutsche Kultur im Preussenlande* which appeared in 1931. One of the more interesting contributions was an historiographical review by Erich Maschke, whose pre- and post-Second World War work are models of source criticism. However, in this context Maschke was liberated from the tedium of footnotes. Surprisingly, he accorded Treitschke's essay lavish praise. Treitschke had managed to combine a sense of 'a masculine, state-oriented will' with a dramatic style that resulted in 'a masterpiece of historical literature that has not been superseded, or only enlarged, after two generations'.[57] Modern source-critical methods had stabilised the wilder flights of Enlightened and Romantic historians. But, Maschke observed, a new era was dawning in which under pressure of national necessity, 'weapons would be forged from the sources' for the 'struggle of existence'.[58]

In view of this professional encouragement, lesser talents could dispense with the sources altogether. Käthe Schirmacher (1865–1930), who made a name for herself as a founder of *Verband fortschrittlicher Frauenvereine*, author of feminist tracts and member of the Eastern

Marches Association before the First World War, included a section on the Order in her book *Unsere Ostmark* (1923). Interestingly, she began with the observation that since the 'main trends' in the history of the Order were well known, she could dispense with the details. Such details as there were came from Treitschke's essay which, she remarked, was the 'deepest' history of the Order that had yet been written.[59] The historical task of the Order was to dam the 'wildly agitated, restless Slav and semi-Slav flood'. The various eastern marcher principalities were 'a German dike association', or 'bridgeheads in the whirling flood'.[60] As for the Order itself, it proclaimed the total surrender of the individual to something greater than himself.[61] Schirmacher's singular discovery was that the Knights had returned to Prussia to raise 'supermen'. Quite how this was to take place remains a mystery, as the avowedly celibate Knights had female settler companions who, our authoress severely observed, 'found no place with mere prettiness and tenderness'.[62] Throughout, the book demonstrates an almost pathological Polonophobia as well as a nauseating preoccupation with sadistic evisceration.

The myth of the Order also played a part in the thought processes of the leaders of some of the völkisch societies of the Republic. The Artamanen League was founded in 1923 by Willibald Hentschel, Bruno Tanzmann and Wilhelm Kotzde. It functioned as a sort of employment exchange – although the genuinely unemployed were excluded lest they lower the tone – providing cheap youth labour to undercut and hence drive out migratory seasonal labourers from Poland. Practical experience on the farms was to prepare the members for the day when they would man fortified peasant settlements in the east.[63] Like the Knights, the Artamanen espoused a conventual and spartan lifestyle involving the renunciation of tobacco, alcohol and casual sexual relations, a life, in other words, that was the antithesis of that pursued in the degenerate and Jew-dominated big cities. There the similarities with their medieval model ended, for once established on their farms the members were set to work 'for Volk and race' by producing healthy peasant children.[64] In 1928 Kotzde published a history of the Order that began with the preaching of the First Crusade in 1095. Evidently, at the Council of Clermont Urban II had managed to 'arouse both the other-worldliness and love of adventure of the Nordic peoples'. Medieval migrations eastwards represented 'the selection of the healthiest blood and the most active parts of the people who created a piece of new Germany in the Ordensland'.[65] The latter was 'an outpost of Germanism against the growing Slav ethnic flood' or, more simply, 'the armed watch in the east'. As for the 'higher civilisation' that the Knights brought with them, this was 'no longer merely Christian, but specifically German'. After Tannenberg, in which 'many a German breathed his last under the dagger of a slant-eyed Asiatic', 'the land lay open to the eastern hordes'. The alliance between the Prussian Stände and the Poles was an example of 'disregard for their duty to the Volk'.[66]

The fact that the Artamanen attracted later Nazi figures such as Heinrich Himmler or Rudolf Hoess raises the difficult question of the relationship between the myth of the Order and Nazi organisations. The difficulty arises from the fact that although leading Nazis were obviously aware of the advantages of stressing historical continuities for present and future political objectives (a point made explicitly in *Mein Kampf*), historical precedents – whether real or imagined – were extrinsic to a world view in which the contestants in the larger struggle were inevitably the same. Certainly, as a political pragmatist Hitler did not fail to miss the importance of the myth of the Order to foster links with the conservative elites. In August 1933 he spoke at a meeting to honour Hindenburg held within the Tannenberg memorial at Hohenstein, while in *Mein Kampf* he invoked the Knights to legitimise his belief that territorial claims would have to be made at the expense of Soviet Russia: 'this meant that the new Reich must again set itself on the march along the road of the German Knights of old, to obtain by the German sword soil for the German plough and daily bread for the nation'.[67] How he envisaged the Knights becomes clear from remarks he made in May 1942. They did not 'wear kid gloves' but came armed with the sword as well as the Bible. His commanders in the east should be crusaders for the National Socialist world view.[68]

The castles of the Order also served as symbolic prefigurements for the National Socialist *Ordensburgen* which were constructed in the mid-1930s under the auspices of Robert Ley's *Deutsche Arbeitsfront.* Although the connection was explicitly denied by both Ley and the architect Klotz, the historical model was clear enough to outside visitors.[69] The *Ordensburgen* were training institutions for young National Socialist German Workers' Party (NSDAP) members with seven years' post-school experience who had demonstrated during this time 'an unwavering sense of community'. The trainees were to circulate between the romantically situated fortresses of Crössinsee (Pomerania), Vogelsang (Eifel) and Sonthofen (Allgäu) over a five-year period, culminating with six months at the Reichsordensburg of Marienburg. They spent their time acquiring military and sporting skills while pursuing a pseudo-academic curriculum that included racial studies and both pre- and contemporary history. The aim was to mass-produce future leaders to replace the generation that had had the benefit of rude experience. They were also a criticism of the traditional forms of higher education, which were perceived as being class-bound and excessively specialised.[70]

Reality did not accord with this meritocratic high-mindedness. The *Ordensburgen* were embodiments of National Socialist narcissism. The colossal architecture and rules on alcohol consumption contradicted attempts to recreate the beery camaraderie of the *Sturmlokal*, and the asceticism of the barracks was designed for the edification of the curious staying at the neigbouring, purpose-built hotels.[71] They also failed to achieve their aims. A report entitled 'Führers of the Future' filed by a *Manchester Guardian* correspondent in November 1937 does not suggest that the trainees were being put in the way of learning political dexterity. 'Heavens', the correspondent exclaimed, 'what an education! . . . You are only forming brawn here, not brains!' 'We distrust words and phrases: we prefer action', was his guide's reply.[72] Ley's aims were also hampered by a failure to integrate graduates into career structures and by the reluctance of other Nazi leaders to allow educational reproduction to come under any rival institutional aegis. The SS in particular ensured that those marked out for high office by attendance at the SS-Junkerschule at Bad Tölz had bloodied their hands during a practical period at Dachau. When they took their midnight oaths to Hitler, they were part of the apparatus of terror in ways that Ley's 'solid chaps' were not.[73]

Alfred Rosenberg's employment of the myth of the Order was less straightforward since it concealed a critique of NSDAP organisation. His Marienburg speech of 27 April 1934 contained most of the clichés about the Order that were rife in the literature considered above. The Order was a bulwark against 'the forces that pressed forward from the east', an inspired idea in the mind of Hermann von Salza, 'the first Führer of the Order', who was concerned to 'secure and extend German *Lebensraum*'. The Order's decline was attributed to its 'bloodless asceticism' and the treason on the part of Grand Master Michael

Küchmeister, 'the Erzberger of that time'.[74] However, this was merely a conventional preamble to the suggestion that the National Socialist movement should abandon the medieval lord–vassal principle in favour of the (higher) principle embodied in the military religious orders. It should adopt a form of a fascist senate along the lines of the Italian Gran Consiglio. Drawing back from the implication of this, Rosenberg added that Hitler would have the sole right to approve such a system and could either associate or nominate his own successor.[75]

The Order also figured prominently among the ideological properties of Heinrich Himmler. In 1936 he published a pamphlet, *Die Schutzstaffel als antibolshewistische Kampforganisation*, which consisted of brief histories of the French, Russian and German revolutions, selected highlights from the 'national story' and some discussion of the morality of the SS men. These subjects were reached in a roundabout way via sections on primitive communality, the sacrosanctity of field-mice and farmyard rats, astronomy, the oldest plough and the significance of runes. Following a few sections on notable figures or events from the Germanic Dark Ages – the set pieces of nineteenth-century school history books – Himmler employed the history of the Order to illumine 'the way to obedience'. The crusades represented the migration 'of German blood to the desert sands of the Far East'; the military orders were 'the school of obedience, subordination and authority of the state'. The Knights were a selection of the most noble blood that had been proven in battle, a *Führerschicht* destined to dominate peoples 'who were not of the same value as our people'.[76] He returned to the Order in a piece entitled 'Heralds of Eternal Greatness' which appeared in two NSDAP or SS journals. The article was constructed around the paradox that 'when people are silent, the stones speak' or, in other words, that monuments embody past societies. The castles of the Order – the 'germ cell of the Prussian–German state' – were evidence of higher German civilisation. He concluded with the thought:

> The stones have not spoken in vain . . . the fields are again German. Monuments are always built by people. People are children of their blood. As the blood speaks, so the people build. With joy we see our buildings today and are proud to have played a part in their construction. Through them the Führer will speak to future generations.[77]

The SS needed some form of historical legitimation, both as a way of justifying their rapid rise to power and because historical models may have had a greater consensus-building potential within the organisation than some of the more arcane branches of pseudo-science patronised by the SS leadership. The desiderata for any historical model were that it should not be too specific and that only those values that the SS could put to use should be abstracted from the historical prototype concerned.[78] Thus, one might emulate the obedience of the Jesuits; but the central tenets of Christianity, which might let moral imperatives get in the way of action, were allowed to fall by the wayside. Parenthetically, one might note that it was illegal for an SS man to describe himself as an atheist (they were 'presumptuous, swollen-headed and stupid and not suitable for us'), because atheism betokened an unhealthy lack of community spirit and an equally unhealthy disbelief in life's higher purposes.[79]

A similar ambivalence governed the ways in which the SS regarded the Order. Its organisational efficiency, aristocratic composition, loyalty to an idea, subordination of the individual to the whole, 'corpse-like obedience' (the metaphor occurs in the Order's own Rule) and mission in the east were all laudable. However, certain crucial aspects of the model were repugnant. Celibacy, for instance, was 'a false example to Germanism, an unhappy teaching of Asiatic Christianity' which led to 'a denial of the clan' and 'a dissipation of the blood'.[80] Moreover, for Himmler, the Middle Ages – in contrast to still earlier periods – were automatically suspect on account of the perceived power of the Roman Church. The Order was just one of a number of masculine, elitist and doggedly purposive societies including the Japanese Samurai, the Jesuits, Tito's partisans and Soviet Commissars that were pressed into service to provide some spurious historical lustre for an organisation pursuing fundamentally ahistorical goals. It is important to realise the distance suddenly being travelled from Treitschke at his most rabid, or Prussian *Polenpolitik* at its most ruthless. 'Our task', Himmler wrote in 1942, 'is not to Germanise the east in the old sense, that means by imposing the German language or laws, but to make sure that only people of true German blood dwell in the east.'[81] A year later he lectured a group of senior SS commanders in Posen on the qualities that they needed to perform their tasks. Extolling a sort of 'decent' unfeelingness, he observed:

> It is absolutely wrong to project your own harmless soul with its deep feelings, our kindheartedness, our idealism upon alien peoples. This is true, beginning with Herder, who must have been drunk when he wrote the *Voices of the Peoples*, thereby bringing such immeasurable

> suffering and misery upon us who came after him. This is true, beginning with the Czechs and Slovenes, to whom we brought their sense of nationhood. They themselves were incapable of it, but we invented it for them.[82]

Present compassion, he insisted, would mean a legacy of racial treason. For at the dark core of this world view lay a preoccupation that was fundamentally antithetical to change as such. In an historical novel of the time, the heroes are not the Knights – dismissed as 'chaff in the wind' – but the peasants

> who wander through the centuries in an unending, similar chain, from father and mother, son and daughter, grandson and granddaughter, and who are certain in dying that through the eyes of our children and our children's children we will behold the stirring and growth of the fruits of our labours and the rain and sun on German fields.[83]

The SS man, too, stood in a similar transcendental continuum. With that typical millennia-spanning portentousness that one finds in Himmler's writings, a writer in the SS house journal noted:

> Our existence, so closely confined between life and death, experiences at the same time through history an immeasurable expansion. It teaches us to feel like a link in a chain which stretches from millennia and stretches into millennia so that in our consciousness the legacy of the past and the duties of the future merge into an indissoluble unity which establishes a law for the struggles of the present.[84]

The sources for this view of human existence are beyond the realm of medieval history upon which this chapter has concentrated.

CHAPTER TWO

Albert Brackmann, *Ostforscher:* the years of retirement

In a recent study of the auto-co-ordination of the German universities, Bruno Reimann drew attention to a form of post-Second World War apologetic writing that deflects critical inquiry by concentrating upon the second-rate and the marginal – the racial anthropologists grafted onto faculties – rather than upon the central figures of scholarly life.[1] Albert Brackmann (1871–1952), was firmly on the inside track. The scion of a family of pastors, scholars and patricians (his mother was an Ebersdorff) from Hanover, he studied theology and history in Tübingen, Leipzig and Göttingen. Specialising in the editing of sources on relations between emperors and popes, he joined the staff of the MGH at twenty-seven, became an *extraordinarius* in Marburg in 1905 and was called to the chair of history at Königsberg in 1913. Declared unfit for military service, his experiences in a hospital and then helping refugees, collecting contemporary documents and in 1919 supplying a memorandum refuting article 92 of the Versailles Treaty, contributed to his decision to study the history of the Germans in the east.[2] After a short spell in Marburg, from where he contributed leaders to the *Königsberger Allgemeine Zeitung*, Brackmann moved to Berlin in 1922. He retained an honorary professorship there after becoming general director of the Prussian State Archives in 1929 and commissary leader of the Imperial Archive in 1935. Along the way, he accumulated membership of the Prussian and Bavarian academies, the learned society of Göttingen and three historical commissions, as well as the central directorate of the MGH, co-editorship of the *Historische Zeitschrift* (1928–35) and editorship of the series *Deutschland und der*

Osten.[3] He also had access to high places, a ramified network of academic contacts and a regiment of grateful former pupils. The historical profession discovered the dominant ruler not only in its historical manifestations long before 1933.

An academic pluralist on this scale ineluctably attracted the attention of Walter Frank, himself in the business of empire-building, although on the basis of casting himself and his colleagues in the role of a committed troop much put-upon by an entrenched liberal 'guild'. By no stretch of the imagination could Brackmann be described as a liberal. He belonged to the German People's Party (DVP) from 1919 to 1925, and to the German Nationalist People's Party (DNVP) thereafter. He supported the Eastern Marches Association from 1926, and in 1933 the Dahlem group of the National Socialist German Workers' Party (NSDAP) was in touch with him concerning possible donations to their funds.[4] Like the majority of conservative historians, of whom it was once said that 'they easily lose the ability to move their heads because of always looking backwards, so that if any movement at all is possible, only movement to the right remains', Brackmann was not well disposed towards the Weimar constitution.[5] In a letter to Professor Otto Becker in September 1931, he observed that from the centre in Berlin he could see the baleful effects of parliamentary factionalism. He preferred the rule of the few, along the lines of the Roman senate or 'better still in the form of the Venetian Council of Ten'. This could be brought about by bolstering the power of the President who would introduce these changes. Brackmann's head invariably turned upwards for solace in difficult times.[6]

But for Frank, Brackmann was a dangerous liberal. In 1936 Frank managed to push this 'pillar of liberal and pro-Jewish academicism' (for a Jewish scholar, Dr Sergei Jakobson had been drawing a research grant from the Dahlem *Publikationsstelle* since 1931), into premature retirement.[7] This did not herald a period of senescent self-reflection. As Frank wore himself out and got on others' nerves with campaigns based upon character assassination and bibliographic blackmail, Brackmann continued his organisational and historical work and was courted by the new regime. No other victim of Frank's received the *Adlerschild* of the German Empire or telegrams from Hitler, Göring, Frick and Ribbentrop upon reaching the age of seventy.[8]

For there was not much in Brackmann's *œuvre* that the Nazis found wanting. In some ways, he was more ideologically attuned than his colleagues. For example, in 1933 he edited a book entitled *Deutschland und Polen*, which was designed to coincide with the international historical congress in Warsaw. In the preface, which was an attempt to bring history into line with the new course heralded before the Hitler–Piłsudski Non-Aggression Pact, he described the book as an attempt to set aside the polemics of the moment because the historian 'is not a judge of the past or a law-maker for the future but a servant of the truth'.[9] In this case, the new truth, which clearly perplexed one of the hardened nationalistic contributors in Königsberg, was subsidised by 10,000 RM from the Prussian and Imperial Interior Ministries and the Foreign Office.[10] Dropping a contribution on art history, Brackmann observed that the criteria for inclusion were governed by the book's 'political aims'.[11] Somewhat later, in 1935, he supplied a reference for Dr Richard Drögereit, who had helped with the English translation and wanted to study Anglo-Saxon charters in the British Museum. He sent Drögereit four copies of *Germany and Poland* for distribution as 'unobtrusive propaganda' among English academics.[12] But as the contents of the book demonstrate, it was difficult to revise the prejudices of many decades overnight. With some monotony, the nineteen contributors stressed the continuity of German settlement in eastern Europe despite the Germanic migrations; the inability of the Slavs to form coherent states; the existence of a West–East 'cultural gradient' and, as Hermann Aubin put it, the historical mission of the Germans to 'civilise the sub-Germanic zone';[13] the existence of a time-transcendental *Drang nach Osten*; and Poland's role – to use a cliché used here by Hermann Oncken – as Germany's 'Irland-Ulster'.[14] In August 1933, Brackmann sent a dedicatory copy to Hitler. He hoped that the 'hochzuverehrender Herr Reichskanzler' would accept his work – which 'corresponded' with Hitler's Reichstag speech of 17 May 1933 – as 'an external token of our gratitude for the intelligent and success-promising way in which you have also grappled with these most difficult questions of our internal and foreign policy'. The Chancellor received the book 'with pleasure'.[15] In Poland, where apart from a few papers like *Prawda Katolika*, reviewers aired their profound misgivings, the book was confiscated by (badly informed) customs officers.[16]

Brackmann's services to the Nazi regime were not confined to the furnishing of his own books. Reviewing his own achievements to an audience of professors in 1937, Brackmann noted how 'fortunate' it had been that Soviet scholars (working on the collected works of Marx and Engels in exchange with Germans working in the USSR on the correspondence between Wilhelm I and the Czar) had relayed police records to a Magdeburg Communist Party paper. That ended the archival treaty of 1928 and the Russians were banned from the archives.[17] The doors could also close against the enemy within. As is well known, Brackmann sealed the fate of Eckart Kehr.[18] But having left the archives, in his capacities of chairman of the North-East German Research Community (NODFG) and as an editor of series of books and journals, he was a convenient, if sometimes reluctant, channel for ironing out any ideological difficulties in the work of his contributors.

Those affected could not be classed as members of any academic 'resistance'. In 1937, he suggested that his friend and NODFG colleague Hermann Aubin might like to substitute the word 'settlement' for 'colonisation' when writing about the Germans in eastern Europe, as he had been informed by the authorities that 'colonisation' was to be avoided at all costs. It had pejorative and rootless connotations that might be overcome by the use of the words 'regaining' or 'resettlement'.[19] He wrote in similar terms to the historical geographers Hans and Gertrud Mortensen (University of Göttingen), who were producing a three-volume history of the settlement of East Prussia. As convinced National Socialists, the Mortensens were surprised to discover further ministerial objections to the third volume of their work. For in the joint appeal to the Mortensens' patriotism that he drafted with the Interior Ministry, Brackmann pointed out how unfortunate if the book also failed, inadvertently, to stress the German 'cultural achievement' in the region.[20] Although Mortensen assured Brackmann that 'he would never publish or make known anything that could damage Germany or the German people even if it was the scholarly truth', the point he and his wife were making was too subtle for the censors. Namely, that the fifteenth-century Lithuanian 'refugees' had been allowed by the German Order to settle in a wilderness which none the less clearly belonged to the territories of the Order. By destroying the idea of East Prussia as a Lithuanian *Urheimat*, they believed that they had found an answer to the problem presented by past and present (irrefutable) Lithuanian *numerical* dominance in the area.[21]

Brackmann and his subordinates were also consulted on the matter of who received grants to study which subjects. For example, in 1937 the *Deutsche Forschungsgemeinschaft* requested an opinion on an application made by Dr Paul Wirth, who wanted to study the linguistic geography of the terms used by Sorbian fishermen, weavers, beekeepers, potters and rope-makers.[22] In a confidential report, one of Brackmann's subordinates noted that in general 'it is not desirable that works on the Sorbian language should be published from the German side. The Sorbian language should remain as unnoticed as possible and its decline not be impeded by increased academic study.' The work might inadvertently deliver proof to the Poles and Czechs of the 'Germanisation' of the Sorbs.[23] At *no point* was Wirth's project considered upon its academic merits. On 25 August 1937, he was informed that a grant for his project 'was not possible at the moment'.[24]

By way of contrast, large amounts of money from the Interior Ministry's *Osthilfe* funds were channelled through the NODFG to scholars active in eastern Europe. Kurt Lück was a young man whom everyone wanted to help. In March 1932, Brackmann canvassed various ministries in person to find a way of subsidising the star-in-need in Posen. Brackmann found him a grant, put Lück in the way of reworking Erich Schmidt's *Geschichte des Deutschtums in Polen*, and later the *Publikationsstelle* (PSte) recommended Lück's work to the Foreign Office as suitable for use by two American academics. Kurt Lück was born in Kolmar (Posen) in 1900. After completing his doctorate in 1924, he served several prison sentences for anti-Polish agitation. The titles of his books speak for themselves: *Deutsche Aufbaukräfte in der Entwicklung Polens* (1935), *Der Mythos vom Deutschen in der polnischen Volksüberlieferung und Literatur* (1938) and *Deutsche Gestalter und Ordner im Osten* (1940). It was a brief but meteoric career that ended for the Waffen-SS Hauptsturmführer at the hands of Soviet partisans on 3 March 1942.[25] By that time, the *Ostfront* was casting a long shadow over Brackmann's ex-pupils and colleagues. Noting that 'it is now almost as bad as in the World War', he regretted the loss of the medievalist Karl Kasiske on an intelligence operation outside Leningrad, and Dr Fritz Morré (whom he fondly remembered appearing at his seminar in 1931 'in a brown shirt') who also fell 'in spirited action for Führer and Vaterland' with the SA in Russia.[26]

Erich Maschke (Professor of Social and Economic History at Heidelberg from 1953 to 1969) was another promising young historian in need in the early 1930s. Although his dissertation was published in 1928 and his *Habilitationsschrift* on an aspect of papal taxation in medieval Poland appeared the following year, he and his wife had serious financial difficulties on a stipend of 61 RM per month. Brackmann arranged a monthly grant of 300 RM (tax free), from the publications fund of the Geheimes Staatsarchiv, the forerunner of the PSte.[27] Working on the history of the Germans in Poland, Maschke was collecting historical evidence on 'subjective national and cultural identity' from Polish sources.[28] In order to pursue this matter in the Polish archives, Maschke applied to Brackmann for an additional travel grant of 300 RM in 1934. There was a problem about the wording of the application to the Polish authorities, for the PSte connection would put them on the alert. It was a choice between 'Studies on the History of Germanism in Poland' and 'Studies of Social and Economic History in Poland'.[29] Brackmann thought the former 'too obvious'.[30] In the end, Maschke opted for 'Structural Changes in the Demographic Development of Poland under the Influence of German Law', under which loose camouflage he would publish something to satisfy the Poles before his real work emerged 'as a supplement'.[31] Appointed to the chair of history at Jena in 1935, Maschke had little time to cancel payment of his grant or to report on research subsidised by the PSte since 1932. For since arriving in Jena, he had been much in demand as a political educator for both the NSDAP and the Storm Troopers (SA), of which he was a member.[32] Despite these difficulties, Brackmann invited Maschke to join the board of the NODFG as an academic advisor in March 1939.[33] Reviewing his published output, Maschke remarked that in his essay 'Towards a Cultural History of Germanism in Poland' (1935), 'under a deliberately chosen colourless title I wanted to investigate the coherence of blood and settlement in the growth of Germanism in Great Poland and sought to show that from its roots Germanism exhibited a self-contained national identity'.[34] For blood had become a mystic causal agency in his work. Discussing the history of the Piasts in *Der Schulungsbrief*, Maschke noted that 'since the ruling class in these countries was of Nordic race, like the Polish Piasts who were demonstrably of Viking origin and in whom German blood became ever stronger through numerous marriages with German princesses, they could carry out the process of Germanisation quickly and obviously without the use of force'.[35] The Jews appeared in a discussion of the Hanseatic League. The merchants of the Hansa were community conscious and not the fragmented and atomised creatures created by modern economic liberalism. However, the Jew 'lived from usury and all legal measures, all uprisings by the outraged and impoverished masses did not prevent him from acquiring riches by bleeding the people'. In the same vein, so to speak, the decline of the German Knights could be ascribed to celibacy or a denial of 'fresh access of blood for the Führerschicht'.[36]

In September 1939, Brackmann could reflect proudly that both the NODFG and the PSte in Dahlem had become 'the central agencies for scholarly advice for the Foreign Office, Interior Ministry, Army High Command, parts of the Propaganda Ministry and a number of SS departments'. A position of influence had been reached in which his advice concerning future frontier adjustments would be heard with respect.[37] He had been in contact with the SS since at least 1937, when he informed the SS candidate for his former directorship of the whereabouts of archival materials that might yield 'some important sidelights towards a characterisation of Herr Walter Frank'.[38] Himmler deputed Heydrich to have a particular deposit investigated. By November 1938, Brackmann was in direct contact with Himmler. Like the SS archaeologists, he was interested in the imperial tombs at Quedlinburg. An inscription the SS had discovered, concerning Otto III's appointment of his aunt to a deputyship while he was in Italy, led Brackmann to the conclusion that use of a similar word to describe Boleslaw of Poland in 1000 had important 'implications' for the early history of the Polish state. He requested photographs and in June 1939 sent Himmler a copy of his own findings.[39]

Apart from a common interest in the Ottonians, Brackmann was also an author for the SS Ahnenerbe organisation. In September 1939, SS-Untersturmführer Dr Kaiser informed him that he would be paid a total of 500 RM and royalties of 10 per cent for a 40–60-page booklet entitled *Krisis und Aufbau in Osteuropa*. According to their agreement, the booklet was to be a form of 'intellectual liquidation' of the Poles, a reckoning before world history, for 'Weltgeschichte = Weltgericht'. The themes to be stressed were that the Germanic peoples' claim to an original *Lebensraum* in the east were justified both by continuous settlement and by cultural superiority. A *Drang nach Osten* had always existed despite 'Roman Christian' efforts to lure the Germans westwards in order 'to kill German self-consciousness'. Indeed, a continuum of intent in the east, from Heinrich I by apostolic succession to Bismarck, had only been broken by the late Wilhelmine and Weimar governments (they were thinking of Caprivi). Under Adolf Hitler the continuum was restored.[40] To prevent any authorial deviations resulting from Brackmann's dotage, parts of the manuscript were relayed to SS Standartenführer Professor Dr Six of the SS Security Service (SD) for comment.[41] Apart from the SS indisposition towards Roman Catholicism, there was not much here that was not latent in *Deutschland und Polen* in 1933.

Brackmann fully lived up to the expectations of his publishers. Embellished with quotations from Kurt Lück and Adolf Hitler, the booklet reflects some of Brackmann's more enduring preoccupations. Stressing the continuation of a *Restgermanen* presence after the barbarian migrations, Brackmann observed that the Slavs had filtered through in the form of medieval 'seasonal workers' to labour for the Indo-Germanic ruling class as though they were the antecedents of the *Ostarbeiter* on East Elbian estates or in the factories in the Ruhr.[42] Describing the Frederickian colonisation of West Prussia, in which the King recognised the value of working subjects, he remarked that 'through Frederick the Great a particular Prussian characteristic was created that recognised nothing higher than duty and incessant work. In this respect, Prussia was the forerunner of the new Germany in which similarly only those people who fulfil their duty within the community have value'.[43] As for Poland, weakness meant trouble. The Flottwell era was an example of how to proceed; Austrian concessions in Galicia or hesitant employment of the Expropriatory Laws of 1908, the converse.[44]

The booklet satisfied the SS publishers. The initial print run was 30,000 of which 7,000 were purchased by the army. The SS sent Brackmann a Christmas present. Like any author, he was worried about the reviews, which in this case meant the NSDAP and the *Völkische Beobachter*. However, indefatigably, he soldiered on with more work and was glad that a sub-branch of the PSte had been opened in Warsaw at the behest of Hans Frank.[45] For the conquest of Poland opened up fresh roads of power for the retired *Geheimrat*. It resulted in an extended network of research institutes, increased funds, more patronage to exercise and further committee meetings to dominate. He was the obvious person to consult concerning recruitment to Hans Frank's Institut für deutsche Ostarbeit (IdO) in Cracow and inevitably made his voice heard on the panel to award the institute's 'Copernicus Prize'.[46] The first academic leader of the IdO was a former employee, Dr Gerhard Sappok, for whom Brackmann had been a referee in 1937 when Sappok sought the post of leader of the branch of the German

Academic Exchange Service in Warsaw. The job required someone 'absolutely politically reliable'.[47] Among Sappok's achievements in Cracow, before being sacked for being an in-house spy for the Brackmann circle, was a memorandum on the reworking of street-signs, to obliterate those recalling 'anti-German personalities, events or Jews'.[48]

Operating in this company resulted in a certain loss of perspective and disorientation of values for the Herr General-Direktor (as his subordinates called him long after he had ceased to be anything of the sort). In November 1939, he informed the Nazi editor of the *Historische Zeitschrift* of his willingness to write an essay on German–Polish relations. An earlier confrontation with historians in Posen had been held up by the outbreak of war and now he no longer felt the need to publish it in the same form, because some of the Polish historians had been arrested. A revised version might grace the journal where it could demonstrate the 'guilty involvement' of Polish scholars 'in the events that now lay behind us'.[49] Through Sappok, operating in France until his disappearance while buying a loaf of bread in Autun, Brackmann tried to secure the Bibliotheka Polska for the PSte, as the latter required a complete Polish library for its extended field of operations. In October 1940, he informed Aubin that the Einsatzstab Rosenberg would hand over *one* Polish library in return for increased co-operation in other areas. 130,000 books were duly deposited in Dahlem.[50] The SS-Sonderkommando 'Gruppe-Künsberg' was also active in the book trade. In May 1942, three cases of books (253 volumes on Russian intellectual history), in October, seventeen cases and in February 1943, seven more cases (for the NODFG) were ready for collection by Brackmann's staff from a store in the Hardenbergstrasse.[51]

By that time Brackmann was involved in the business of relocating people. In a letter to Professor Walter Kuhn in 1943, he stressed the importance that the authorities attached to short and reliable descriptions of the process of 'Germanising' populations of foreign national origin.[52] As the leading expert on historical settlement, both then and subsequently, Kuhn was actively involved in the planning of the relocation of ethnic Germans from Galicia and Volhynia. In a report to the chief of the SD emigration office in Łódź, he endeavoured to tally both the historical and the present circumstances of the migrants (whom he put in categories according to their racial value) with the climatological and soil conditions prevailing in the Reich. A few village communities where incest was evident or which were 'infected' by the 'spiritual sickness' of sectarianism needed to be broken up upon transportation. His correspondent, SS-candidate, Dr Gradmann, agreed that the effects of incest were shocking, 'since a great percentage of the children are idiots' and that the sectarian villages were 'a health hazard'.[53]

But the difficulties of ethnicity were by no means alien to Brackmann. He only needed to think of Professor Otto Reche, the racial expert on the committee of the NODFG and professor of racial studies at Leipzig. Since what follows brings an eminent historian into direct contact with a pathological racialist, the relationship must be considered in some detail. Reche, who had been receiving Interior Ministry funds via the NODFG since 1935, bombarded Brackmann with a flurry of letters in the autumn of 1939, enjoining Brackmann to use his political contacts on Reche's behalf.[54] Reche, a Silesian who, 'as a schoolboy had given a lecture to the class on the natural antipathy between the Germans and *Slawentum*', was desperate to make his talents available to the regime.[55] He was worried that a too liberal definition of ethnicity would result in 'a linguistically-Germanised mishmash with strong Asiatic characteristics'. The Germans needed *Raum* and not 'Polish lice in the fur '.[56] Although over sixty and therefore past military service, Reche was sure that Brackmann would help him find a home for his strange abilities which included, *inter alia*, a memorandum on the abolition of the word 'Russia'. Fearing the 'suggestive' power of 'Mütterchen Russland', he wanted to stimulate ethnic separatism within the USSR through a book called *Der Vielvölkerstaat Osteuropas*. He believed in *divide et impera*.[57] The object of Brackmann's solicitude – which involved hurried meetings at the Anhalter Bahnhof and visits to ministries – was Reche's memorandum 'On the demographic-political securing of the German East'. Brackmann, who also did not want Polish lice in his fur, tried to tell Reche that Minister Frick was too busy with vital economic questions to consider Reche's proposals. His rather literal correspondent deplored the fact that 'despite the exclusion of the Jews, we still cannot get away from the Jewish way of thought that the economy is destiny'.[58] Brackmann then suggested that the man of the moment was not Frick but SS-Obergruppenführer Lorenz, and Reche need not fear that he was soft on the Poles for 'soon one will try to push out as many Poles as possible in order to get a pure German frontier population'. The only problem concerned where the eight million Poles were to go, for *Restpolen* was by then overcrowded. Brackmann had the impression that similar ignorance prevailed in the circles around Hitler.[59]

The matter of 'Wohin mit den Polacken' also taxed Reche. He thought that the Ukrainians should be shoved eastwards.[60] Brackmann informed him that the NODFG and the PSte were directly involved in resettlement plans and that their charts and maps adorned the walls of SS-Obergruppenführer Lorenz's office.[61] Recently, it had been said that 'without our collaboration, the work of redefining frontiers would not have been possible'.[62] Eventually, Reche managed to locate the man he had been seeking. With SS-Gruppenführer Pancke of the Race and Settlement Main Office (RuSHA), he could discuss 'the racial political side' of the problem.[63] He was a seeker of absolutes.

This activity on behalf of a demented anti-Semite was not entirely unqualified. Forwarding Reche's memorandum to the Interior Ministry, Brackmann observed that 'next to many points one must put a question mark'. However, all in all, 'it still seems valuable to me to listen to one of our leading racial researchers on the matter'.[64] This was no isolated occurrence. In August 1942, the Interior Ministry wanted to initiate anthropological studies of the Sorbs in Upper Lusatia and wrote to the PSte enquiring who might be suitable to carry out the work. In October, Brackmann suggested to Reche that he might like to use doctoral students to investigate 'the racial composition of the present-day Wends'. Reche was the logical choice, as he had been investigating the peasants around Bautzen for some eight years. But he was reluctant to press on, as most of his assistants had been called up and he felt 'overburdened by work to the limits of my endurance'. In addition to his academic tasks, Reche was advising a number of state and NSDAP offices and providing expert opinion on racial pedigree for civil and military authorities and the courts.[65]

To discover where the drift of Reche's work led in his own field of history, Brackmann had to look no further than the first volume of his own massive *Festschrift*. Grappling with the problem of the Nordic influence among the West Slavs, Reche noted that 'in the eastern *Raum* [races] are intermingled so strongly that in many respects they more or less resemble one another; one only has to think of a common tendency towards shorter- and broader-shaped heads, lower and broader facial formation, of the accentuation of the cheekbones, of primitive nasal formation, of thick taut hair'.[66] However, he was making progress, not among the quick, but among the long-since dead. Inevitably, there was much work to be done, amidst the skulls in the Germanic and *Urslav* graves. He concluded that the first Polish state must have been founded in an area of strong, residual *Restgermanen* settlement. Maybe, he asked himself, there had never been a Slav period in history *at all.*[67] What Brackmann thought of this imaginative solution to his life's work is unknown. He read the essay 'with great interest' and thought that it was 'an extraordinarily important foundation for all further work' in the field.[68] For though he sailed so very close to this particular current, neither his scholarly reputation nor his standing with the regime obliged him to enter this inner circle of conviction. Consequentially, at the end of a long life, Albert Brackmann could survey his ravaged country, secure in the knowledge that through his pupils and academic clientele – Aubin, Kuhn and Erich Keyser to name but three – succession in *his* kingdom was in safe hands. In the year of Brackmann's death, Aubin and Keyser produced the first volume of the *Zeitschrift für Ostforschung*.

CHAPTER THREE

'See you again in Siberia': the German–Soviet war and other tragedies

On Saturday 21 June 1941, the German panzer commander Heinz Guderian visited forward positions overlooking the Russian fortress at Brest-Litovsk. Built on the confluence of the Bug and Muchawiec, the town consisted of four islands, ringed by a high earth rampart. Soviet defences along the river stood unattended. Within the fortress, Red Army soldiers drilled to the tunes of a military band. The town was usually garrisoned by 8,000 soldiers, but this weekend the force stood at 3,500 because of leave or assignments elsewhere. At midnight, the Berlin–Moscow express train crossed the Bug in the direction of Brest, with a Soviet grain train rumbling over the frontier in the opposite direction somewhat later.[1] German deserters who relayed the information that an attack was imminent were ignored, and in some cases shot.[2]

In fact, warnings that something grave was afoot had been flowing in for months. Since February, the Soviet ambassador in Berlin, Dekanozov, had reported to Molotov on German preparations for war. Molotov probably downplayed the threat because of his role in making the 1939 Non-Aggression Pact. Careerism, hierarchy and the caution endemic among the Soviet Establishment meant that Dekanozov did not express his fears directly to Stalin.[3] Soviet foreign intelligence services also presented confused and confusing impressions. Agents in Berlin and Tokyo, or from various branches of Soviet secret intelligence, gave conflicting dates for a future invasion. Even when the People's Commissariat of Internal Affairs (NKVD) resorted to such stratagems as simultaneously locking German diplomatic couriers in the elevator and a bathroom of the Hotel Metropol in order to photograph the contents of an attaché case in their bedroom, the information gained was mixed. A letter from Schulenburg, the Russophile and conservative German ambassador, to Foreign Minister Ribbentrop, confidently anticipated resolving any conflicts, while also reporting that his embassy staff was being reduced to a minimum as German diplomats prepared to evacuate the Moscow embassy. A Soviet agent who attended a cocktail party at the embassy, scouting locations for listening devices, noted that packers had removed many of the decorations and paintings.[4] According to Stalin's most recent Russian biographer, Stalin set great store on the relative prices of mutton and fleeces in Germany, since he calculated that without sheepskin coats for the winter the Germans could not possibly attack.[5] Information from British intelligence sources, as well as from Soviet spies operating within it, bore the taint of attempts to inveigle Stalin in an intra-imperialist war.[6] After all, when the British had predicted a German invasion of the Soviet Union for May, the Germans had in fact attacked the British on the island of Crete.

When in May 1941 Schulenburg told Dekanozov of Hitler's plans to attack the Soviet Union, Dekanozov relayed the news to Molotov who in turn informed Stalin. The latter commented: 'We shall consider that disinformation has now reached the level of ambassadors.' In mid-June, an intelligence source in the Luftwaffe reported that the final preparations for an attack had been made. Stalin scribbled the response: 'Comrade Merkulov, you can send your "source" from the staff of the German airforce to his fucking mother. This is not a "source", but disinformation.'[7] Two days before the invasion. Deputy Chairman Mikoyan received information from the chief of the port of Riga that all twenty-five German merchant ships there were preparing to sail on 21 June regardless of whether they had loaded or unloaded their cargoes. He told Stalin that this highly unusual action could only be preparation for war. Stalin replied that since Hitler would regard detaining the ships as an act of provocation they should be allowed to put to sea.[8] Massive troop concentrations and ominously regular Luftwaffe overflights were also discounted as attempts by Hitler to bluff Stalin into yet further concessions to his German allies. When on 21 June Dekanozov sought out Beria to inform him that an attack would commence the next day, Beria told Stalin the ambassador would be called to account for 'bombarding' them with disinformation. On the same day, Beria dismissed a report from the head of military intelligence that 170 German divisions were massed on the frontier, with the marginal comment: 'My people and I, Iosif Vissarionovich, firmly remember your wise prediction: Hitler will not attack us in 1941.'[9] By two in the morning, attempts to forward information from further deserters proved impossible, since German special forces had already cut the telephone lines. From three o'clock onwards, the toscin sounded and the bleary-eyed denizens of Moscow ministeries, many nursing hangovers from Saturday evening, scurried back to their desks. Shortly after retiring, following a long Politburo session, Stalin was woken to take a telephone call from Zhukov informing him of the German attack.

Operation Barbarossa, the greatest land invasion in modern warfare, commenced at that hour with a barrage from thousands of guns and waves of dive-bombers whining through the dawn sky. By late morning, the Luftwaffe had destroyed 890 Soviet aircraft, most of them caught unawares on the ground. By 12 July, some 6,857 Russian aircraft had been put out of commission, with the loss of 550 German aeroplanes.[10] The NKVD had decided to relocate and reconstruct the airbases, which meant that fighter aircraft were conveniently concentrated on relatively few functioning airfields. The Luftwaffe also roved above the roadways, bombing and machine-gunning fleeing soldiers and civilians on the ground. Although Luftwaffe historians tend to highlight the daring annihilation of stationary aircraft, it is well to note what they did to towns. A Russian historian who survived a raid on Minsk recalls:

> On the morning of 24 June 1941, a Tuesday, I saw it myself, a squadron of 96 aircraft flew over Minsk. They bombed the town all day long. The entire centre was destroyed. Only a couple of large buildings were left standing. Everything else in the centre was in ruins. When this bombing began that morning I was in the Pedagogical Institute. We were at work. During the bombardment we crept into the cellar. And then, when we came out, what did we see there! Burning houses, ashes, ruins. And corpses everywhere in the streets. People wanted to get out of the town during the bombing. But they could not flee quickly enough since the streets were jam-packed. And those who were outside were mown down by low-flying German aircraft.[11]

A few hours after Guderian had watched Soviet troops drilling in Brest, submersible tanks from his 18th Panzer left their jumping-off positions to negotiate thirteen feet of water in the river Bug with the aid of water-proofing, developed earlier for the invasion of England. Simultaneously, Brest was hit with about 5,000 shells and bombs per minute. Attacking the fortress from three directions, German forces anticipated capturing it within eight hours. In the event, the Russian garrison held out for a month as Army Group Centre bypassed this local difficulty en route for Smolensk. Seventeen of Brest's 3,500 defenders survived. The German army made similarly rapid progress elswhere, partly because Stalin had decided to move his fortifications westwards from the old 1939 borders. The new fortifications were not complete, for the NKVD failed to supply sufficient convict labour from its concentration camps, while the old fortifications had been dismantled.[12]

Recent Russian biographers of Stalin disagree on whether Stalin went into a blue funk or remained completely in control as befitted the self-styled 'Man of Steel'. Dmitri Volkogonov claims that 'Stalin had never had so great a shock in his life', while Edvard Radzinsky details a constant round of meetings, many of them devoted to identifying scape-goats to blame. Having initially ordered his generals not to respond offensively to what he persisted in regarding as 'provocation' by a few maverick German generals, for each flash of reality required some commensurately implausible explanation, Stalin retired to his dacha at Kuntsevo, remarking 'All that Lenin created, we have lost' or, in its more vulgar form, 'Lenin left us a great inheritance and we, his heirs, have fucked it all up.'[13] It seems that his two-day absence from the Kremlin was inspired by a reading of a play about Ivan the Terrible in which the Tsar feigned sickness in order to see which of his boyars would be disloyal, rising from his sick-bed to strike them down. A timely absence also underlined Stalin's indispensability to the rest of the ruling elite, a tactic borne out when Molotov organised a sort of Politiburo pilgrimage to his dacha requesting Stalin to return to work.[14]

The invasion force was both vast and multinational. Over three million German and Axis troops, including Croats, Finns, Romanians, Hungarians, Italians, Slovaks and Spaniards, divided into three Army Groups, teemed across the frontier in the direction of Leningrad, Moscow and the Ukraine. Each of Hitler's allies had their own, partially interrelated, expansionary or revanchist motives for attacking the Soviet Union. The Finns sought to continue the Winter War in order to regain territory lost under the Peace of Moscow of 12 March 1940.[15] It was a separate war within a war, fought according to conventional rules, and including the possibility of a separate peace. With a keen eye on Hitler's promises to Finland, the revanchist Romanian regime sought the restoration of Bessarabia and North Bukovina, and territory reaching towards Soviet Moldavia.[16] Hungarian participation was in turn both the product of fear that Hitler would reward his loyal Romanian ally by rescinding control of Transylvania (ceded to Hungary in 1940), and an attempt to neutralise the fascist Arrow Cross, advocates of total conformity with German policy, by adopting aspects of their agenda. The Germans helped along the Budapest decision-making process by bombing Kassa and claiming that this was the work of the Red Air Force.[17] By contrast, Hitler regarded the presence of 62,000 Italian troops in the Corpo di Spedizione Italiano in Russia as a mixed blessing. Sent by Mussolini with much accompanying fanfare about an anti-Bolshevik crusade, Hitler had no illusions about why they were in Russia, namely as 'harvest hands' in the forthcoming division and spoliation of conquered territory. Less tangible support came from the German churches whose prayers accompanied the advancing armies and whose view of the enemy was distinctly un-Christian. Rarely failing to take a side swipe at the irreligious aspects of the Nazi regime, Protestant and Roman Catholic clerics none the less vigorously denounced the godless heathens in the Kremlin. In a telegram to Hitler dated 30 June 1941, Protestant clerics wrote:

> You, my Führer, have banished the Bolshevik menace from our own land, and now summon our nation, and the nations of Europe, to a decisive passage of arms against the mortal enemy of all order and all western–Christian civilisation. The German nation, including all its Christian members, thanks you for this deed. The German Protestant Church accompanies you in all its prayers, and is with our incomparable soldiery who are now using mighty blows to eradicate the source of this pestilence, so that a new order will arise under your leadership.

Roman Catholic clerics, including such notable opponents of the Nazi regime as Bornewasser of Trier or Galen of Münster, spoke colourfully of a 'hotbed of people who through their enmity to God and their hatred of Christ have almost degenerated into beasts', or the 'Bolshevik colossus, this murdering, soul-destroying, nation-destroying monster', or of 'the liberation of the deeply religiously inclined Russian people from the twenty-four years of Bolshevik pollution and partial destruction'.[18]

In the months before 'Barbarossa', maps were scoured and memories probed in order to construct a working view of the enemy. From the deep past, Caulaincourt, Ségur and Clausewitz were trawled for historical precedents. From the recent past, former Freikorps fighters such as Erwin Dwinger, or Reichswehr officers who had studied air, gas and tank warfare with the Soviets in the 1920s, were questioned about their experiences.[19] As was the case before the invasion of Poland, a host of academic 'experts' on the east (*Ostforscher*): economists, geographers, historians, linguists and racial scientists, crawled out of the woodwork to offer their detailed knowledge of Russia or the Soviet Union. As we shall see, it was the hour of the experts.[20]

Inevitably, all of this information both reflected, or was combined with, longer-term perceptions and deeply entrenched stereotypes of the 'east' or the 'Russians'. Nineteenth-century liberal and socialist Germans lived in the shadow of the knouts and sabres of the Tsars's reactionary, semi-barbaric 'Cossack' armies. Twentieth-century German conservatives remembered a particularly brutal Russian occupation of their East Prussian rural bastion during the First World War, when: 'The Russian army resembled migrating rats who in times of great destruction, forsake their hiding places in the Siberian tundra in order to eat bare the settled lands. Ever fresh hordes come forth in a brown milling mass from the seething steppe.'[21] They also deeply, and justifiably, feared the 'Asiatic' terror of Lenin and his accomplices, conveniently confusing it with the febrile sectarian revolutionism they had brutally crushed in Berlin or Munich. They were certainly not alone in this since even the sectarian revolutionist Rosa Luxemburg had complained about the 'Tartar-Mongolian savagery' of Lenin's Bolsheviks. In sum, regardless of admiration for the stoic peasants as mediated by Tolstoy, or the psychological sophistication of Dostoevsky, something at once inferior and threatening lurked out there in the east.

Hubris and a series of derogatory metaphors first coined by Baltic German Russophobes before the First World War were apparent during the planning stage at the very highest levels. Jodl remarked to Warlimont: 'the Russian colossus will be proved to be a pig's bladder; prick it and it will burst', while Hitler was reported as saying: 'the Russian Armed Forces are like a headless colossus with feet of clay'. Most German generals were fixated with a rapid and devastating campaign of eight to ten weeks' duration against an opponent whose commanders allegedly thought in rigidly schematic terms and whose men were demoralised, slow-witted helots.[22] The disastrous Soviet record in Finland and Poland seemed to confirm this view. Much less attention was paid to the 1938–39 Far Eastern campaign or to such factors as climate, distance and logistics. The minority of German commanders who did not share this optimistic view seem to have confined themselves to ambiguously ironic remarks, notably when Rundstedt bade farewell to Ritter von Leeb on 4 May 1941 with the ominous words: 'Well then, see you again in Siberia.'[23]

The success of the initial German attack seemed to confirm the majority view. The Axis advance was so rapid that as early as 3 July the Chief of General Staff, Franz Halder, noted in his diary that: 'the Russian campaign had been won in the space of two weeks'. His mind was already racing ahead to denying the Soviets the economic resources for future recovery; to Britain, that on-going irritant; and to finding a possible thrust through the Caucasus to Iran. This over-confidence was reflected in Hitler's decision of 14 July 1941 to switch armaments priorities from the army to the navy and Luftwaffe.[24]

Optimistic initial assessments were gradually belied by conditions on the ground. Heavily laden infantrymen slogged along poor roads and tracks, covered in sweat and dust, and plagued by stinging insects, towards destinations that only served to underline how vast the country was. The rigours of forced marches in the summer heat were duly superseded by the mud from the autumn rains, miring men, vehicles and horses alike. Something of the sinister vastness of a fitfully beguiling landscape was caught by Manstein, the German commander on the southernmost front:

> I now found myself in the vast expanses of the steppes, which were almost entirely devoid of natural obstacles, even if they did not offer any cover either . . . The only variety was offered by the small rivers, the beds of which had dried up in summer-time to form deep, steep-banked fissures known as balkas. Nevertheless, the very monotony of the steppes gave them a strange and unique fascination. Everyone was captivated at one time or other by the endlessness of the landscape, through which it was possible to drive for hours on end – often guided by the compass – without encountering the least rise in the ground or setting eyes on a single human being or habitation. The distant horizon seemed like some mountain ridge behind which a paradise might beckon, but it only stretched on and on. The poles of the Anglo-Iranian telegraph line, built some years before by Siemens, alone served to break the eternal sameness of it all. Yet at sunset the steppes were transformed into a dazzling blaze of colour.[25]

By 6 October the problems of mud were compounded by the first light falls of snow. Wheeled vehicles could only advance by being shunted or towed by tracked craft, and even chains and towropes had to be dropped from the air in the first indication that the German army was ill equipped for the ordeal ahead. With temperatures down to −8°C and falling in early November, machine guns jammed, telescopic sights proved useless, engines had to be de-iced with fires underneath, tanks without calks slid around, while the intense cold penetrated thin denim uniforms and worn leather boots. Sartorial confusion reigned, with many German soldiers increasingly dressed in captured Russian fur hats, overcoats and felt boots, with insulation provided by newspapers, to protect themselves from what by early December had become temperatures of −32°C. Such shelter as existed – assuming it had not been booby-trapped by the retreating Russians – was equally lethal since the foul air encouraged respiratory illnesses and lice. Of course, these harsh weather conditions also applied to the Russians, who in the eyes of ordinary German soldiers seemed as though they were being collected from nowhere, given vodka and a weapon, and then thrown, wave-like, into virtually suicidal attacks. As they advanced deeper into the desolation of the Russian winter, the German army shed any vestigial human curiosity or sympathy for the Russian population, whose material civilisation was analogous to that of a backward country, and replaced it with a dull, uncomprehending hatred for this alien people.[26]

The failure to anticipate appalling climatic conditions, and the strategic errors, were now compounded by co-ordinated Soviet resistance, and a desperate effort on the Soviet home front, although in this war home and fighting fronts were inextricably confused. Having already dissipated his armour between three armies stretched along a front whose width reached 1,500 miles with a depth of 1,000 miles at maximum extent, Hitler diverted much of the flanking armour from the central Moscow front either south, to take the Donets Basin and Crimea, or north to put pressure on Leningrad. Remonstrations from commanders who wished to prioritise the assault on the Soviet capital were met with the remark: 'My generals know nothing about the economic aspects of the war.' Although major victories were achieved in the south (while Leningrad was subjected to close investment), notably the taking of half a million Soviet prisoners at Kiev, ill-equipped and exhausted German troops were then thrown into the long-range haul against Moscow precisely when conditions were least propitious.

Stalin rapidly reasserted his grip on the shambles his own policies had largely created. Typically, he wheeled out Molotov in the first radio appeal to the Soviet people, thus distancing himself from the catastrophe of the Non-Aggression Pact. On 3 July Stalin himself came on the wireless, his low, toneless voice accompanied by deep and weary breathing and frequent sips of water. The contrast between the even delivery and the tragedy that was unfolding apparently moved many people and, via clear instructions regarding scorched earth policies and partisan warfare, left them with the impression that there was ultimately someone in charge. The opening form of address struck an unfamiliar personal and indeed religious note: 'Comrades, citizens, brothers and sisters, fighters of our Army and Navy! I am speaking to you, my friends!' Acknowledging that 'a serious threat hangs over our country', he proceeded to justify the Nazi–Soviet Pact:

> A non-aggression pact is a peace pact between two states, and that was the pact that Germany proposed to us in 1939. No peace-loving state could have rejected such a pact with another country, even if scoundrels like Hitler and Ribbentrop stood at its head. All the more so, as this Pact did not in any way violate the territorial integrity, independence or honour of our country.[27]

The violations of Baltic, Finnish or Polish integrity, independence and honour by Soviet forces were lost in the ether. Amidst all the references to heroic resistance to imminent enslavement by 'German princes and barons', for the ideology could not comfortably accommodate invading armies consisting of Bavarian farmboys or butchers and carpenters from Darmstadt or Düsseldorf, Stalin characteristically warmed to the subject of the fight against the enemy within, still mysteriously omnipresent despite the horrors of the 1930s:

> A merciless struggle must be undertaken against all deserters and panic-mongers . . . We must destroy spies, diversionists and enemy paratroopers . . . Military tribunals should immediately try anyone who, through panic or cowardice, is interfering with our defence, regardless of position or rank.

In subsequent weeks and months, the resort to state terror was as instinctual as it was real. Generals such as Korobkov or Pavlov, whom Stalin blamed for his own mistakes, were shot for criminal negligence. Other able commanders, such as Meretskov, named by Pavlov under torture as part of a putative anti-Soviet conspiracy, were temporarily arrested and then three months later sent to command armies. This was not a unique experience. One of the most able commanders, the Russo-Pole Rokossovsky, who had been imprisoned and tortured in August 1937 was only released in March 1940 following the debacle of the Soviet–Finnish war, proved that talent was in short supply. He went to his command via a spell in a sanatorium.[28] Grotesquely, General Kachalov was tried in absentia for desertion in October 1941, notwithstanding his having been killed by a German direct hit in August. The mistake was not rectified until 1956, his family having borne until then the mark of a 'traitor to the Fatherland'.[29] A further twenty generals committed suicide following the failures of that summer. Taking advantage of emergency wartime conditions, Stalin also executed the remnant of suspected opponents who had somehow survived the purges of the late 1930s. As they fell back from the advancing Germans, the NKVD systematically executed political prisoners and all those serving ten or more years in gaol. In the Ukraine, NKVD killers slaughtered 1,000–2,000 political prisoners in Lutsk; 837 in Sambir; 500 in Dubno; 3,000–4,000 in Lviv; 850 in Drohobych; 1,500 in Stanyslaviv and so on. Order No. 270 of 16 August 1941 criminalised the families of officers and communists taken prisoner, and deprived the families of lesser ranks who met the same fate of access to rations and welfare.[30] Those who entered captivity, wounded and unconscious like General Ponedelin, would disappear into the gulag system after years of German captivity to be shot long after the war. Men who had escaped encirclement or imprisonment were sent to mine-laying units or NKVD screening camps. NKVD 'Special Sections' were used to weed out 'unreliable elements' and to keep Red Army troops at gunpoint on the frontline. On 25 July the NKVD rounded up and shot 1,000 'deserters'. In another notorious incident, they disarmed a large number of Red Army soldiers who had evaded encirclement, and who were then massacred by the Germans while en route to an NKVD screening centre.[31] The NKVD was also active in shooting all Germans in its north Russian and Siberian concentration camps, and in uprooting 650,000–700,000 ethnic Germans, deporting them to Kazakhstan and Siberia. If they survived journeys in cattle trucks lasting three months (and on one train alone 400 children died), the male deportees were sent down the mines while their families lived in fenced-in camps ringed with NKVD watchtowers. Community dignitaries were simply shot. In order to rationalise their own murderousness, in August 1941 the Russians dropped parachutists masquerading as German troops on Volga German settlements, who then asked villagers to hide them as the putative vanguard of the invading Wehrmacht. Anyone falling for this ploy was subsequently shot, as were villagers caught with swastika flags in the house, flags which the communists had helpfully distributed to these people in 1939 to celebrate the Hitler–Stalin Pact.[32]

With the advance on Moscow slowed by the weather and by dogged Russian resistance, Hitler – whose mind thought in feet and inches of captured ground – simply rejected advice in favour of tactical retreat. Isolated far from the front in his 'Wolf's Lair' at Rastenburg, and surrounded by cronies with no responsibilities beyond concurring even with the way he mispronounced foreign names such as 'Tschemberlein' or 'Eisenh-o-wer', Hitler received his senior commanders like 'a magistrate in a police court'.[33] Generals who advocated tactical withdrawal were sarcastically rebuffed: 'Sir, where in God's name do you propose to go back to, how far do you want to go back? . . . Do you want to go back 50 kilometres; do you think it is less cold there?'[34] On 20 December 1941, Guderian flew to Rastenburg to remonstrate along the same lines. The ensuing conversation was a typical example of Hitler's autodidactic, self-validating, pseudo-populist reference to his own worm's eye experience of earlier conflicts. As Manstein noted, 'although Hitler was always harping on his "soldierly" outlook and loved to recall that he had acquired his military experience as a front-line soldier, his character had as little in common with the thoughts and emotions of soldiers as had his party with the Prussian virtues which it was so fond of invoking'.[35] Almost before Guderian had even spoken, he sensed an unfriendly atmosphere in the dim light of the conference room:

HITLER: If that is the case [withdrawal] they must dig into the ground where they are and hold every square yard of land.

GUDERIAN: Digging into the ground is no longer feasible in most places, since it is frozen to a depth of five feet and our wretched entrenching tools won't go through it . . .

HITLER: In that case they must blast craters with heavy howitzers. We had to do that in the First World War in Flanders.[36]

It was no use pointing out that conditions in Flanders were otherwise; that shells were limited; and that such a strategy would lead in Russian conditions to a few tub-sized craters in the frozen ground. The discussion moved on to whether the objectives were worth the human sacrifice. When Guderian suggested that they were not and spelled out the casualties and inadequate equipment, Hitler responded:

> I know that you have not spared yourself and that you have spent a great deal of time with the troops. I grant you that. But you are seeing events at too close a range. You have been too deeply impressed by the suffering of the soldiers. You feel too much pity for them. You should stand back more. Believe me, things appear clearer when examined at longer range.[37]

Manstein also provides astute insights on Hitler as a would-be warlord:

> He was a man who saw fighting only in terms of the utmost brutality. His way of thinking conformed more to a mental picture of masses of the enemy bleeding to death before our lines than to the conception of a subtle fencer who knows how to make an occasional step backwards in order to lunge for the decisive thrust. For the art of war he substituted a brutal force which, as he saw it, was guaranteed maximum effectiveness by the will-power behind it . . . Despite the pains Hitler took to stress his own former status as a front-line soldier, I still never had the feeling that his heart belonged to the fighting troops. Losses, as far as he was concerned, were merely figures which reduced fighting power. They are unlikely to have seriously disturbed him as a human being.[38]

While Hitler was pondering the 'longer range' from the vantage point of Rastenburg, Stalin lived up to his grim reputation as the bureaucrat's bureaucrat by centralising ultimate (civilian) control of the war effort in the State Defence Committee (the only soldier present was Voroshilov) and military power in the Supreme Command or *Stavka* which he also chaired.[39] He could match Hitler not only in brutality and personal rudeness, but also in holding forth with irrelevant details from his capacious memory, albeit displaying his mastery of the nomenklatura rather than Hitler's well-known *rage de nombres.* Like Hitler, he also made catastrophic interventions in military dispositions usually by ordering ill-prepared counter-offensives. Ultimately, however, Stalin listened to the advice of professionals, effectively adjudicating between various alternative proposals, which his generals then wisely attributed to his strategic genius, while his opposite in Berlin followed the dictates of destiny and providence.[40] One can all too clearly imagine Hitler's mad monologues and tirades, in contrast with Stalin's menacingly laconic presence, with that impassive pock-marked face silently puffing on a pipe or sipping lemon tea. Whatever temperamental dissimilarities, the two dictators shared an indisposition to visit the fighting fronts, and a total indifference to casualties or other losses, including in Stalin's case, the capture and death of his son Yakov, an event shrugged off and never recalled in conversation.

It would be wrong to over-personalise the Soviet war effort. A political culture replete with all-powerful Party bosses and used to rhetorical battles, campaigns and Stakhanovite-style shock work quickly adapted to the exigencies of total war. The movement of strategic plant eastwards had in any case been on-going since the late 1920s. An Evacuation Council supervised the removal of some ten million people eastwards and the relocation of a strategically vital plant. This was urgent since the area conquered by the Germans contained 40 per cent of the Soviet population; 60 per cent of its arms industry; 38 per cent of its cattle; 60 per cent of its swine; 63 per cent of its coal; 71 per cent of its iron ore; 57 per cent of rolled steel production and so forth.[41] It was not an unrelieved success story; only seventeen out of sixty-four steel works were removed from the Donets Basin, and before one is tantalised by Soviet statistics, one should recall the role of *gulag* labour. But there were enough successes. For example, in late December 1941 the Zaporozhstal steel works in the Ukraine was removed to near Chelyabinsk in the Urals, with the job being completed in six weeks despite the need to heat the ground to lay foundations or the fact that cement froze. Some 1,500 major installations were evacuated by the end of 1941, using a million or so railway wagons as transport. This mass evacuation of plant and labour was accompanied by the conversion of consumer manufacturing industries so that bicycle factories turned out flame-throwers, or typewriter makers turned their skills to automatic weapons. Gigantic plants, such as 'Tankograd' at Chelyabinsk, used mass-production techniques to manufacture vast numbers of mechanically uncomplicated T-34 tanks, the standardised weapon which would play such a part in rolling back Hitler's more sophisticated, yet fatally variegated, armoured spearheads.[42] In 1941 a fifth of Soviet weaponry had come from the east; a year later the fraction was three-quarters. While the factories went eastwards, in October and November 1941 about eight divisions of troops, 1,000 tanks and 1,000 aircraft from the Soviet Far Eastern command were shipped westwards, once the spy Richard Sorge had confirmed that the Japanese were going to attack in the Pacific rather than towards the Soviet Union. These fresh troops were carefully husbanded while citizen militias, often consisting of what Stalin contemptuously called the 'four-eyed intelligentsia', were used to plug gaps in the front.

Hitler's attack on the Soviet Union managed to bestow upon the communist regime a popular legitimacy that was at best notional at its inception, and which it had certainly forfeited even among many believers during the terroristic depredations of the 1930s. Although many citizens of the Soviet empire undoubtedly welcomed the Germans as liberators with, as we shall see, some groups better represented in the Wehrmacht than the Red Army, German policy equally rapidly disabused people of residual illusions. German atrocities against civilians and prisoners of war left the Soviet population with no alternative to rallying to Stalin's calculating appeals to simple patriotism, a strategy already prefigured in the doctrine of 'Socialism in One Country'. The latter was now lent historical resonance through reference to great composers, writers and Tsarist generals. For security reasons, the twenty-fourth anniversary celebrations of the October Revolution were held in the depths of the Mayakovsky underground station on the night of 6 November rather than in the Bolshoi Theatre, although the interior of the latter was recreated in the station for the benefit of newsreel cameras. Sandwiches and soft drinks were distributed from a stationary train while Stalin and the Politburo arrived on another.[43] In his address, to an audience of NKVD men, Stalin said:

> It is these people without honour or conscience, these people with the morality of animals, who have the effrontery to call for the extermination of the great Russian nation – the nation of Plekhanov and Lenin, of Belinsky and Chernyshevsky, of Pushkin and Tolstoy, of Gorki and Chekhov, of Glinka and Tchaikovsky, of Sechenov and Pavlov, of Suvorov and Kutuzov![44]

The following morning Stalin spoke at a march past on Red Square, with heavy snow grounding German bombers while German troops stood only thirty miles away. With NKVD radio operators atop of Lenin's tomb maintaining contact with their brigade defending Moscow, and an emergency hospital set up in the GUM department store, Stalin invoked the heroes of the Russian past:

> The war you are waging is a war of liberation, a just war. May you be inspired in this war by the heroic figures of our great ancestors, Alexander Nevsky, Dimitri Donskoi, Minin and Pozharsky, Alexander Suvorov, Michael Kutuzov!

A regime that had ostentatiously installed Museums of Atheism in cathedrals suddenly had no qualms reopening churches, with monks collecting money to fund tank regiments, a policy which resulted a few years later in the re-established Patriarch offering prayers for the tyrant in the Kremlin.[45] The author of the 'Godless Five-Year Plan' was soon authorising a tour of the miracle-working icon of Our Lady of Kazan through beseiged Soviet cities. In September 1941, Stalin again restored another aspect of the past he and his colleagues had obliterated when he authorised the creation of Guards Divisions in which crack troops were paid double the usual soldier's salary. Although Stalin's diplomatic miscalculations and refusal to pre-empt the German attack had played a major role in the catastrophe, henceforth he was personally associated with each victory in the 'patriotic war' (defeats were ascribed to others), lending his own name to a 'doctrine' of military strategy, and feted abroad by people such as British press barons who should have known better. We should be careful, too, not to project back onto the wartime period what we have since learned about the imperial corruption of the former Soviet Union. However unpalatable one may find it, this system could draw on the naive enthusiasm of millions of ordinary people, who – despite all the evidence to the contrary – were convinced they were making the world a better place. How else does one account for the epic labours of 'accelerators', 'three hundreders' and 'thousanders' who increased their own productivity by these Stakhanovite percentages? There is also probably much in the novelist Vasily Grossman's view that many Russians saw the war as a chance to correct the abuses and horrors of the communist system, even though most of them were probably generic:

> Nearly everyone believed that good would triumph, that honest men, who hadn't hesitated to sacrifice their lives, would be able to build a good and just life. This faith was all the more touching in that these men thought that they themselves would be unlikely to survive until the end of the war; indeed, they felt astonished each evening to have survived one more day.[46]

The system could also rely upon terror and the ghosts consigned to its moral depths. Beria's NKVD took a leading role in the evacuation of plant and the production of munitions. As a defence industry official put it: 'Everyone in the plants and offices and institutions directly or indirectly connected with armaments and munitions was gripped by dread fear. Beria was no engineer. He was placed in control for the precise purpose of inspiring deadly fear.'[47] The gulags also provided a captive workforce: 39,000 prisoners for weapons and ammunition production, 40,000 to build aircraft and tanks, over 448,000 to construct railways and so forth. Even here, Solzhenitsyn reports that prisoners were infected by a sense of patriotism: 'Coal for Leningrad', 'Mortar shells for the troops', being the slogans. Hundreds of thousands of others were conscripted into penal battalions, to be expended clearing minefields and other obstacles. Whether they felt the pull of patriotism remains unrecorded.[48] We should also remember that matériel equivalent to about a tenth of Soviet production was sent to Russia, at great human cost, by convoy from Britain and the United States of America.

The failure of Operation Typhoon before Moscow was followed by several fractious scenes at Hitler's headquarters during the planning and execution of the 1942 summer campaign. When Halder responded sharply to what was tantamount to a charge of cowardice, Hitler exploded: 'Colonel-General Halder, how dare you use language like that to me! Do you think you can teach me what the man at the front is thinking? What do you know about what goes on at the front? Where were you in the First World War? And you try to pretend that I don't understand what it's like at the front. I won't stand that! It's outrageous!'[49] Having parried over-ambitious Soviet winter offensives, Hitler scaled down his ambitions for the 1942 summer campaign – in itself an indication of how things had changed since the three-pronged thrusts of 1941 – to a major push southwards towards the oilfields of the Caucasus with a simultaneous punch eastwards at the Soviet forces on the Don. Having taken Stalingrad, Hitler could then either send this army south to Astrakhan or direct it northwards towards the rear of Moscow.[50] With the offensive in the south failing to bring Soviet forces to battle, and Marshal Budenny despatched to check their momentum, Hitler connived with Stalin in transforming the struggle for the city which bore the latter's name, and which was bound up with his early history, into a real and talismanic battle of wills. Having already vowed to rase Leningrad and Moscow to the ground, Hitler proclaimed his intention of murdering all Stalingrad's male citizens and deporting women and children on the grounds that its 'thoroughly communistic inhabitants were especially dangerous'.[51] This was to be no ordinary battle.

While Hitler entrusted the advance on Stalingrad to Paulus, a colourless middle-class military bureaucrat with little combat experience,

Stalin summoned Marshal Georgi Zhukov, whose military career stretched back to the First World War, and included the Russian and Spanish Civil Wars, the battle of Khalkin-Gol in Mongolia, and latterly, the defence of Leningrad and the repulse of the Wehrmacht before Moscow. It was not an even match.[52] With a keen eye for enemy weaknesses, Zhukov devised a plan which involved holding Stalingrad while launching a massive pincer movement to isolate Paulus's Sixth Army from potential relief.[53] It was the first of what were to be a succession of Soviet operations planned with enormous care and thoroughness, conceived on an ever vaster scale.[54] Responsibility for retaining Stalingrad itself fell on General Vasiliy Chuikov, a thick-set jolly Russian with a mouthful of gold teeth, who had been recalled from a military attachéship in China, whither he had been despatched for his disastrous role in the campaign against Finland. Conscious of black marks in his copybook in a culture which frequently punished failure by firing squad, Chuikov rose to the occasion, with the wider strategic dispositions in the hands of the brighter Zhukov.

With a record acquired the previous year of brutal depredations against Ukrainian civilians (entire cities were starved and so-called partisans hanged) as well as complicity in the murder of Ukrainian Jews, 6th Army set off to dislodge the Red Army from Stalingrad into the Volga.[55] Whereas a year before they had enjoyed the bountiful produce of the Ukraine, deliberately denied to the starving inhabitants of Kiev and Kharkov next to whom they settled like uniformed locusts, they now crossed the barren and inhospitable steppe, fitfully followed by herds of cattle, and with instructions to live off a land that bore nothing. The railway links were repeatedly cut by Russian saboteurs.

At the end of the line stood one of those bleak and windswept Soviet cities, with its back to Asia. The city was comprehensively bombed on 23 August by 600 German aeroplanes, with 40,000 civilians killed.[56] But bombs and tanks proved to be of limited use in a town whose elongated shape and huge factories, grain elevators and railway stations, made a decisive blow difficult, while providing ample cover for its defenders even when gutted or in ruins. Tank crews spent hours pounding shells into buildings, prevented by limited gun elevation from bringing down the upper floors, while unable to make much impact on the enemy scurrying around in the cellars and sewers. Around every corner lurked a Russian tank or artillery piece, while from above came the risk of grenades. Supplied from the opposite river bank, the Soviets stayed within hailing distance of their German opponents, to minimise the value of German airpower, while maximising their own skills at close-quarter combat with grenades, tommy-guns and the knife. Their sharpshooters were so adept that the Germans felt obliged to call upon the services of the super-sniper Heinz Thorwald, head of the sniper training school at Zossen. After a few days and nights during which Thorwald shot several Russians, he momentarily revealed his position under a sheet of metal in no-man's-land, and was duly killed by his Soviet counterparts.[57] The Soviets fired shells and salvoes of Katyusha rockets from the east bank of the Volga, over the heads of the pockets of Russian soldiers in the city, and onto the Germans in the city centre. At night they ferried over reinforcements, including fit young guardsmen: 'All of them young and tall, and healthy, many of them in paratroop uniform, with knives and daggers tucked into their belts. They went in for bayonet charges, and would throw a dead Nazi over their shoulder like a sack of straw. For house to house fighting, there was nothing quite like them. They would attack in small groups, and, breaking into houses and cellars, they would use knives and daggers.'[58]

The 6th Army exhausted itself in countless major and minor offensives in the ruins of the city (with the Russian counter-attacking at night), never apparently latching onto the strategy of working their way along the river bank from both north and south to cut the Russians off from the 'ant heap' of activity across the Volga. Back in Moscow, its fate was being sealed. In the Kremlin on the morning of 13 November, Zhukov outlined to Stalin the finely tuned plans he had been developing for a massive counter-offensive. According to Zhukov, the meeting went well, with Stalin silently puffing his pipe and stroking his moustache to signal his approval.[59] Stalin concluded the meeting with the words: 'Return to Stalingrad tomorrow morning and make a check that troops and commands are ready to start the operation.' At 6 a.m. on 20 November, the Russian defenders of Stalingrad heard the muffled thud of gunfire through the foggy dawn. Zhukov had launched a massive pincer offensive, code-named 'Uranus', whose effect was to encircle Paulus's forces, cutting them off from outside relief at a depth that facilitated the manoeuvring of Russian reinforcements against any approaching hostile force.

Instead of encouraging Paulus in his initial desire to evacuate the city as quickly as possible, Hitler ordered him to stay put. The 300,000 troops in Stalingrad were supposedly to be supplied from the air, even though the Luftwaffe was in no position to airlift the minimum daily requirement of 500 tonnes of fuel, food, medicines and munitions. Manstein was brought in as commander of the new Army Group Don. He also insisted that Paulus remain in Stalingrad until relief came in the shape of Operation Winter Tempest consisting of the bulk of 4th Panzer Army under Hermann Hoth. With Hitler refusing, and Paulus reluctant to countenance a simultaneous breakout, Hoth's armoured thrust petered out against stiff Russian resistance.[60]

The effect of these operations was to leave a quarter of a million men cut off from all hope of relief, without adequate supplies, and encircled by superior forces, under a dysentery-ridden commander whose strong point was not initiative in a crisis. As weather conditions deteriorated, and the Soviets took the airfields, the supplies landed inside the 'Cauldron' dwindled to 100 tonnes a day, with a corresponding reduction in the number of wounded making the return journey. With the capture of Gumrak airfield, supplies had to be dropped in canisters, with soldiers lying down in cross-shaped formations in a pitiful attempt to give these measures some semblance of accuracy. Although the pre-Stalingrad record of 6th Army suggests they were far from being blameless victims expended by a callous and incompetent leadership, the ordinary soldiers obviously underwent a protracted and terrible ordeal which it would be churlish to disparage. Men with complicated stomach wounds were simply set aside to die by overworked field surgeons since lengthy operations were a luxury and their stretchers would take up too much space in relief flights. Fingers, toes and ears damaged by frostbite were amputated with minimal anaesthetic and no after-care.[61] With their clothing infested by fleas and lice, and mice running over their faces at night, sometimes eating frozen toes, the soldiers of 6th Army also had to deal with hunger. Letters home spoke of how, having adjusted to a diet of horsemeat, they were next reduced to cooking cats: 'The day before yesterday we slaughtered a cat. I can tell you, although I would never have thought it possible, it tasted wonderful.' Men made lame jokes about being so thin that they could dress and undress behind a broom handle as their thoughts focused obsessively on a small piece of bread.[62] Food became an obsession. In a letter to his mother dated 8 December 1942, a soldier wrote:

> Because of supply problems, our rations have been halved. Some days there is only 50 grams of bread, which means a bite in the morning and a mouthful in the evening. Since yesterday, the daily bread ration

> has been raised to 250 grams. Everything depends upon the weather, since when it is foggy our transport planes cannot fly because of the danger of freezing up. Lunch isn't what it should be for this time of year. Thin like water. One sits at meals, already thinking about the next meal . . . Every crumb of bread, which before one would have swept off the table, has become precious. I've never learned to value bread as I have during recent weeks. Potatoes, yes potatoes, seem to me like images in a dream! The soil here yields nothing edible: only steppe.[63]

On 15 January 1943, a young soldier called Hermann wrote:

> Cold and hunger wear down even the best soldiers. Just like last year, the number of cases of frostbite on feet and hands has risen. The Russians are dropping a lot of propaganda leaflets, and each day call upon us to surrender since our position is hopeless. But we're not entirely without hope, even if we can see that we have no meat to eat. We've still got two horses, but then that's that. We've even cooked lungs ourselves, simply to have something in our stomachs. I eat only once a day – at midday. After I've spooned down my watery soup, I quickly swallow my bit of bread with sausage or butter, then I eagerly await tomorrow's lunch.[64]

Christmas and New Year were evocatively burdensome when spent in a dimly lit bunker or frozen hole in the ground, listening to the Christmas carols which the Russians malevolently broadcast through loudspeakers. Writing on 30 December 1942, a soldier described the homesickness and loneliness they were all experiencing:

> This year we had a sad Christmas without mail or a tree, no candles, indeed nothing that signified Christmas at all. I don't know how often I heard the words Germany or home spoken on Christmas Eve, but it was very frequent. I am lying in a bunker with a twenty-two-year-old. The lad cried on Christmas Eve like a child, I tell you we all had tears in our eyes when we heard there was no mail. Although I am only just twenty-one myself, I gritted my teeth and said: 'perhaps the mail will come tomorrow', even though I didn't believe this myself.[65]

While the National Socialist leadership purveyed an image of 6th Army heroically expiring in battle like the Spartans at Thermopylae, the reality was a vast number of men starving to death in miserable makeshift shelters. The erstwhile spearhead had degenerated into an atomised mass of hungry beggars. Remonstrating with a Luftwaffe officer on 19 January 1943, Paulus said:

> As commander of an army what should I say when a man comes to me and begs: Herr Colonel-General, a piece of bread? It's already the

> fourth day on which the men have had nothing to eat . . . We can't retake a position any more, because the men are collapsing with exhaustion . . . The last horses have been eaten . . . Can you even imagine that soldiers are falling upon the old corpse of a horse, cutting off the head and eating the brains raw?[66]

On 31 January, the Russians closed in on Paulus's headquarters in the Univermag store. A German officer hailed a young Russian lieutenant with the words: 'Our big chief wants to talk to your big chief.' After protracted exchanges, Lieutenant Yelchenko was admitted to the building, where he came across Paulus, lying sick and unshaven on an iron bed. Yelchenko said: 'Well, that finishes it.' The forlorn Field-Marshal Paulus nodded in agreement. 90,000 German soldiers began the long march into captivity, from which 6,000 would return alive a decade later.

Wider Soviet offensives that winter, and the successful German counter-thrust at Kharkov in mid-March, resulted in mutual exhaustion and a ragged frontline, whose most anomalous feature was the Soviet salient around Kursk. This salient preoccupied military planners on both sides during the lull in fighting brought on by the spring thaw.[67] Opinion on the German side was split between advocates of back- and forehand strategies. In the former scenario, the German army would await an inevitable Soviet breakout from the salient, for the reconquest of the Donets and the Ukraine was surely too tempting a target, then wear them down with countless defensive battles before launching their own limited offensive. The forehand strategy, which enjoyed Hitler's support, involved concentrating Germany's rather diminished resources for a limited offensive while the Russians were still refitting after the winter. Similar debates took place on the Soviet side. While Stalin advocated a full-scale offensive, many of his commanders pressed for an attritionist defensive posture prior to a massive counter-offensive. In the end, they prevailed.

Hitler's constant postponment of what was code-named 'Citadelle' was due to his worries about an immanent Allied landing in the Mediterranean, and to the conflicting counsels of his generals. Having studied reconnaisance photographs of the Soviet defensive positions, General Model requested more tanks. Guderian, the new Inspector-General of Armoured Troops, who could see no point in an offensive in the east that year, muddied the waters further, by arguing that the new tanks coming on stream, such as the Panther and Tiger, needed further evaluation before being committed in such a crucial battle. These protracted debates and the ensuing instructions were closely monitored by the British code-breakers at Bletchley Park, so that Hitler's final decision to authorise 'Citadelle' reached Stalin rather quicker than it did his own generals.

These delays enabled the Soviets to develop their response very carefully. The Red Air Force, which specialised in the artillery-style air offensive, disposed of nearly 3,000 aircraft at Kursk, including the formidable Ilyushin II-2m3 equipped with anti-tank bombs and cannon which could rip through most armour. Over forty dummy airfields, replete with fake aircraft and control towers, confused the Luftwaffe as to where the real Red Airforce strength lay. On the ground, the Kursk salient was turned into a fortress. The Soviets laid over a million mines, at a density of about one per foot, and set up 500 miles of barbed-wire entanglements, some of it electrified. Complex networks of trenches, gun emplacements and wide anti-tank ditches, built with the help of 300,000 civilians, completed the conversion of the salient into a formidable series of obstacles, whose defensive echelons stretched back over 100 miles. At the points where they anticipated German attacks, the Russians had as many as 150 heavy guns per mile. Much of the build-up of over a million troops took place at night, under strict blackout and with disembarkation away from obvious targets such as stations. Communications were limited to ten-second bursts of radio traffic impossible to intercept. Partisans were let loose on the German railways, with each attack causing bottlenecks and hence tempting targets for Russian bombers.[68]

After much prevarication, Hitler finally set 4 July as the date for 'Citadelle', on a battlefield the size of Wales. Various attempts were made to disguise the timing, for example by ostentatiously sending Manstein to decorate Antonescu in Bucharest, and then quietly flying him straight back to the Kursk front. Both British intelligence and German deserters gave the Russians the exact day and time of the attack, enabling Zhukov to launch a massive artillery barrage at 2.20 a.m., ten minutes before the German artillery strike. The German advance, when it came, reflected the mistake of waiting months for the latest types of armour. Many of the new Panther tanks belched flames from their exhausts before grinding to a halt with burned-out engines. Clusters of heavily armed Tigers could blast the lighter T-34s at long distance, but were easily out-manoeuvred, surrounded or susceptible to a shell (or ramming) at point-blank range. Perhaps equally worryingly, German radio interceptors noted that, in contrast to what they had experienced in 1941, Russian commanders were not signalling their superiors with the panicky refrain: 'Am under attack, what should I do?'[69]

Probably the most decisive engagement during this vast battle took place on the southern bend of the Kursk salient in the orchards and wheat fields of the small town of Prokhorovka. German armour under General Hoth, including such fearsome formations as 'Totenkopf', 'Das Reich' and the 'Leibstandarte Adolf Hitler', penetrated the Soviet front before exhaustion and Russian resistance forced them to a halt. Both sides paused, with the Russians committing a fresh tank army from their reserves to meet Hoth's attack. The two armies literally collided hull to hull on the morning of 12 July, oblivious to the thunderstorms overhead. The battlefield was so tight (about three square miles) and the concentration of armour so dense that both commanders rapidly lost control of their formations, as tanks careered around in the wheat fields, churning up clouds of dust to add to the exhaust fumes and explosions. Any advantages of weight and firepower enjoyed by German armour were lost in point-blank combat against an enemy that never gave up, and whose tank drivers (including women) steered according to the directions indicated by the tank commander's feet resting on their shoulders. Over 300 German tanks were destroyed that day alone. Russian veterans admit to taking few prisoners in a fight where neither side gave or expected any quarter. By nine o'clock at night the battle was over. Any lingering doubts about where the strategic initiative now lay were over too, as Soviet offensives became bolder, spurred on by the evidence of German atrocities in the territories they reconquered, and largely dictating the pace of events.

The military history of the German invasion of the Soviet Union barely conveys the prolonged nightmare which enveloped that empire, nor does it explain the hatred which added a special viciousness to the conflict on both sides. Many wars include episodes of brutality and inhumanity, especially when they involve 'irregulars', but this is rarely either premeditated or systemic. The German campaign in the Soviet Union was both. As a final reckoning between two antagonistic non-democratic political systems based on the delusion that they could remodel mankind, and as a biologistic campaign against Bolsheviks,

Jews, Gypsies and Slavic 'Untermenschen', the war in the east had a fundamentally different register from that in the west. The line between conventional and ideological warfare was erased long before the fighting commenced, and compounded by conditions on the ground. This applied to the treatment of captured enemy combatants or – since the boundaries were in any case blurred by both sides – of enemy civilians. These themes will be discussed in turn below.

A few bleak facts and comparisons may illustrate the fate of Soviet prisoners of war. During the First World War, some 1,434,500 Russians were captured by the German army; 5.4 per cent of them died in captivity. Between the 1941 invasion and 1945, some 5.7 million Red Army soldiers were captured by the Germans and their allies. 930,000 of these men and women were recovered alive from German prisoner of war camps in January 1945. As many as a further one million prisoners had been released during the war, many of them more or less voluntarily serving the Wehrmacht in either combat or auxiliary capacities. Another half a million had managed to escape or had been liberated by the Red Army. The remainder, consisting of about 3,300,000 prisoners (or 57.5 per cent of the original total) had died in captivity. The record of German prisoners of war in Soviet hands was equally bleak, although not statistically commensurate. Of the 3,155,000 men captured, 1,185,000 (or 37.5 per cent of the total) died while in captivity. By contrast, of the 232,000 British or American soldiers in German hands, 8,348 (or 3.5 per cent of the total captured) had died by 1945.[70]

The juridical relationship between Germany and the Soviet Union was unclear, which probably 'legitimised' German atrocities at a level so academically rarefied that it is almost irrelevant. The Soviet Union had not ratified the 1929 Geneva Convention on prisoners of war, nor had it expressly acknowledged the 1895/1907 Hague Laws of Land Warfare. Although this meant that the German government considered itself bound by no international obligations towards Russia, this was not strictly juridically true, since both sides were bound by the well-established conventions of warfare as they had evolved since the early modern period. These stipulated that prisoners of war were entitled to humane treatment; with clothing, food and shelter roughly on a par with that enjoyed by one's own reserve army troops. Matters were therefore not quite as ill defined as the Germans maintained. The Soviet Union had also ratified the 1929 Geneva Convention on treatment of captured enemy wounded. One should also note that Soviet attempts to subscribe formally to the Hague Convention in July 1941 via Swedish intermediacy were deliberately frustrated by the German leadership.[71]

Those involved have advanced more or less cogent reasons why such a vast proportion of Soviet prisoners of war died. The system was suddenly overloaded by vast numbers of prisoners. Soviet soldiers had low levels of resistance because the Red Army had been operating in areas where Stalin had ordered the destruction of all plant and foodstuffs. Atrocious weather and epidemic diseases devastated the prisoner population. All of these things were partially true, but they fall well short of the whole truth.[72] What is missing is human agency and intentionality within this exculpatory fog of contingent circumstances.

In a war which was meant to be won in weeks, the treatment of prisoners was accorded low priority. Military planners knew that massive battles of encirclement would yield commensurately large numbers of captives. The large number of prisoner fatalities was therefore firstly a product of decisions to keep the majority of prisoners in Russia, in areas which were being systematically stripped of resources to feed the German army, and where in order not to impair German military effectiveness provision of food, shelter or transport would be minimal. This was compounded by another salient feature of National Socialist thinking, namely that entire peoples had differential racial values. This view of things was carried over into its treatment of prisoners of war as well as of the burgeoning foreign labour force. British and American prisoners were treated relatively well (not least because their governments would have carried out reprisals against German prisoners), Flemings were treated better than Walloons, Frenchmen better than Poles and so on. Russians occupied almost the lowest rung in this hierarchy, being regarded as literally expendable. Instructions on the treatment of Russian prisoners of war, issued on 16 June 1941, were saturated with National Socialist ideology, and were designed to prohibit even minimal human relations between prisoners and their guards or German civilians. Any signs of 'resistance' were to be 'ruthlessly eradicated'. This was a world away from the relatively decent conditions experienced by British or American prisoners of war in Germany. In the case of the Russians, there was no reciprocity.

Since the ruthless exploitation of Russia's resources was intrinsic to Hitler's war aims, and to the maintainance of both military and domestic morale, the deliberate starvation of the enemy population, including prisoners of war, was factored into the planning of the invasion and occupation. If German civilian planners such as Backe could countenance the deaths of '*x* million people through starvation' with all too evident equanimity, so their military equivalents had resolved that Red Army prisoners would receive rations well below the minimum necessary to sustain life. Thus Red Army prisoners received 20 grams of millet or bread, or 100 grams of millet without bread per day as they trudged forlornly back through Belarus. In August 1941 these *ad hoc* arrangements were replaced by consolidated rations equivalent to 2,100 calories per day for prisoners who worked and 2,040 for those who did not. These levels were rarely attained except in the paper world of military bureaucrats. In September, a committee chaired by Göring decided that in order to stabilise or improve the wartime rations of the German civilian population, it would be necessary to reduce the rations of 'Bolshevik prisoners'. Unembarrassed by his own pinguidity, he also made a few off-the-cuff suggestions about eating cats and horses.[73] Soon after, the Quarter-Master General Eduard Wagner reduced the rations of non-working prisoners to 1,500 calories per day, i.e. two-thirds of the minimum necessary to stay alive. The effects of this were catastrophic. Even the commandants of concentration camps complained that 5 to 10 per cent of the Russians they were sent were actually half-dead or dead on arrival, thus denying them the pleasure of executing them. In a prisoner of war camp in Silesia, men were eating grass, flowers, raw potatoes or each other. Columns of hungry and exhausted men were lucky if their route passed crops such as sugar beets, rotting because the refineries had been blown during the Soviet retreat. A German industrialist visiting the Ukraine to organise the takeover of a steel plant recorded.

> Endless columns of prisoners passed by. In one case, there were 12,500 men guarded by only thirty German soldiers. Those who were unable to walk were shot. We spent the night in a small village because we were stuck in the mud. There we found a transit camp, where we witnessed how at night the prisoners cooked and ate their comrades who had been shot by our sentries for indiscipline. The prisoners' food consisted of potatoes from the villagers. Each man received at most two potatoes a day.[74]

Russian prisoners walked to captivity partly because the Soviet railway network was widely cast, but also because those in charge of returning empty trucks and wagons steadfastly refused to have them occupied by dirty, lice-ridden prisoners. This meant that prisoners had to march distances of over 500 kilometres driven on by guards who shot them by the wayside when they could go no further. This was sometimes done in full public view, as for example in Smolensk in October 1941 where 120 Soviet prisoners were mown down in the town centre. It made a very poor impression on the civilian population, with word of beatings and shootings spreading like wildfire. The Axis war correspondent Curzio Malaparte, who wrote much of his book *Kaputt* while in the Ukraine, has left us a haunting description of the fate of a group of Soviet prisoners. On one occasion he was present at what were cynically dubbed 'lessons in the open' in a kolkhoz of a village near Nemirovskoye. A group of Soviet captives were lined up in the farmyard, soaked through by the incessant rain. Some were big, crop-haired farmboys; others lean, stern-looking artisans and engineers. A short, corpulent German corporal, employing the benign tones of a schoolmaster, began to set them a reading test. Those who passed would work as clerks; those who failed would work in the docks or on the land. Old copies of *Izvestia* and *Pravda* were distributed to groups of five men, who then read from the sodden newsprint. The majority who failed to read fluently were sent to the left; the literate minority passed to the right. All of which was accompanied by much jocularity on the part of the prisoners, with calls of 'Clerks!' or 'Stones on the back!' from the respective groups, and arch asides by their captors. And so it went on for about an hour until eighty-seven men were on the left and thirty-one on the right. The latter group were then marched off to a wall where they were shot by the waiting SS. The colonel in charge explained: 'Russia must be cleared of all this learned rabble. The peasants and workers who can read and write too well are dangerous. They are all communists.'[75]

Some German commanders, such as General Tettau, ordered a stop to these practices; others, such as Reichenau, positively encouraged them. When the winter made marches impossible, the prisoners were shipped in open railway goods wagons. This brought no relief since their trains had no priority, and moved at a snail's pace as civilian and military bureaucrats in the occupied territories exchanged cables, letters, memoranda and telephone calls regarding the appropriate forms and permissions. If their trains halted in towns and villages, they might also be fortunate enough to fight one another over potatoes and bread thrown in by sympathetic civilians. Many simply froze to death.

In one case, 1,000 men died on a train somewhere along the 200-kilometre journey from Bobrujsk to Minsk. The use of covered cars made little difference since these were unheated. In early December 1941, it was reported that 'between 25 and 70 per cent' of prisoners were dying in transit.[76]

The prisoner of war camp system was multi-layered. In front-line areas, prisoners were confined in Army POW Collection Points; in rear areas, in POW transit camps (Dulags); and in civilian- or Wehrmacht-administered territories, in Stalags and Oflags for men and officers respectively. Conditions in these camps were appalling. In so far as preparations had been made, these involved fencing off open-air sites. Penned in, prisoners were handed a few implements (including cooking pots) with which to dig holes in the ground which they then covered with whatever materials were available. Huddled together in the summer heat or freezing cold they were prey to lice, pneumonia, typhus and other diseases. Hitler expressly declined a Red Cross offer of vaccination materials. The SS volunteered the simpler solution of shooting the sick prisoners. Maltreatment of prisoners was condoned and encouraged by the army leadership. In a summary of regulations governing treatment of prisoners, General Reinecke began with the bald statement: 'Bolshevism is the deadly enemy of National Socialist Germany.' Every soldier was to exercise extreme distance and 'correct' coolness towards these prisoners. Any dissent was to be dealt with instantly with the bayonet, riflestock or a bullet. There was a shoot to kill policy in the case of escapees, with no shouted warnings, or warning shots. Order within POW camps was to be preserved by a selected group of Russian prisoners armed with clubs and whips. In a bizarre endeavour to distinguish between military violence and brutality, Reinecke stipulated that German troops were not allowed to use either.[77]

These directives were a relatively late addition to an earlier complex of criminal orders designed to transform the invasion of Russia into ideological war against 'Jewish-Bolshevism' rather than a conventional military conflict. We must go back some months to uncover the lines of responsibility. While the war's moral parameters was determined by Hitler, they were given authority, detail and legality by senior Wehrmacht officers, notably Halder. Of course, the politicisation of the German army was an on-going affair rather than something that suddenly occurred in the context of the invasion of Russia. Senior German soldiers had aided and abetted the murder by the SS of Röhm and his associates in 1934, and senior officers had ordered the 'eradication' of communists in the Sudetenland by the military police in 1938 and the summary shooting of Czech and German political exiles by the regular army in France in 1940. Many of them also tacitly approved the depredations of the Einsatzgruppen in Poland, or like Jodl, Keitel or Reinecke were actively involved in disseminating National Socialist ideology for military consumption. The expansion of the officer corps from 3,800 in 1935 to 35,000 professionals (and an equivalent numbers of reservists) by 1941 may well have diluted and subverted their core values. This was in the twofold sense that the new recruits were merely functional professionals bereft of external moral reference points, whilst their sheer numbers and social dilution made the enforcement of informal codes of behaviour through close contact between social equals more difficult.[78] The Wehrmacht did not arrive in Russia either 'unpoliticised' or with an unblemished record.

Although planning for 'Barbarossa' had commenced in June 1940, directives on the conduct of the war only began to flow after March 1941, as if Hitler wished to see how the initial decision was received before revealing just how far he was about to go in realising his ideological objectives. Dealing with a traditionalist body of men who had to be handled carefully, he preferred to introduce his own values, by stages, a few at a time. Sketchy preliminary directives passed back and forth between Hitler and his senior generals from December 1940 to March 1941, with Jodl raising the question of collaboration with the SS in the 'rendering harmless' of Bolshevik cadres and commissars, and hence the exclusion of these people from military jurisdiction. At two conferences attended by military leaders on 17 and 30 March 1941, Hitler's stark views on the conduct of this war were recorded, and internalised, by Halder:

> The intelligentsia appointed by Stalin must be exterminated. The leadership apparatus of the Russian empire must be destroyed. The use of the most brutal violence is necessary in the Greater Russian region. Ideological ties do not really hold the Russian people tightly together. It will collapse if one gets rid of the functionaries.[79]

Speaking to 250 senior officers in the Reich Chancellory on 30 March, and tactically confining his remarks to political rather than racial issues, Hitler gradually revealed the cards from the deck on his table, pitching his remarks in a way that would appeal to his thoroughly anti-communist audience:

> Communism is a tremendous danger for the future. We must get away from the standpoint of soldierly comradeship. The communist is from first to last no comrade. It is a war of extermination. If we do not regard it as such, we may defeat the enemy, but in thirty years' time we will again be confronted by the communist enemy. We are not fighting a war in order to conserve the enemy . . . Fight against Russia: destruction of the Bolshevik commissars and the communist intelligentsia . . . It is not a question of court martials. The leaders of the troops must know what is involved. They must take the lead in the struggle. The troops must defend themselves with the methods with which they are attacked. Commissars and the GPU people are criminals and must be treated as such. That does not mean that the troops need get out of hand. The leader must draw up orders in accordance with the sentiments of his troops. The struggle will be very different from that in the west. In the east toughness now means mildness in the future. The leaders must make the sacrifice of overcoming their scruples.[80]

Although some of those present later claimed to have been outraged by aspects of this two-and-a-half-hour talk (waiting for Hitler to leave the room before murmuring their responses) the reality was that they hurried away to turn his words into legal forms, providing that they had not independently initiated similar measures already. On 26 March – i.e. four days before the conference at which Hitler spoke – the Quarter-Master General Wagner came to an agreement with the Chief of the Security Police and SD, Reinhard Heydrich, which was endorsed and issued as an order by Field-Marshal Brauschitsch a month later, regarding the operational space to be allotted to the already notorious SS Einsatzgruppen. Under the terms of this directive, 'On Co-operation with the Security Police and SD in the Eastern War which is Envisaged', the latter were empowered to carry out 'executive measures' against enemy civilians involved in 'anti-German and anti-state activities' in Army Group Areas, and a rather more restricted range of functions in Army rear and operational areas.[81] In other words, activities which had appalled some German officers in Poland (including ironically Wagner himself) were to be tolerated on a much vaster scale (against a deliberately loosely defined group of victims), provided this did not interfere with military operations. This may have been a way of keeping the Wehrmacht's uniform clean, but its effect none the less was to leave it looking very shabby. This was not the only instance of formal military and SS co-operation.

With the role of the SS carefully defined, so as to preclude any disputes about respective competences, army commanders next turned to the question of military jurisdiction. The latter only applied to disciplinary matters within the German army. In other words, hostile civilians (including those who distributed leaflets or refused to obey a German order) were denied any rights, and indeed could be killed with impunity by German soldiers without resort to legal process and merely subject to the approval of an officer. As the drafts of this directive did the rounds, Halder insisted on including collective reprisals against places where it was impossible to establish quickly the identity of an individual sharpshooter or saboteur. This reflected a long Prussian tradition of extreme measures against suspected enemy irregulars which has so far not been properly investigated. Clearly aware of the dark forces that these orders could unleash, the High Command tried to re-establish some vestiges of control by prohibiting arbitrary individual outrages lest they lead to anarchy and the moral brutalisation of all and sundry. This was a case of having one's cake and eating it. A revised final version of this directive was authorised by Keitel on 13 May 1941.[82]

The final element in this complex of criminal orders was the so-called Commissar Order of 6 June 1941. Recent research has demonstrated that senior generals, including once again Halder, formulated this infamous directive, by which civilian and military Communist Party functionaries were to be identified (by their starred, hammer and sickle lapel badges) and murdered by the army either on the spot or in rear areas. Effectively, the army was assuming the functions hitherto performed by the Einsatzgruppen, namely the killing of an entire group of people solely by virtue of their membership of that group and without formal process. The general intention, essayed earlier by both the Nazis and the Soviets in occupied Poland, was to destroy the ruling elite of the country concerned. Inevitably, there were weasel attempts to justify this in terms of the 'Asiatic-barbarian' manner in which such cadres would treat German prisoners, or by arguing that the Red Army would swiftly disintegrate without these political fanatics. The supposed cruelty of the enemy – which was real enough in some instances – justified the Wehrmacht's indiscriminate, systematic and wholesale resort to carnage. These measures were also quietly extended to so-called 'politruks', i.e. more lowly Party functionaries attached to individual companies.[83]

Since it was not unknown for lower-level officers to ignore the Commissar Order, and therefore for commissars to filter back into the POW camp system, in mid-July 1941 a conference was convened to deal with this problem, whose participants included General Reinecke and SS-Gruppenführer Müller of the Reich Security Main Office. Although the Abwehr representative Lieutenant-Colonel Lahousen mentioned both the ill-effects on military morale of the shooting of commissars (and the resultant effect upon Soviet readiness to capitulate), Reinecke argued that the officer corps had to abandon the ethics of the 'ice age' in favour of National Socialist values.[84] Sensing an opportunity, Müller volunteered the services of the SD both to identify potential victims and to kill them at one remove from the military. According to directives issued on 8 September, POW camp commandants and their intelligence officers were to co-operate with the SS security agencies. Profound objections to this were raised by the foreign branch of the Abwehr. It contravened international law; it would affect military discipline and morale; it would give the Russians a propaganda victory on a plate; and it would mean that the Wehrmacht would be formally responsible for people another agency was killing. Approving and covering these measures, Keitel explicitly rejected the Abwehr's hankering for outmoded 'chivalrous warfare'. These agreements and directives necessarily involved, and indeed stipulated, smooth co-operation between the POW camps and the SD. However, matters were not always so smooth in practice.

The general drift towards officially licensed, and potentially inflationary, criminality was rounded off by the broad brushwork of the 'Guidelines for the Conduct of the Troops in Russia' issued in May 1941, part of which read:

> This struggle requires ruthless and energetic action against Bolshevik agitators, guerrillas, saboteurs and Jews, and the total elimination of all active or passive resistance. The members of the Red Army – including prisoners – must be treated with extreme reserve and the greatest caution since one must reckon with devious methods of combat. The Asiatic soldiers of the Red Army in particular are devious, cunning and without feeling.[85]

These orders were fed down the chain by senior commanding officers, several of whom unreflectingly elided Jews with Bolshevism. Thus, on 2 May 1941, General Erich Hoepner, who would end his days in 1944 swaying from a length of piano wire because of involvement in the Bomb Plot, wrote:

> The war against Russia is an important chapter in the struggle for existence of the German nation. It is the old battle of Germanic against Slav peoples, of the defence of European culture against Muscovite-Asiatic inundation, and the repulse of Jewish-Bolshevism. The objective of this battle must be the destruction of present-day Russia and it must therefore be conducted with unprecedented severity. Every military action must be guided in planning and execution by an iron will to exterminate the enemy mercilessly and totally. In particular, no adherents of the present Russian-Bolshevik system are to be spared.[86]

Field-Marshal von Reichenau gave his directives a more explicitly hard-line anti-Semitic edge on 10 October 1941:

> The main aim of the campaign against the Jewish-Bolshevist system is the complete destruction of its forces and the extermination of the Asiatic influence in the sphere of European culture. As a result, the troops have to take on tasks which go beyond the conventional purely military ones. In the eastern sphere the soldier is not simply a fighter according to the rules of war, but the supporter of a ruthless racial ideology and the avenger of all the bestialities which have been inflicted on the German nation and those ethnic groups related to it. For this reason, the soldiers must show full understanding for the necessity for the severe but just atonement being required of the Jewish sub-humans.[87]

And so did Field-Marshal Manstein, who relayed Reichenau's orders to other armies in his group, or General Hoth, whom we have already encountered, who in November 1941 instructed his troops:

> Every sign of active or passive resistance or any sort of machinations on the part of Jewish-Bolshevik agitators are to be immediately and pitilessly exterminated . . . These circles are the intellectual supports of Bolshevism, the bearers of its murderous organisation, the helpmates of the partisans. It is the same Jewish class of beings who have done so much damage to our own Fatherland by virtue of their activities against the nation and civilisation, and who promote anti-German tendencies throughout the world, and who will be the harbingers of revenge. Their extermination is a dictate of our own survival.[88]

Estimates of how many commissars were killed range between 140,000 and 580,000.[89] That the Commissar Order was widely implemented is not doubted even by those who draw attention to low-level exceptions within larger military formations. The one alleged large-scale exception to this rule, namely General Hans-Jürgen von Arnim's 17th Panzer Division, is apparently contradicted by the evidence of his divisional record. Sometimes, moral indignation was combined with overt anti-Semitism – the two are not mutually exclusive – as reflected in the remarks of another Panzer officer, General Lemensen, regarding the shooting of prisoners of war, deserters and criminals:

> This is murder! The German Wehrmacht is waging this war against Bolshevism, but not against the united Russian peoples. We want to bring back peace, calm, and order to this land which has suffered terribly for many years from the oppression of a Jewish and criminal group . . . A Russian soldier who has been taken prisoner while wearing a uniform and after he put up a brave fight, has the right to decent treatment . . . This instruction does not change anything regarding the Führer's order on the ruthless action to be taken against partisans and Bolshevik commissars.[90]

On a lower level, there is evidence that individual officers disapproved of the ways in which the SS went about selecting political and racial 'undesirables' among prisoners of war. In November 1941, the commandant of Dulag 185 at Mogilev, Major Wittmer, refused to hand Jewish prisoners of war over to an Einsatzkommando, which resulted in a formal complaint from its commander to SS-Obergruppenführer Erich von dem Bach-Zelewski. The Major said that he had no orders to hand over Jews, and as far as he was concerned that ended the matter. He also disapproved of another of this SS officer's local initiatives, namely the instant liquidation of all young males who could not explain what they were doing on the roads on the grounds that they were a priori 'asocial' or 'partisans'. The SS officer conceded in his report that Wittmer had no hestitation in having mutinying Soviet prisoners summarily shot, but he needed to evince more ideological resolution on the 'Jewish Question'. Nothing appears to have come of his refusal to co-operate with the Einsatzkommando or of the complaint to Bach-Zelewski.[91] A further example of obvious Wehrmacht discomfort with the activities of the SS comes from Bavaria. Captain Wilhelm H. was an Abwehr officer in the POW camp Stalag VIIA at Moosburg between September 1939 and March 1944. In September 1941 he was instructed to co-operate with a team of Gestapo men from Munich who would be arriving to select victims from among the camp's 1,500 to 2,000 Russian prisoners. Asked by Wilhelm H. how he proposed to do this, given that he knew neither Russian nor anything about its political system, the Gestapo leader said that this was none of the Captain's business. What actually counted was numbers; the fulfulling of quotas, percentages and targets. Soon 200 Russians were en route to Dachau. The Gestapo leader later complained to another army officer, Major Meinel, that his men were psychologically finished by the shootings they had carried out, thus giving the game away as to the fate of the Russian prisoners in Dachau.[92]

We know relatively precisely what happened to Russian prisoners of war once they reached the concentration camps of Buchenwald, Dachau, Flossenbürg, Gross-Rosen, Mauthausen, Neuengamme, Sachsenhausen and Auschwitz. At Sachsenhausen, the Inspector of Concentration Camps Theodor Eicke explained to camp staff that Hitler had decreed that 18,000 Soviet commissars were to be shot in retaliation for shootings of German prisoners in Russia. They met their end in circumstances which reek of deviousness and moral squalor. A shower-room in one of the barracks was equipped with a height-measuring device whose sliding head-level concealed a slot through which prisoners were shot in the back of the neck by men concealed in a box behind the wall.[93] In Buchenwald, Russian captives were taken to a converted riding stables, undressed and led individually into a medical examination room. Blaring music from a gramophone drowned out the sound of what followed from the next group of victims. Members of 'Kommando 99', dressed in medical white, manoeuvered the victim to a measuring device through which concealed shooters killed them with a 7.65-millimetre pistol. Non-Russian prisoners then had precisely three minutes to remove the corpse and to hose down the walls and gutters. Each shooter killed eight people in succession (thus empyting their magazines), and the action only paused to allow for the clearing of the mortuary after every thirty-five to forty victims.[94] In Mauthausen, the Russians were issued with soap and towels and then gassed in pseudo-shower chambers, in Auschwitz or Gross-Rosen they were killed by an injection of phenol or hydrocyanic acid administered to the heart by doctors or medical orderlies. Other uses for Soviet prisoners included an incident at Shitomir in August 1941 when a group of them were shot with captured Red Army dum-dum bullets so that German military doctors could accurately observe, and write up, the effects of these munitions on the human body.[95]

Although no serious scholar contests the premeditated and systemic criminality of the war in Russia, it would obviously be misleading and unfair to argue that it was all-pervasive. Nine or ten million German men fought on the Eastern Front for more or less longer periods of time.

Their experiences were myriad: changing tank tracks and servicing engines; more or less passive and prosaic occupation duties; the nerve-racking pursuit of partisans in forests and swamps; intense fire-fights bringing and giving death or serious injury; captivity or desertion; as well as politically or racially motivated mass murder on a scale that is almost incomprehensible. One recent account stresses such factors as the general demodernisation of warfare on this front; the ways in which massive casualties destroyed the loyalties of micro, primary, groups, leaving soldiers with nothing to identify with other than the macro group of race and nation; the interplay between extremely harsh military discipline and the sanctioning of atrocities against civilians and enemy prisoners; and finally, the fact that 'Hitler's Army' had massively internalised the dictator's racist perspectives.[96] However, this does not explain why, for example, naval U-Boat crews seem to have evinced similar levels of fanaticism. Other accounts, which seek to correct an over-schematic translation of ideological fanaticism into action, themselves run the risk of distortion by highlighting essentially anecdotal instances of 'slipper soldiers', who having lost all vestiges of martial bearing or purpose, sat by the stove drinking vodka with the local partisan commanders.[97]

Accounts which stress ideological motivation begin with the degeneration of a modern mobile war into one of demodernised attrition in conditions that resembled the Western Front in 1914–18. Casualty rates were also enormous. During the first six months of fighting, the Ostheer lost three-quarters of a million men, rising to a million casualties by March 1942, of whom a quarter were killed or missing. The crack Gross Deutschland Regiment began the campaign 6,000 strong; by the end of 1941 it had sustained 4,070 casualties; by February 1942 it consisted of three officers and thirty other ranks. By December 1941, 6th and 7th Panzer Divisions consisted of respectively 180 and 200 men, while 18th Panzer Division numbered four infantry battalions.[98] Such massive casualty rates meant that formations increasingly consisted of hurriedly assembled strangers lacking the close regional or social bonds which normally knitted soldiers together. In the face of obvious enemy superiority in generalship, materials and manpower, the German troops were held together by ferocious military discipline that punished even minor infractions, let alone desertion, panic or self-mutilation, by firing squad. Some 15,000 men were executed by court martial on the Eastern Front, with hundreds of thousands more sentenced to penal battalions or terms of imprisonment. This should be contrasted with the forty and 100 British and French soldiers respectively executed during the Second World War.[99]

Compensation for draconian combat discipline consisted of virtual licence to do with others what one liked. German troops practised self-help by simply stealing food, livestock, draught animals, wagons, clothing and felt boots, regardless of the hardships this entailed for the civilian population. Even the pack animals were fed with the straw from the roofs of peasant houses. They also indiscriminately looted the contents of houses, as is evident from a report in November 1941 from Rear Area 582: 'The items stolen include, for example, handscarves, cushion covers, tablecloths, handtowels, men's trousers, curtain material, men's jackets, all types of cloth, men's coats, bedspreads, samovars, wristwatches, children's underwear and clothing, mourning-dress, women's and children's shoes, women's clothing, ladies' underwear, etc.'[100] In some places, the scale of what vanished suggests a form of organised criminality. Thus in Vitebsk during late 1941, 188 cows were stolen, as well as 15 tonnes of salt, and a million sheets of plywood. In other places the military vandalised plant and machinery, or destroyed such resources as fish stocks by fishing with hand grenades, in what were forms of delinquency. The slightest resistance was dealt with by extreme violence.

Military brutality was also influenced by the conditioning these soldiers had undergone both while growing up in Nazi Germany, and in the form of ideological instruction during their time in the army. Although one should exercise due caution when discussing such a vast number of men, from different backgrounds, generations and political or religious persuasions, it would be surprising if many of them did not ardently believe in Volk, Reich and Führer, in Germany's superior right of conquest and dominance, or in the inferiority (racial or cultural) of other peoples. Such sentiments were common to many peoples at the time, and it is both anachronistic and a form of inverse racism to imagine that Germans (or others) were somehow immune to it. Nor did the Germans have a monopoly of hatred of the enemy. In a 1942 article entitled 'The Justification of Hatred', the Soviet war correspondent Ilya Ehrenburg proved adept at the dehumanising stereotyping of the enemy:

> This war is unlike former wars. For the first time our people face not men but cruel and vile monsters, savages equipped with every technically perfected weapon, scum acting according to rule and quoting science, who have turned the massacre of babies into the last word of state wisdom. Hatred has not come easily to us . . . We hate the Nazis because we love our country, the people, humanity. In this lies the strength of our hatred and also its justification. When we encounter the Fascists we realize how blind hatred has laid waste the soul of Germany. That kind of hatred is alien to us. We hate every Nazi for being the representative of a man-hating principle, we hate him for the widow's tears, for the crippled childhood of the orphans, for the pitiable hordes of refugees, for the trampled fields, for the annihilation of millions of lives. We are fighting not men but automata in human likeness. Our hatred of them is the stronger because outwardly they appear to be men, because they can laugh and pat a dog or a horse, because in their diaries they indulge in self-analysis, because they are disguised as human beings, as civilised Europeans.[101]

What distinguishes this account from its German analogues is firstly, that the Russians had to unlearn their received respect for German cultural and technological superiority, as symbolised by Ehrenburg's own story of a group of collective farmers marvelling at a captured German cigarette lighter in the shape of a revolver: 'That's culture!'; and secondly, that Ehrenburg was careful to differentiate between Nazis and Germans, hoping indeed that 'The German people will also live, once purged of the hideous crimes of the Nazi decade.' The Germans had no respect for Russian civilisation and intended to, and did, kill millions of them. Such distinctions mattered.

It is certainly not hard to find evidence of the 'Herrenmensch' mentality among the ordinary German soldiery, especially if one looks in quasi-official Nazi compilations of opinion. Collections of letters from soldiers recycled for propaganda purposes are unsurprisingly suffused with racism, as for example when a private wrote home in August 1941:

> What would have happened to cultural Europe, had these sons of the Steppe, poisoned and drunk with a destructive poison, these incited sub-humans, invaded our beautiful Germany? Endlessly we thank our Führer, with love and loyalty, the saviour and historical figure.

A lance corporal wrote:

> Only a Jew can be a Bolshevik, for this blood-sucker there can be nothing nicer than to be a Bolshevik . . . Wherever one spits one finds a Jew . . . As far as I know . . . not a single Jew has worked in the

> workers' paradise, everyone, even the smallest blood-sucker, has a post where he naturally enjoys great privileges.[102]

The close identity of these letters with crude Nazi racial hatreds and their relentless uniformity of outlook should give us pause for thought. Letters recently discovered in Moscow, which came from captured German military post offices, prisoners of war or the dead, speak a different, more personal language, as they thought about their families or the prospect of violent death in the weak light of candle-lit bunkers.

The overwhelming majority of these letters, many of them painstakingly written by men for whom grammar, spelling and the articulation of emotion were an unaccustomed effort, were concerned with what was happening at home. These men did not write about Jews or any Russian civilians; they wanted news from their parents, wives, girlfriends, siblings and children, or they imaginatively recreated what they were themselves missing. When they discussed the war, this largely took the form of describing physical exertions and privations such as forced marches, lack of food and shelter or problems of personal hygiene. The enemy did not figure especially large in these descriptions, except as an unwelcome element of danger that periodically intruded into the permanent quest for food and warmth. In a letter to a friend called Ludwig, dated 18 November 1942, a soldier called Ernst gave a vivid account of life in a hut in the suburbs of Stalingrad:

> Dear Ludwig
> The spectre of the Russian winter has not yet appeared – perhaps it is still on the way from the far Kirghiz steppe? We can still take −16 degrees. The day before yesterday it snowed for the first time, while tonight the wind turned a downpour to ice. I ventured out today – it was classic – like going skating. Nothing much was missing, and a vehicle had fallen into a ditch.
>
> Thank God, the onset of cold weather means we've seen the back of swarms of flies. It still hums with them, however these 'flies' are not affected by the seasons, and the Bolsheviks certainly not.
>
> We've taken up quarters in a hotly contested suburb of Stalingrad. Hopefully we'll spend the winter in solid huts, which we are doing up. First, we've given the hovels a thorough clean, since dirt is considered a social virtue in this paradise. We've hammered and sawed away, swinging the paint brush too, so that the interior now seems pleasant. The stove gives out a cosy warmth. We sit here in our corner in the evening, which makes being here bearable.
>
> As soon as we moved into the hut, the guerrilla war against lice and fleas commenced in earnest. How it itches and pinches, creeps

> and crawls, burning your skin when the enemy attacks. Each morning begins with a battle of extermination, and then all through the day tearing one's shirt away from the body to hunt them more freely. It's impossible to get rid of these brutes, despite washing.
>
> Naturally I am flabbergasted about Willi. Presumably he's got engaged in the meantime? He's surely met the love of his life. 'She may be late in coming, but she comes nevertheless.' Doubtless he will have to give up some of his dearest old customs. I doubt whether his intended will be able to handle beer late into the evening. Dear Ludwig, send my best wishes to Willi. I wish him all happiness with his beloved.[103]

Having covered the weather, sledging, fleas and Willi's amours, Ernst turned to the Russians. His comments on 'Der Russe' were not without an element of grudging admiration:

> Stalingrad still hasn't fallen. You may well have been wondering about that. We don't since we are hard by the edge of events. The Russian fights ferociously over every meter. Naturally, Stalin has deployed his elite troops here, i.e. almost exclusively political commissars and officers. They each have to be done to death. And also the Russians have a masterly grasp of how to camouflage and defend themselves in the ruins of the city. This battle has already cost much blood. Still, by the end of this year, the west bank will have been cleaned out.

As the war progressed, the predominant sentiment was to return home alive. As Herbert wrote to his parents in January 1943:

> I will be pleased if I don't see this thrice damned Russia ever again, since in time it is enough to finish off anyone. Like almost all of my comrades I only have one wish: to get out of this workers' paradise and never to hear of it or see it again. We all have only one desire: peace and quiet and enough to eat, and then they can all kiss our arses.[104]

Others reflected on life, death and salvation in what amounted to pre-combat final testaments. In January 1942 a soldier called Sim wrote to his sister Duna about matters he did not wish to share with his pregnant wife Lotte lest it adversely affect her health. Recently transferred to combat duties, this deeply religious man wrote:

> There is a reason why I am writing this letter to you, in the eventuality that God does not pass me by with the bitter chalice of death, for then, as soon as you receive the news, you can relay this letter as my farewell greeting above all to Lotte, but also to all the others . . . Believe in Jesus Christ – there is no one else who can remove the sting of dying. God knows, how very close I am to Lotte and Klaus. It feels like a sword going through my heart when I think about you all, and

> that I may not see you again, and what distress Lotte and you will feel, what bitterness, and grief! . . . But I know that if we do not see each other on Earth again, we will see each other when Jesus Christ summons us to the last judgement. I need to say all this to you, both to remind and warn you not to dismiss this message out of hand, never betraying our Lord, and living according to how the Lord of life and death set down in the scriptures. If this is not the case, then we will never see each other again, then death will really be a hideous visage, and then one's entire life will have been a pointless egotistical struggle.[105]

The military campaigns in the Soviet Union were the means to realise a vision of territorial expansion which would bring both long-term economic security and perpetual racial renewal. Of course, there were many different emphases, and indeed, variant visions which were much more pragmatically sensitive to circumstances in the Soviet Union. The political influence exerted by their proponents, and such similarly labile factors as the course of the war, also affected German debates about the future of the occupied eastern territories. Although some historians have concentrated on the 'modernising' destructive fantasies of sundry middle-echelon technocratic planners, it is important to remember that other Germans (not least in the military) had quite a subtle grasp of the political realities of the Soviet Union, and advocated other policies. Curiously enough, a recent exhibition in Hamburg devoted to German military criminality particularly in the Soviet Union, while assuming the liberal moral high ground towards the old soldiers, itself subconsciously mirrored the Nazis' treatment of that country as an 'object', by reducing the Russians to 'victims', and totally ignoring such themes as collaboration between certain nationalities and the Germans, or those in the army who advocated more pragmatic alternative policies. No doubt the crimes of the Wehrmacht should be de-mythologised in this fashion, but – provided we are all clear on these moral essentials – does this have to be at the cost of nuance and an understanding of conditions in the Soviet Union?[106]

Hitler's views on Russia were characteristically unsubtle. Judging from his *Table Talk*, the record of his nightly ruminations on prehistoric dogs, an Aryan Jesus or such random *obiter dicta* as 'tarts adore poachers', delivered to a largely captive audience, Hitler was simultaneously drawn to, and repelled by, 'the east', that shorthand term for that undifferentiated vastness that lay beyond Germany's eastern border before 'it' metamorphosed into the Orient. His constructive fantasies included vast roads raised on ridges so that the icy winds would clear the snow, while the traffic passed Kreis's tenebrous monuments to the (German) dead; or double-decker trains speeding carefree German Labour Front holiday-makers to the beach resorts of the Black Sea. The 'space' would be settled and shaped by veteran soldier-farmers from Germany, together with Danish, Dutch, Norwegian and Swedish settlers in the north 'by special arrangement'. The settlers were to enjoy large farms; officialdom handsome headquarters; with 'palaces' for the regional governors. German colonial society would be a literal and metaphorical 'fortress', closed to outsiders, since 'the least of our stable-lads must be superior to any native'. The negative features of this vision predominated, with crassness co-mingled with callousness. Although Hitler repeatedly and explicitly took British rule in India as his exemplar – 'Our role in Russia will be analogous to that of England in India . . . The Russian space is our India. Like the English, we shall rule this empire with a handful of men' – his notion of colonial rule was like something he had read in a lurid book about the more squalid British (or German) African colonies than about centuries of complex British involvement in the sub-Continent, which left its imprint on everything from cuisine to cricket.[107] The Russians were 'a mass of born slaves, who feel the need of a master'. Outsiders (i.e. the Germans) had introduced the principle of organised society to peoples accustomed to behaving in the antisocial manner of 'rabbits'.[108] A lack of civilisation was to be encouraged: 'no vaccination for the Russians, and no soap to get the dirt off them . . . But let them have all the spirits and tobacco they want.'[109] Callousness and crude exploitation characterise virtually everything Hitler said about Russia. On 17 October 1941 he remarked: 'We're not going to play at children's nurses: we're absolutely without obligations as far as these people are concerned. To struggle against the hovels, chase away the fleas, provide German teachers, bring out newspapers – very little of that for us! . . . For the rest, let them know just enough to understand our highway signs, so that they won't get themselves run over by our vehicles!'[110] Economic intercourse would be of the most rudimentary kind, a matter of scarves and glass beads for the natives: 'At harvest time we will set up markets at all the centres of any importance. There we will buy up all the cereals and fruit, and sell the more trashy products of our own manufacture . . . Our agricultural machinery factories, our transport companies, our manufacturers of household goods and so forth will find there an enormous market for their goods. It will also be a splendid market for cheap cotton goods – the more brightly coloured the better. Why should we thwart the longing of these people for bright colours?'[111] Future rebellions would be suppressed by dropping 'a few bombs on their cities'; while, *mutatis mutandis*, every year a 'troop of Kirghizes' would be paraded through Berlin 'to strike their imaginations with the size of our monuments'.[112] Although there was nothing here except a desire to destroy, exploit and overawe, this 'vision' would set the parameters for policy in occupied Russia.

A crucial meeting held on 16 July 1941 between Hitler, Bormann, Göring, Lammers, Keitel and Rosenberg illustrates the deciding voice of Hitler in questions of major policy. The meeting ran from three in the afternoon until eight at night with one break for coffee. Hitler began by expressing his annoyance with a Vichy newspaper which had had the temerity to suggest that the invasion was a 'European war', the implication being that there would also be European dividends for the clients of the victors. He insisted that there was no need to make German goals explicit, 'the important thing is that we ourselves know what it is we want'. There were to be no self-limiting public declarations of policy, 'all the necessary measures – shootings, resettlement etc. – we will and can do despite this'. There was to be no 'seesaw policy' (*Schaukelpolitik*), but rather the remorseless pursuit of a single goal, permanent German hegemony and the eradication of any other military power west of the Urals. He had learned this single-mindedness from the English, who in India also showed how they never staked all on any given indigenous ruler. No Slav, Chechen, Cossack or Ukrainian was to be allowed to carry a gun. In this 'Garden of Eden' bombers would suppress revolts, and any Slav who even looked askance at a German could be shot dead. Keitel and Göring joined in the tough talk. Göring brushed aside Rosenberg's interjections about culture and the universities of Kiev as fripperies which got in the way of the primordial quest for food; Keitel spoke of individual and collective reprisals for sloppiness or failure to prevent acts of sabotage. Control visibly slipped away from Rosenberg as more forceful players messed up his personnel plans for the dominion he notionally ruled as Minister for the Occupied Eastern Territories. Thanks to Göring, and Hitler who made the final dispositions, the lapsarian Marxist Erich 'the Red' Koch, rather than Sauckel, was despatched to the Ukraine.[113]

Although, in practice, this was the only game in town, it is of more than academic interest to explore other possible options. Describing the latter as 'alternatives' would be to misconstrue entirely the balance of forces within the Nazi 'polycracy', or the shared goal of permanent German dominance.[114] Some players displayed a greater understanding of the unpopularity of Soviet rule or of the profound ethnic and religious fissures in many parts of that vast empire than was evident in this discussion. There were also diplomatic considerations, such as Finnish fellow-feeling for the Estonians, or Turkish concern for the (Moslem) peoples of the Caucasus which influenced German policy in these areas around the margins.[115] Some German policy-makers also thought in terms of driving a wedge between the Kremlin and the Russian population along the lines of the slogan 'Liberation, not Conquest'. Others shared Hitler's rampant Russophobia, but combined this with an appreciation of the ethnic heterogeneity of the Soviet Union. Rosenberg envisaged a protectorate over Lithuania, Latvia, Estonia and Belarus; an enlarged and notionally independent Ukraine; some sort of Caucasian federation; and, corralled by this cordon sanitaire, a revived, but reduced, 'Muscovy', whose expansionary dynamic would be redirected towards Asia and which would serve as a dumping ground for 'undesirables'.[116]

The Ukraine has had a bad reputation in western circles fixated with a few thousand Ukrainian SS men but ignorant of, or indifferent to, what happened to its huge population during the Second World War, which included the destruction of 700 cities and towns and 28,000 villages and the deaths of nearly seven million people, including virtually all Jews. The former Soviet Union (aided by 'Nazi-hunters' in the American Office of Special Investigations) eagerly fostered the wholesale criminalisation of Ukrainian exiles, largely because until 1953 it had to contend with Ukrainian nationalist guerrilla fighters, with whom it liked to think the exiles were linked in a common 'imperialist' plot. In 1945, 27,000 Red Army soldiers and policemen were deployed in the Ukraine to crush what amounted to an anti-Soviet revolt.

Any residual goodwill towards the Germans in the Ukraine, whether from émigré separatists or peasants offering bread, salt and flowers, and prompted in the western Ukraine by the experience of eighteen months of Soviet occupation, including the deportation of 1.2 million Poles, was rapidly squandered as these representatives of a higher culture behaved as 'Herrenmenschen'. Although various German agencies had long-standing contacts with Ukrainian émigrés, for example the

Abwehr with Mel'nyk and Bandera's respective branches of the Organisation of Ukrainian Nationalists (OUN), Hitler's scepticism towards these circles (probably justified given the extent of NKVD penetration) resulted in the paradox that they were banned from even entering the occupied areas. When Bandera's supporters tried to declare a Ukrainian state centred on L'vov on the back of the German invasion, this lasted all of a week, with Bandera himself being arrested and sent to Germany. Galicia did not become the kernel of a Ukrainian state, but rather a province added to the German-ruled Polish Generalgouvernement. In order to nullify Polish statehood through the promotion of ethnic rivalries, Galician-Ukrainian cultural autonomy was encouraged by the Germans, while paradoxically it was ruthlessly repressed in rump Ukraine itself. Parts of the Ukraine were handed over to Romania, and Koch set up shop in the small town of Rivne rather than Kiev to underline the nullity of Ukrainian statehood. From 1942 onwards, the peasantry of the western Ukraine flocked to the Ukrainian Insurgent Army (UPA), fighting a complex triangular war against the Germans and Soviet and Polish partisans, a war which was still going on eight years after liberation happened in western Europe.[117]

In the Baltic States of Estonia, Latvia and Lithuania, the Germans similarly encountered peoples with massive grievances against the Soviet Union. During their occupation of the Baltic States between 1940 and 1941, the Soviets killed or deported an estimated 34,250 Latvians, nearly 60,000 Estonians and 75,000 Lithuanians in the interests of 'Sovietising' these subtly distinctive societies.[118] Harking back to an ahistorical version of the Hansa and the Teutonic Knights, the Nazis thought in terms of 'Germanising' the 'racially suitable' members of the indigenous population, coupled with extensive German colonisation and the deportation of 'undesirables'. Those nationalists who thought the Germans had come as liberators were rapidly disabused. On 24 June 1941, after German tanks had arrived in the night, Lithuanian nationalists in Vilnius established a Citizens' Committee in anticipation of independence. A rather irritated German official reported to Lieutenant-General Wilhelm Schubert that the nationalists were acting as if they were 'absolutely equal partners in the territory liberated from the Russians' and 'as if the Germans had only gone to war with the Russians in order to liberate Lithuania and to grant it independence'. The official had rapidly disabused a certain

Professor Jurgutis (the Foreign Minister of former Lithuania) of any dreams of independence, sharply reminding him who was boss.[119] As German casualties in the east mounted, the issue of enhanced Baltic autonomy and future independence became intertwined with the establishment of Baltic SS units, with the Latvians and Estonians offering to co-operate in return for political concessions. The latter came to nought.

German rule in occupied Soviet territory consisted of areas of military and civilian control. Behind the front lines, with a depth of 15–25 kilometres, lay the 'Army Rear Areas' of another fifty or so kilometres, and then 100 kilometres more of the 'Army Group Rear Areas'. Military occupation policy varied greatly depending on the officers in charge, the attitude and composition of the population, and whether German interests were short- or long-range, extensive or limited. Thus, in Army Group Centre's Rear Area officers such as Schlabrenndorff, Gersdorff or Tresckow actually rebuilt primary and specialised schools, while in the Caucasus, where Hitler's interest was limited to oil, officers slipped into place by Stauffenberg at the High Command of the German Army (OKH) restored religious freedom to Buddhists, Muslims and Orthodox Christians, while accelerating the conversion of the *kolkhozy* into co-operatives.[120] Lest one purveys too roseate an impression of military rule, it is important to remember that the concessions to minorities were not extended to Gypsies, Jews or the mentally ill, who were systematically slaughtered, or to the surrounding Slavic populations, who along with the non-Russian minorities, were subjected to the full depredations of an army that lived off what they produced.

Behind these necessarily labile layers of military administration lay two vast civilian-controlled Reich Commissariats, notionally subordinated to Rosenberg's Berlin-based Ostministerium (OMi), whose sobriquet *Cha-ostministerium* reflected its improvised incoherence. Rosenberg was only notionally in control of either Koch in Rivne (or rather Königsberg, where he preferred to reside) or Heinrich Lohse in Riga, since these unreconstructed Party bullies enjoyed direct access to Hitler. Screaming sessions and the construction of coalitions to outdo one another at the highest level characterised the relationship between Koch and Rosenberg, a relationship mirrored in the Baltic in the simultaneous feud between Lohse and his nominal subordinate in Tallin, Generalkommissar Litzmann. Further inroads into Rosenberg's fictive empire were made by Göring's multinational economic agency; Sauckel's control of forced labour procurement; Speer's munitions apparatus; and Himmler's grim racial warriors, the Higher SS- and Police Leaders whose orders came directly from Berlin. The quality of the German administration in the field was not high, with a huge influx of abrasive bullies and losers from the more populist branches of the National Socialist German Workers' Party (NSDAP), who were accurately described by the term 'Ostnieten' or 'eastern nobodies'. Guidelines telling them how to behave are instructive. Germany lacked England's long imperial tradition of transforming young people into 'Führernaturen'. The Germans were to be 'comradely among themselves, responsible to their superiors, and authoritarian towards their subordinates'. One must not explain oneself to a Russian for 'he can talk better than you since he is a born dialectician and has inherited a philosophical disposition', and Germans should conceal their own mistakes. The Russians were effeminate and sentimental, thus explaining why they had pleaded with every foreign conqueror 'Come and rule over us!' The Germans were to show no weakness, either in the form of tears or convivial over-indulgence, and were to be totally impervious to either 'charm' or 'corruption, denunciation and byzantinism'. The Russian could stand just about anything: 'since his stomach is flexible, no false pity'. It was no use whining to superiors, instead: 'Help yourself, then God will help you!'[121] The reality of occupation officialdom was far removed from these injunctions to personal austerity. Modestly endowed German bureaucrats could strut about, whip in hand, among the 'natives' or 'niggers' as Koch called them. Secretaries in the bloated administrative capitals enjoyed salaries that were three times those of an army lieutenant. Corruption was rife, with the Ukraine becoming the 'junk market of the Reich'. German officials and their families acted as conduits for commodities such as salt, cheap jewellery, unfashionable shoes and garish dresses sent by their relatives in the Reich, which were then exchanged with the Ukrainians for eggs, oil, bacon, ham and so on, and despatched, illegally, via rail or post back to the Reich.[122] In the sticks, 14,000 agricultural leaders – as these upwardly mobile former farmers were called – braved the partisans in order to be mistranslated by their interpreters, or misled by Soviet collective farm functionaries and resentful Russian peasants.[123]

Germany had gone to war with one of the most ethnically and confessionally diverse societies in the world. This fact was potentially encouraging. Although half the Soviet population were ethnic Russians, and three-quarters Slavs, the remaining quarter of the Soviet Union's population consisted of over 100 different nationalities. Many of these peoples had substantive grievances against the Soviet regime, regarding Lenin's guarantees of national autonomy as worthless. A few examples must suffice. In the Ukraine, scene of the greatest horrors brought about by collectivisation, the NKVD massacred thousands of nationalist prisoners held in their prisons and concentration camps shortly before the Germans arrived. Further south, the Crimean Tatar Muslim clergy and intelligentsia were decimated in the 1920s and 1930s in an anti-intellectual and anti-clerical campaign, while between 30,000 and 40,000 peasants were deported in the interests of collectivisation.[124] The ethnically heterogeneous, yet distinctive, Cossacks were closely identified by the Bolsheviks with the Tsarist and White regimes, and hence were subjected to policies whose effect was to destroy their traditional way of life. Similarly repressive policies were pursued by the Bolsheviks towards the nomadic Mongolian Kalmyk herdsmen. The regime enforced sedentarisation, substituting clay huts for tents, while reducing individual ownership of livestock (a mark of social prestige) from treble to single figures. 5,000 Kalmyk intellectuals were liquidated, including the poet Amur-Sanan, and their Buddhist monasteries and temples were closed and pillaged. In the summer of 1942, the NKVD helped themselves to two million cattle, with Kalmyk guerrilla groups formed shortly afterwards to prevent this.[125] Surely there was a legacy of hatred here which any invader could build on?

Initially, Hitler was adamant in his opposition to using indigenous forces, other than as 'Hiwis' or auxiliary volunteers, who were simply integrated as non-combatant supply troops. The steady depletion of the German army in Russia gradually brought about a change in policy regarding eastern combat forces, promoted by more enlightened officers in Foreign Armies East of the Wehrmacht High Command, such as Reinhard Gehlen, Alexis von Roenne, Wilfried Strick-Strickfeldt and Stauffenberg who realised that the war in Russia also had to have a political dimension. Local commanders also improvised contingents of 'eastern troops'. Beginning with a directive dated 17 December 1941, six national legions were formed, of Armenians, Azerbaijani, Georgians, North Caucasians, Turkestanis and Volga Tatars, consisting of fifteen battalions in late 1942 and another twenty-one battalions in early 1943.[126] There was also a 3,000-strong Kalmyk cavalry corps.

This came about largely through the commitment of individual German officers, such as the forty-year-old former architect Dr Doll, whose swastika armband apparently reminded his Kalmyk troops of a Buddhist health symbol and who encouraged the Kalmyk rich in Elitsa to feed their poorer compatriots. Mayoral elections were held in Kalmyk settlements, collectivisation was immediately terminated, and individuals were allowed to own as much livestock as they wished. Their military effectiveness was limited to intelligence-gathering and detecting acts of sabotage. Judging from reports on their daily activities, the Kalmyks' forte was checking railway lines for loosened or missing ties and concealed explosive charges which they then notified to the nearest German authorities, thus averting massive German military casualties. Following Doll's death in July 1944, the Kalmyks were absorbed into a Caucasian formation of the Waffen-SS.[127] The Waffen-SS indeed became the leading, if reluctant, supporter of indigenous forces, with its depleted ranks being more than replenished with Latvians, Estonians and, from 1943 onwards, Ukrainians, in the revealingly named SS Volunteer Division 'Galicia'. The SS also assumed control of 238,000 indigenous auxiliary police and anti-partisan forces in the two Reichkommissariats, providing them with ideological instruction in the notorious Trawnicki training base near Lublin. One of these SS-backed groups – the Brigade Druzhina – which took part in Operation Kottbus under former Red Army Lieutenant-Colonel Vladimir Rodionov, subsequently slaughtered its German component and then redefected en masse to the Soviets.

Cossack troops were sporadically deployed on the Eastern Front by the Germans from the summer of 1941 onwards. The German 14th Panzer Corps was perplexed to discover that the Soviet 9th Army they were attacking was being simultaneously assaulted by a mysterious force situated in their rear. This turned out to be Nicholas Nazarenko's Don Cossacks. A survivor of Soviet labour camps, Nazarenko indignantly told the Germans who wished to disarm his troops that he had been fighting the Bolsheviks since 1918. Another Cossack, Major Ivan Kononov, persuaded the entire Soviet 436th Regiment to desert to the Germans, largely it seems because the Bolsheviks had hanged his father and shot his mother during the last stages of the First World War. Keeping Cossack émigré leaders at arm's length, lest they seek substantive political changes, the Germans appointed one of their own as overall commander of Cossack forces. Helmuth von Pannwitz had grown up within sight of Tsarist Cossack troops on the Russo-German Polish border. A professional cavalry officer and Freikorps veteran, Pannwitz served with enormous distinction on the Eastern Front and was rewarded with the task of organising the disparate Cossack hosts. Apart from the support of Kleist and Zeitzler, Pannwitz found an unlikely ally in the shape of the SS whose race 'experts' now decided that the Cossacks were not Slavs but misplaced 'Aryan' Goths. Based at Mielau in East Prussia, Pannwitz oganised a Cossack Division, replete with such exotic Atamans as Nicholas Kulakov, who, having lost both legs during the Civil War in 1920, spent the next twenty years in hiding under his own house, carving wooden legs, until his liberation by German forces. The Cossack Division was then entrained for Yugoslavia to fight the Balkan manifestation of the Bolshevik menace.[128]

But collaboration was far from being the exclusive preserve of either non-Russian or marginalised Slav ethnic groups such as the Cossacks. Only very recently have Russian historians begun to explore the realities of occupation that lurked behind the self-serving ideology of the Great Patriotic War. An untold number of communist officials simply switched allegiances in a predictable demonstration of how an amoral prediliction for control, power and terror outweighed any nominal ideological antipathy.[129] About one million Russians also had varying degrees of involvement with the German armed forces, the majority being unarmed auxiliaries or 'Hiwis' after their German acronym, but with up to a quarter of a million as combat troops, some of which we have already encountered. The most notorious instance of collaboration with the Germans is associated with General Vlasov and the Committee for the Liberation of the Peoples of Russia.

Andrei Andreyevich Vlasov was born in 1900, into a peasant family with thirteen children. As he wrote in his 'Open Letter' of March 1943, Vlasov was a typical product of the Soviet system, who had not been personally 'harmed' by it in any way. He served in the Red Army during the Civil War, rising quickly through the ranks to the post of company commander. He joined the Communist Party in 1930, and in 1938 was sent to China to promote the Soviet dual strategy of support for Chiang Kai-shek against the Japanese, and for the communists against their own ally. He bravely commanded Soviet forces during the breakout from Kiev and then in the defence of Moscow. On 24 January 1942 he was promoted to Lieutenant-General and awarded the Order of the

Red Banner. In the spring he was despatched to the Volkhov Front, to command the 2nd Shock Army which was intended to relieve the pressure on Leningrad. High level disagreements about precisely who was in charge of the Front resulted in the encirclement of Vlasov's troops who were then poorly supplied and forbidden to withdraw. Ordering his troops to disperse and survive as best as they could, Vlasov himself spent weeks wandering around in a forest.

Before his capture by the Germans in a hut on 12 July 1942, Vlasov probably turned over in his mind the factors which made him collaborate. According to the 'Open Letter':

> I realised that none of those things for which the Russian people had fought during the Civil War had been achieved by Bolshevik victory. I saw what a difficult life a Russian worker led and how the peasant was forcibly driven to join the collective farms. Millions of Russian people disappeared, having been arrested and shot without trial. I saw everything Russian was being destroyed, that time-servers were being given positions of command in the Red Army, people to whom the interests of the Russian nation were of no importance.[130]

He had also accumulated many negative impressions of Stalin's Russia, including people deported as kulaks for owning a cow; the lies one was supposed to live for the sake of personal advancement; the faces missing from the officer corps when he returned from China; and finally, the lives expended on the Volkhov Front, and the fate awaiting any commander who had lost an army. Far from being an unreconstructed reactionary (anti-Semitism was after all something he shared with Stalin), Vlasov wrote that he wanted to 'complete the national revolution'.

Detained in a VIP camp at Vinnitsa in the Ukraine, Vlasov had a series of meetings with high-level German officials who were drawn to Vlasov's suggestion of a Russian National Army to liberate the country from Stalinism. Paradoxically, many of these prisoners thought that they had more freedom in a Nazi prison camp than they had as free men in the Soviet Union. Although German military propagandists were mainly interested in using Vlasov's name to encourage desertion from the Red Army, sympathetic German 'minders', notably Strick-Strickfeldt, indulged Vlasov's growing political ambitions by organising both the distribution of his Smolensk Declaration and the speaking tours of the occupied areas. The Smolensk Declaration was a curious combination of anti-Stalinism, liberal reform proposals and misrepresentation of Nazi policy. The guiding thoughts were eternal friendship and peace with honour with Germany, and happiness for the Russian people. Bolshevism and Stalinism were not only held responsible for the recent military disasters, but in an eccentric inversion of Marxist agentail theories of fascism, were represented as being the instruments of Anglo-American capitalists bent on the economic spoliation of Russia. The description of Nazi goals in Russia was partial in the extreme:

> Germany, meanwhile, is not waging war against the Russian people and their Motherland, but only Bolshevism. Germany does not wish to encroach on the living space of the Russian people or on their national and political liberties. Adolf Hitler's National Socialist Germany aims to organise a 'New Europe' without Bolsheviks and Capitalists, in which every nation is guaranteed an honourable place.[131]

The 'New Russia' would be constructed on the basis of the abolition of the kolkhozy; the restoration of private commerce and ownership; freedom of thought; social justice; and workers' rights that were to include employment, education, leisure and an untroubled old age. Attempts to convert these heady goals into reality with a Russian Liberation Army were stymied by the hostility of Hitler and Himmler to the idea of arming Slavs, a view apparently confirmed by high desertion rates among existing eastern troops. Himmler seems also to have been incensed by a remark from Vlasov, whom he called 'a Bolshevik butcher's apprentice', to the effect that he would soon be playing host to the Germans in Russia. Vlasov was put on ice, in slightly sordid union with his second (bigamous) wife, the widow of an SS officer. As far as Hitler was concerned, the only legitimate function for Vlasov or the Red Army officers in the camp at Dabendorf was to encourage desertions from the enemy. This was quite literally so in the run up to 'Citadelle', where for weeks the latter were deployed in Operation Silver Lining, broadcasting to their compatriots through loudspeakers so powerful that they could be heard miles away. Hitler clearly saw that if he allowed Vlasov an army, the latter would use this to lever political concessions which totally contradicted Nazi war aims in Russia. The worsening situation on the Eastern Front at least changed Himmler's mind. He met Vlasov in September 1944 and, favourably impressed by this tall and rather unworldly figure, authorised him to form a division of Russian troops and to publish a manifesto. This was made public in Prague, the last Slav city in German hands, although no prominent Nazi leaders turned up for the ceremony. In January 1945, Vlasov was given command of two severely depleted divisions which he wished to preserve for a future Anglo-American war on Soviet communism, but which the Nazis regarded as cannon fodder. Vlasov was detained by the Red Army while trying to reach American lines, and after torture and a perfunctory trial in camera was hanged as a traitor in post-war Moscow. Broadly speaking, while the Nazis were willing, opportunistically, to exploit 'native' forces to make up for their own loss of manpower, this never translated into a change of policy towards the occupied Soviet Union. This does not lessen the personal tragedy of Vlasov and his supporters, who through choice and force of circumstances, had to operate in the unforgiving zone between two murderous dictatorships.

Economic and military necessity, as well as ideological rigidity, also stalled attempts to reform the Bolshevik socio-economic order in ways which might have appealed to the mass of the indigenous population. As we have seen, Hitler's conception of future German–Russian economic relations was based upon colonial exploitation. Practical concerns ensured that there was no more than cosmetic tinkering with the institution of the collective farm or *kolkhoz*, while the state farms (*sovkhozy*) and tractor depots were simply taken over by the Germans. Crudely executed Russian-language propaganda posters depicted happy peasants liberated by German arms from the burden of collectivisation, entering with outstretched arms into a fabular world of 'the free farmer on his own land'.[132] In reality, decollectivisation, with all of the decentralisation and dislocation that entailed would have massively complicated access to food, one of the reasons why the Bolsheviks had introduced collectivisation in the first place. As State Secretary Backe, one of the most vocal opponents of reform, remarked, if the Soviets had not established collective farms, the Germans would have had to have done it for them. Not everyone shared this view. A loose and heterogeneous group of pragmatists, consisting of diplomats, economists and intelligence officers, recognised the danger of alienating the rural population and pressed for reforms. These were eventually implemented on paper. The Agrarian Decree issued in February 1942 was an unsatisfactory compromise between these opposed views. It simply renamed the *kolkhozy* as *obshchinnoe khoziaistvo* (communal economies) which in an uncanny echo of Marxist deferred gratification were to be a 'transitional form' ('Übergangsform') before the nirvana of wholesale re-privatisation.[133]

The slogan was: 'Have patience.' Minor concessions to the peasantry included granting their small household plots private and tax-free status (in usufruct rather than ownership) and unlimited livestock. These reforms were stymied by Hitler's hardline satraps in the east. Speaking in Rivne in late August 1942, Erich Koch said:

> There is no liberated Ukraine. Our aim must be that every Ukrainian labours for Germany, not that we benefit the people here. The Ukraine has to deliver what is lacking in Germany. If this people work ten hours a day, then eight of those hours has to be work for us. All sentimental reservations have to be set aside. This nation must be ruled with an iron fist so that it assists us in winning the war. We haven't liberated it in order to benefit the Ukraine, but rather to secure the living space and food base needed by Germany.[134]

Pre-invasion Nazi industrial strategy for occupied Russia envisaged the elimination through closure or transfer to Germany of all Soviet industry with the exception of extractive industries such as coal-mining or oil. The most primitive forms of colonial exploitation, predicated on the exchange of Soviet raw materials for German manufactured goods, ensued. The failure to achieve rapid victory meant that these simple ideas were superseded by a more nuanced approach involving the re-stimulation of a growing proportion of Soviet industrial capacity. Both large and small Soviet enterprises were reopened or rebuilt in order to satisfy the demands of the German war machine. This was a slow process. Whereas in pre-war Minsk there had been 332 factories with a workforce of about 40,000 people, by October 1941 only 39 factories and 3,378 workers had been reactivated. Forms of multinational control already evident in other parts of Nazi-occupied Europe were translated to the occupied Soviet Union. Overall economic control was exercised by Göring and his State Secretary Paul Korner through the 'Wirtschaftsführungsstab Ost' which also included Backe, Thomas from the High Command of the German Armed Forces (OKW) and Syrup from the Ministry of Economics. The fundamental goals of economic policy were set in a memorandum dated 8 November 1941:

> The highest possible productive surpluses to supply the Reich and the remaining countries of Europe are to be achieved through cheap production and the maintenance of the low standard of living of the indigenous population. In this manner it will not only be possible to broadly satisfy the European demand for food and raw materials, but

> also at the same time to provide the Reich with a source of income which will enable it to cover in a few decades a significant proportion of the debts it has contracted to finance the war while largely sparing the German taxpayer.[135]

A variety of mechanisms were used to harness the industrial economy of occupied Russia to German interests, including direct state ownership; mixed state and private sector continental-wide monopolies for essential commodities; state and private trusteeships where the firms concerned operated a given plant on behalf of the state with the question of ownership indefinitely deferred; and finally, direct private sector control. Equally characteristic of the Nazi economy in general was the presence of major players from the German private sector in what were nominally state-controlled agencies and concerns. The latter were invited to become 'foster-parents' of Soviet firms so that, for example, in August 1942 the IG Farben industrialist Paul Pleiger confirmed that the Krupp concern should assume control of the Asov Steel Works in Mariupol and an engineering works in Kramatorsk. A list of German 'foster-parents', reflecting the position reached in the coal and iron and steel industries by March 1943, included such firms as Bischoff in Recklingshausen, Dortmund-Horder, Krupp, Mannesmann, Siemens-Schuckert and Hoesch AG.[136] The standard business abbreviation 'GmbH' (company with limited liability) was soon cynically referred to as 'Greift mit beiden Händen'.[137] By and large, levels of production were disappointing. Whereas pre-war annual Soviet coal production in the Donets Basin was 90 million tonnes, only 4.1 million tonnes were mined throughout the entire German occupation. Similarly, the iron-ore mines of Kriwoi Rog produced about 12 per cent of what had been achieved under Soviet administration. Occupied Russia supplied the Reich with about one-seventh of what it gleaned from France. Ironically, whereas in 1940 Germany had imported 700,000 tonnes of barley under regular commercial agreements, in 1942 requisition yielded a mere 120,468 tonnes.[138] According to informed observers such as Minister of Finance Schwerin von Krosigk, the restoration of production was hampered by massive over-bureaucratisation, as 'organisations, societies and constructions of every sort shoot out from the ground like mushrooms', and by the influx to the east of a small army of talentless German white-collar workers who then paid themselves vastly inflated salaries while their 'native' subordinates did the work. Instead of yielding surpluses to alleviate the Reich's mounting debt, the occupied Soviet Union was actually having to be subsidised.[139] Further reasons for low Soviet productivity were not explored in this memorandum. Whereas the German occupiers at least had to consider a coherent policy towards the peasantry, industrial labour warranted no such consideration, beyond whether or not to export it forcibly to Germany. The fact that a Russian miner worked at 50 to 60 per cent of the capacity of his German counterpart was not attributed to his receiving an eighth of the latter's wages.

Although as we have seen, some marginal elements in the German regime or the military advocated more pragmatic policies in the Soviet Union, the dominant plans and practice were based on murder and gross exploitation. As in the case of the occupation of Poland, a small army of more or less sane academic 'experts' volunteered their thoughts on the ultimate fate of the former Soviet Union. Puffed up with self-importance, these people flitted in and out of the corridors of power, in a simultaneously ludicrous yet terrifying illustration of the maxim that a little learning is a dangerous thing, especially when that learning consisted of a denatured, functional pursuit of 'relevance', on the part of an intermediary class of 'experts' whose transparent ambition was power for themselves. A dangerous example of this phenomenon was SS-Oberführer Professor Konrad Meyer, a young agronomist whose gift was to convert Himmler's eccentric concerns into coldly technocratic schemes for ethnic cleansing, although we should never mistake the surface 'rationality' for the underlying madness.[140] Apparently Himmler found talking to such people about the thickness of farmhouse walls or the shape of colonial villages a form of relaxation after days spent running a continental police empire.[141]

Having made a name for himself in the context of the expulsion of Poles and Jews from the incorporated territories, Meyer was commissioned to produce a plan which encompassed the vastly augmented area created by 'Barbarossa'. Even within the SS, planning was a congested field. In an inaugural address in October 1941 to senior members of the occupation regime in Prague, the new Reichsprotektor, Reinhard Heydrich, outlined his conception of settlement in the east. There were to be two moral universes consisting of peoples cognate with the Germans who would receive relatively decent treatment; while beyond, in the east, a German military elite would rule Slav 'helots'. A form of human polderisation would ensue, with an outer wall of soldier farmers keeping out the human 'storm flood of Asia', and protecting the ever expanding rings of German settlement behind it.[142]

The Reich Main Security Office of the SS also drew up a global plan for the east in late 1941, whose contents can be reconstructed from a critical commentary by Dr Erhard Wetzel, the desk officer for racial policy in Rosenberg's Ministry for the East (OMi). This plan would have taken thirty years to implement after the end of the war. It covered Poland, the Baltic, Belarus, parts of the Ukraine, 'Ingermanland' (the Leningrad area) and 'Gothengau' (the Crimean peninsular). Its SS authors envisaged 10 million German settlers moving east, with 31 million of the 45 million indigenous inhabitants being relocated to western Siberia. Here Wetzel punctiliously corrected SS arithmetic, since their figure of 45 million both appeared to be too low and included 5 or 6 million Jews who would have been 'got rid of' before the resettlement. The actual population would have been 60 to 65 million, of whom 46 to 51 million would be moved. Deportations were to be percentual according to nationality. Thus 80 to 85 per cent of Poles (or 20 to 24 million people) were to go. Pondering their destination, Wetzel discounted Siberia (which would be weakened as a bulwark against rump Russia), allowed 'one cannot liquidate the Poles like the Jews', and then opted for sending the Polish intelligentsia to Brazil in exchange for ethnic German repatriates while the lower orders would go to Siberia, where, together with other peoples who would be 'pumped in', they would constitute a denatured, 'Americanised' hodge-podge distinct from the Russians. Censuring the SS on their reticence on this last grouping, Wetzel proffered much detailed advice on how to curb Russian fecundity. Apart from mass-produced prophylactics, he suggested the retraining of midwives as abortionists and the deliberate under-training of paediatricians; voluntary sterilisation; and the cessation of all public health measures designed to diminish infant mortality.[143]

The obvious statistical errors and logistical improbabilities in the Reich Main Security Office (RSHA) plan led Himmler to turn to the more practised Meyer. In May 1942, Meyer delivered the memorandum: 'Generalplan Ost: Legal, Economic and Spatial Foundations for Development in the East.' The plan, which exists only in summary form, envisaged the creation of three vast 'marcher settlements' (Ingermanland, Memel-Narew and Gothengau) whose population would be 50 per cent German, and which would be linked to the Reich at 100-kilometre intervals by thirty-six 'settlement strongpoints', whose population would be a quarter German. This plan would take twenty-five years to implement, would involve five million German settlers, and would cost sixty-six billion Reichsmarks.[144] Himmler liked the deliberate exclusion of OMi from the 'marches', but wanted the timescale shortened by five years, the integration of Alsace-Lorraine and Bohemia-Moravia into the plan, and the accelerated 'Germanisation' of the Generalgouvernement and parts of the Baltic. Meyer was commissioned to produce a 'general settlement plan' incorporating these revisions.

If these long-range plans reveal the essential inhumanity of Nazi intentions in the east, day-to-day treatment of the civilian population virtually guaranteed sullen non-co-operation and virulent hatred. Three areas deserve closer attention: the deliberate starvation of large numbers of people; the forced procurement of labour; and the indiscriminate brutality employed in the course of anti-partisan warfare.

The conquest of Soviet Russia was not solely an ideological showdown with 'Jewish-Bolshevism', nor a gigantic form of ethnic cleansing, but also a quest for a secure long-term economic base from which to continue the bid for world power.[145] Since the fields shimmering with wheat of Hitler's imagining proved chimerical, German economic experts, notably State Secretary Herbert Backe, developed the simple expedient of starving millions of Russians by diverting food to the military and the German home front. This was presented as the only way out of a developing crisis whose first symptoms were a cut in the domestic German meat ration, but whose consequences were precisely the same as those elaborated in the 'Generalplan Ost'. In other words, one could arrive at the same desired 'solution' through any number of formulae. The underlying pathology was fundamentally murderous whatever the rationalising gloss put upon it.

Beginning with the fact that Tsarist Russia had exported large agricultural surpluses, Backe attributed the recent decline to both Bolshevik incompetence and the demand represented by a growing and increasingly urbanised population. Surpluses could only be engineered for German use by curtailing consumption, a policy rendered easier by the fact that the main areas of demand in the 'wooded zones' in the north (the industrial cities of Leningrad and Moscow) were far from the Black Earth region in the south which generated the surpluses. 'Absolute clarity must reign' on the fact that these urban populations would starve: 'As a result, *x* million people will doubtless starve, if we extract what we need from the land.'[146]

These plans dovetailed with Hitler's more primitive destructive fantasies towards the populations of cities he identified with Bolshevism, or which he regarded as 'objects' of prestige. On 8 July 1941, Halder recorded in his diary that 'it is the Führer's firm decision that Moscow and Leningrad will be rased to the ground, in order to prevent people remaining there, whom we will have to feed during the winter. The towns must be destroyed by the Luftwaffe. Tanks must not be deployed for this purpose. A national catastrophe which will rob not only Bolshevism but also Moscowdom of its centre.'[147] By early September 1941, Leningrad was isolated from the rest of Russia except for a precarious route across Lake Ladoga. Three million people were trapped inside the city and its suburban environs in what would become a siege lasting 900 days. Intensely suspicious of Leningrad particularism with its shades of Kirov, Stalin disbanded the three-man Defence Council, on the spurious grounds that its functions overlapped with that of the Leningrad Front Command. By prioritising the hasty improvisation of trenches and gun emplacements to check the German advance, the Soviet authorities neglected both the possibility of mass evacuation of non-essential civilians, notably children, and the laying in of food in the event of a siege. Food was actually being removed from the city to supply other unoccupied areas. Rationing was belatedly and incompetently introduced, as well as ghastly substitute foods such as flour adulterated with cellulose or a jelly made from a vast load of sheep guts, whose odour was neutralised with cloves. By the onset of winter, with eighteen hours of darkness and temperatures plummeting to −40°C electricity and central heating ceased, with people reduced to stripping wallpaper in order to cook the glue as a soup or drinking the contents of their medicine cupboards. Some people killed and ate their own cats and dogs, with mustard and vinegar failing to mask the taste, and using the fur to make gloves. The German Army cut the main railway line running into Leningrad, while the Luftwaffe harassed what sea traffic there was across the lake. The hasty improvisation of a 200-mile road circling north of German forces proved futile since it was so narrow, and the snow so deep, that traffic frequently ground to a halt. With Hitler insisting that capitulation would be refused, German generals pondered what to do with the besieged city. The possibilities, discussed in late September 1941, included occupation (rejected because with it would go the responsibility for feeding two million people); a vast electrified fence and machine guns to seal the city off (rejected because the ensuing epidemics might spread to German troops and because the latter were unlikely routinely to shoot escaping women and children); exit routes through which women and children could be sent eastwards or distributed across the countryside, while the rest of the population starved to death (deemed possible); and finally, demolish the city and hand the ruins over to the Finnish ally. It was decided to press on with the siege and bombardment. Bombs and shells rained down on the city, bringing random death to a queue or passers-by. An eye-witness reported:

> I was in the Nevsky once when a shell landed close by. And ten yards away from me was a man whose head was cut clean off by a shell splinter. It was horrible. I saw him make his last two steps with his head off – and a bloody mess all round before he collapsed. I vomited right there and then, and was quite ill for the rest of the day – though I had already seen many terrible things before. I shall never forget the night when a children's hospital was hit by an oil bomb; many children were killed, and the whole house was blazing, and some perished in the flames. It's bad for one's nerves to see such things happen; our ambulance services have instructions to wash away blood on the pavement as quickly as possible after a shell has landed.[148]

In November 11,000 people died, in December 52,000, in January 1942 between 3,500 and 4,000 people a day. The first worrying signs of people going to pieces were when men stopped shaving and women became indifferent to their appearance or ceased menstruating. Ages became confused, with children looking prematurely old, while the bodies of the middle aged became childlike. Even the most routine movement, such as climbing stairs or getting into bed, became a major effort, with the dying simply rocking or slumbering. Corpses were collected and dumped in mass graves excavated from the frozen ground with explosives. Funerals were characterised by an absence of emotion. Apathetic dullness replaced tears. None of this affected the party leaders in the warm and well-lit Smolny Institute, who had their own bakers and confectioners producing cakes and rum chocolates for their exclusive delectation, photographs of which were until recently filed in the archives under the entry 'precision engineering'.

Pressure on the population was eventually relieved by the evacuation of women, children and the elderly and the construction of a route across the frozen lake along which supplies were brought. Fuel lines and electric power were restored in the spring by laying pipelines and cables along the bottom of Lake Ladoga. Over 600,000 people died in the course of the siege of Leningrad, as a result of starvation strategies which were applied to other cities such as Kharkov or Kiev. Through such intangible media as Shostakovich's Seventh 'Leningrad' Symphony, the heroism and tragedy of Leningrad were communicated to a much wider Soviet public.

As was the case in other parts of German-occupied Europe, the forced requisition of labour was also a source of fear and resentment. Russian civilians and prisoners of war were compelled to work for the occupation authorities, the former as a result of a general edict on labour service issued by Rosenberg on 19 December 1941. Although Hitler was initially indisposed to exposing German or other foreign labourers to Soviet workers 'polluted by Bolshevism', he changed his mind because of the enormous calls on domestic manpower made by the war in Russia and a reluctance to conscript German women. Göring established the ground rules for the mass employment of Russians, now ironically lauded for the 'amazing development of Russian industry' under the Bolsheviks. In operational areas, Germans were no longer to be involved in heavy labour on roads or railways: 'German skilled workers belong in the arms industry; shovelling and breaking rocks is not their job, that's why the Russian is there.'[149] The deployment of Russians in the Reich would enable the regime to repatriate other foreign workers who ate more and produced less, while relying less on German female labour. The Russian prisoners of war (and as we have seen, many of them were already dead) were destined for the railways, arms factories, construction, agriculture and the mines. They were to be housed in camps and worked in groups, with no disciplinary sanctions other than reduction of rations or execution. Shoes should be wooden, but underwear was superfluous 'since the Russian is scarcely used to it'. There was little difference in the treatment of Russian civilians, except that they were to be given 'a little pocket money' in lieu of wages. Having belatedly discovered that vast numbers of Russian prisoners of war were dead, labour experts redirected their attention to civilian sources. Together with Albert Speer, Fritz Sauckel, the Plenipotentiary for Labour Procurement, turned towards Russia and the Ukraine. The voluntarist approach soon failed to produce significant results. Of course, in the case of many industrial workers, there was nothing 'voluntary' about their decision to go to Germany, since the occupiers both shut down plant that the Soviets had not disabled, and then pursued policies expressly designed to starve the urban population.[150] Stories also rapidly filtered back – via letters, or the oral testimony of pregnant women and the sick who were simply repatriated to save the cost of caring for them – of the appalling conditions eastern workers could expect inside the Reich. Compulsion gained ground.[151] A young Ukrainian woman described the *modus operandi*:

> It commenced with the arrival of a German called Graf Spreti in February 1942 who came to requisition labour. The Germans held a large meeting in a cinema. A crowd of people went along to see what was going on. Spreti said: 'I would like you citizens of Uman to go voluntarily to Germany to assist the German armed forces.' He promised us paradise. But we already knew what to make of such promises, and asked: 'What will happen if we don't want to go?' Graf Spreti replied: 'In that case we will politely demand despite this that you go.' That was on 10 February. Two days later they went from house to house and took away all of the young people. They took us to a big school and at five o'clock in the morning to the station. There, they shoved us into railway wagons, which were then bolted. The journey became a nightmare lasting several weeks.[152]

German agencies responsible for intercepting and interpreting correspondence between Russian or Ukrainian civilians registered 'a sharp worsening of mood' tantamount to 'a terrified panic' resulting from the coercive requisitioning of labour. One of the letter-writers described what happened in a village on 1 October 1942. It is worth noting not just the violence used, but also the role of the village elder, and the complete indifference as to whether the people taken were physically capable of working.

> You can't imagine what depredations occurred. You can doubtless well recall what we were told about the Soviets during the time of Polish rule: it is as unbelievable now as it was then, but then we didn't believe it. There was an order to muster twenty-five workers, the people designated by the Labour Office received registration cards, but none of them turned up, all of them had fled. The German police appeared and began setting fire to the houses of those who had fled. The fire was intense since it hadn't rained for two months, and the bales of hay were stacked in the yards. You can imagine what happened. They would not permit the people who hurried out to extinguish the fire, hitting and arresting them, so that six farmsteads burned down. The police set fire to other houses, people fell to their knees and kissed their hands, but the police hit them with rubber truncheons and

> threatened to burn the whole village down. I don't know how things would have ended had not I, Sapurkany, gone out into the middle of it all. He promised that workers would be there by morning. While the fire raged, the militia went through the nearby villages, detaining workers in custody. Where they couldn't find workers, they locked up the parents until their children reappeared . . . They are snatching people like the knackers used to catch stray dogs. They have been hunting for a week, and still don't have enough. The workers they caught have been locked in a school, and are not allowed out even to go to the lavatory, but have to do it in the same room like pigs. Many people from the villages went on the same day on a pilgrimage to the monastery at Potschaew. They were all arrested, locked up, and will be sent to work. Among them were cripples, the blind and old men and women. At our annual market, Romanov was there. The village elder came up to him and said that he should come along, but he wouldn't. They bound his hands behind his back, and led him naked to the police. When he was told to get out of the cart, he refused, saying that they should free his hands first. Two guards beat him so much that his skin was broken in three places. His mother and sister screamed, and they were beaten too.[153]

On 12 August 1942 a bullish Sauckel attended a conference in Kiev to encourage inter-agency collaboration and to underline the urgency of his procurement activities. In return, he had to listen to a series of discouraging oral reports from district officials. They had too few men to be able to enter areas in which partisans were active. Ever bolder, the latter were assassinating German officials and those who served them, while abducting entire families. People were afraid to sleep in their own homes. Furthermore, no sooner had one managed to round up a group of workers than they ran away. Of 2,600 men loaded onto one train, 1,000 had jumped out during the journey. Indeed 25 per cent of every transport managed to flee during the journey. One could not rely on the Ukrainian guards to preside over the shipment to Germany of their own people. Other officials were perplexed as to how they were supposed to keep the military supplied with grain or timber, when at the same time they were being required to deplete the labour force. What exactly were the priorities?[154] Even when the diligent SS were brought in to do the job, the results were disappointing. According to a report by the SD and Security Police Chief in Kiev dated 20 July 1942, in the early hours of a Sunday morning, they combed houses, rounding up a total of 1,645 people whose papers were not in order. Although this yielded three wanted (political) criminals, the raid failed to meet its intended objective. Only 255 of those detained could be shipped to the Reich. The rest were able to produce the correct documentation, were too sick to work, or were hurriedly retrieved from the SS by their German employers.[155] In one noteworthy case, even the SS complained how the Labour Offices were requisitioning totally unsuitable people. On 9 December 1942, an SS-Obersturmbannführer reported to his superior that a train had recently arrived in Kiev from Przemsyl laden with 319 Ukrainian workers. They were all seriously ill. Eighty-one had the infectious eye disease trachoma, fifty-four were suffering from tuberculosis and five were blind. What angered the SS officer was how someone had managed to declare these people fit for work, wasting administrative time and scarce transport in order to ship them to the Reich, whence they were immediately returned.[156] Reporting again a few days later, the same SS officer answered his own question by noting how labour recruitment officials were simply assembling entire villages, selecting every third man or woman.[157] Quite apart from how the 'eastern workers' fared in Germany the manner in which they had been brought there was one of the main reasons for the mass alienation of the Russian and Ukrainian civilian population.

So too was the 'dirty war' which was being waged in large parts of the territories behind German lines. In 1937, Stalin terminated all preparations for partisan warfare, fearing that these individualist irregulars might constitute the nucleus of decentralised sources of military power in regions hostile to the Soviet state, or that their very existence constituted defeatism.[158] This decision was hastily revoked on 3 July 1941, although it was many months before Moscow asserted its control over the NKVD, the Communist Party or the Red Army units which sprang into existence, or were cut off, in the occupied territories. The first units, consisting of perhaps a total of 30,000 people spread over a vast area, were not a great success. They lacked food and equipment, notably radios, and their composition (people closely identified with the communist system) did not make them popular with the inhabitants of regions such as the Baltic, Crimea and southern Ukraine which had a history of oppression under Soviet rule. The extremely harsh winter of 1941–2 affected the partisans and Germans alike. Food was not easy to find, and if it was seized from the peasants, this militated against a sympathetic environment, while the absence of foliage and deep snow made the partisans vulnerable to aerial spotting and follow-up search and destroy missions.

German policy was co-responsible for the revival of the partisan movement in the spring of 1942. German treatment of Soviet prisoners of war diminished the advantages of surrender, while German occupation policy alienated populations some of which had greeted the Wehrmacht as potential liberators. As we have seen, the arbitrariness of labour procurement also resulted in large-scale flight to the partisans. Complaining to Sauckel in a letter dated 21 December 1942, Rosenberg wrote:

> Reports I have received enable me to perceive that the increase in the number of bands in the occupied eastern territories is largely attributable to the fact that in the areas concerned, labour procurement measures are regarded as a form of mass deportation, to the extent that those who feel threatened by these measures prefer to take their chances by flight to the woods or by directly going over to the bandits.[159]

Finally, the winter campaign had shattered the myth of all-conquering German invincibility, and hence brought the prospect of a return of Soviet rule. No doubt many people who became, or aided and abetted, partisans made complex calculations about present oppression by an invader whose impetus had stalled, and the return of a regime with a proven capacity for vindictiveness and terror, which was using the partisans to demonstrate its long reach even while its fortunes were at their nadir. This dilemma was summed up neatly by one Russian who was reported as saying: 'If I stay with the Germans, I shall be shot when the Bolsheviks come; if the Bolsheviks don't come, I shall be shot sooner or later by the Germans. Thus, if I stay with the Germans, it means certain death; if I join the partisans, I shall probably save myself.'

In May 1942, regional Party direction of the partisans was replaced by the Red Army's Central Staff for Partisan Warfare under Lieutenant-General Panteleymon Ponomarenko, the First Secretary of the Belarussian Communist Party and a close associate of Stalin. This arrangement gave the appearance of popular Red Army control, while actually centralising unpopular Communist Party direction of the partisan movement. Contact between the partisans in the so-called 'Little Land' and their controllers in the 'Great Land' were increased by the provision of radios as well as commissars and NKVD sections. The reformed partisan bands had a strength of between 350 and 2,000 men and women, with a military command structure and specialist personnel including medics, explosives and counter-intelligence experts. The NKVD Administration for Special Tasks provided training in sabotage and the services of professional assassins. One named Kuznetsov was a confident and handsome Russian who had grown up among exiled Germans in Siberia whom the NKVD infiltrated into diplomatic circles in Moscow. In 1942 he was parachuted into western Ukraine where, disguised as a wounded German supply corps officer, he specialised in the point-blank assassination of German officials. Captured by Bandera's pro-German partisans, Kuznetsov blew himself up with a grenade before the Gestapo managed to interrogate him.[160]

Geography largely dictated the partisans' zone of operations. The steppe afforded almost no cover. The principal mountainous regions in the Caucasus and Crimea were inhabited by peoples who were at best neutral towards the Germans and deeply hostile to the Soviets. Partisans there could also be dealt with by experienced alpine troops. This left the areas of dense forest and swamps around the tributaries of the Pripyat, and further north, the woodlands between Minsk and Smolensk, the forests of the Valdai Hills south-east of Leningrad. In other words, the partisans were effectively confined to an area equal to a third of the German occupied territories.[161]

The initial German response to partisan activities was passive, piecemeal and incoherent in the sense that there was no single authority responsible for security across the entire occupied zone, a situation which reflected the overlapping, and sometimes mutually antithetical, competences of civilian administrations, the Army and SS, as well as different definitions of 'security'. The scale of the problem was immense. Occupying an area which was about one million square miles at maximum projected extent, the Germans opted to protect lines of communication, major towns, supply depots and essential economic resources. The army deployed nine Security Divisions, accompanied by seven battalions of motorised police, consisting of older cohorts led by ageing reserve or retired officers. The SS deployed the four mobile Einsatzgruppen, whose principal activity was murdering civilians for racial reasons, as well as regiments of Ordnungspolizei, various Waffen-SS units, and a series of eccentric formations such as the Sonderkommando Dirlewanger or the Kaminski Brigade whose criminal depredations were increasingly an embarrassment.[162] Even had they been exclusively dedicated to one task, and many of these units were mainly committed to racial-biological warfare, these forces, consisting of perhaps 110,000 men, faced an uphill task in securing upwards of nearly a million square miles of hostile territory.

Like strategic bombing, the military effectiveness of partisan warfare is disputed and difficult to gauge. Elements in both equations are impossible to quantify yet crucial to a person's performance: disturbed sleep in the former case, the need to sleep with one eye open in the latter. Those who claim that the Soviet partisan war had little impact on German military operations are surely missing the point that it caused widespread economic disruption, tied down manpower which could have been deployed elsewhere, and by instilling fear and provoking extreme counter-measures, drove a wedge between occupiers and occupied. Reports from German economic agencies tell of a constant level of disruption which German security forces were unable to prevent. One lengthy report concerning the month of July 1942 recorded a campaign of assassination against low-level collaborators such as village mayors, and that 236 milking depots, dairies and mills as well as 17 per cent of sawmills had been disabled. Milk was being poisoned, explosive devices were slipped into grain about to be milled, and even a visit to the theatre brought the risk that the actors were plotting to blow up the audience. Main roads had been mined while minor routes were totally interdicted. Any sort of work in the forests and woods was out of the question. People who might have once collaborated with the Germans were now unsure of themselves. In what was regarded by the Germans as a revealing, if unamusing, anecdote, these officials reported:

> On 7.7 the forester Malaschtschenko appeared at the Economic Command Post to return his service rifle since this only seemed to him to be a permanent danger to his life. He also requested the issuance of a stamped receipt which he could then show to the partisans during their next attack as proof that he had really surrendered his weapon. This permit was issued in order to protect the forester. The fact that a German agency is forced to issue permits on behalf of the partisans illustrates better than any other example what the situation is at present.[163]

These activities had virtually brought economic activity to a standstill, interrupting vital supplies to the front-line troops. All counter-measures had proved totally inadequate. The dominant German response to partisan warfare was redolent of that of other regular armies frustrated by an invisible opponent and surprised by popular resistance.

First, they endeavoured to use language itself to depoliticise the enemy, referred to now as 'bands', 'bandits' or occasionally 'Franktireur', in revealing acknowledgment of the fact that this sort of warfare had a long Prussian history. Secondly, they enhanced security by guarding railways and main roads, while endeavouring to restrict unauthorised civilian movement. Houses had to display lists of occupants, and anyone caught without a travel permit at night could be shot. A deadly competition ensued to guard or disable railways and telecommunications. The partisans began by simply loosening rails (preferably on a decline), graduating, via magnetic or pressure mines and serial explosives, to charges cased in wood which were difficult to detect. Sprinkling gunpowder confused sniffer hounds. The Germans responded by upping the stakes. Apart from sniffer and tracker dogs, they cleared the undergrowth from beside the tracks; built lines of guardhouses to ensure a rapid response; used trains laden with rocks to trigger explosives in advance; and above all, used repair crews and assiduous rescheduling to minimise any disruption. Thirdly, there were fitful attempts to rationalise the overall direction of anti-partisan warfare, attempts which fell well short of co-ordinating SS and Army activities under a unified command system. SS anti-partisan operations were directed from July 1942 by SS-Gruppenführer Knoblauch of the Reichsführer's Command Staff and from spring 1943 by Generalmajor der Waffen-SS Ernst Rode. Liaison with the military, and overall policy was supplied by SS-Obergruppenführer Erich von dem Bach-Zelewski first as 'Plenipotentiary' and from early 1943, as 'Chief of Anti-Bandit Formations', a title which stopped well short of any control of Army operations in this area. Himmler continued to intervene with platitudinous analyses of the enemy, as well as such suggestions as 'it is self-evident that interrogations, when necessary, are to be conducted with the utmost brutality', or 'Death alone does not mean much to the pig-headed Slav; he reckons on it from the word go. By contrast he is afraid of blows; and above all he fears retaliatory measures against his clan.'[164]

The German occupiers practised the taking of hostages and random reprisals against civilians who had the misfortune to inhabit areas where partisans were active. An order issued by Göring on 16 October 1942, regarding the securing of railways, illustrates the way in which the sort of security measures discussed above easily tipped over into the murder of civilians. Any unauthorised Russian found within 1,000 metres of a railway track was to be shot. Any Russian caught committing acts of sabotage 'was to be hanged from the nearest telegraph pole – in the event that he is captured alive'. Villages closest to where lines were destroyed were to be burned down, while 'the male population is to be shot, and the women and children sent to camps'.[165] Ten days later Göring also ordered the removal of all food and livestock from areas where partisans were active, and the deportation for labour of all able-bodied adults in these areas. No heed was to be paid either to such factors as agricultural production, while children were to be sent to rear area camps.[166]

Active anti-partisan combat, that is the business of taking the war to the enemy, also swiftly degenerated into the indiscriminate and mindless terrorisation of civilians. On 7 December 1941, the High Command of 6th Army announced rather prematurely that partisan activity had to all intents and purposes been 'eradicated' in their sector. The report continued: 'In the course of this action several thousand have been publicly hanged or shot in the Army's area. Experience shows that death by hanging is particularly terrifying. In Kharkov, several hundred partisans and suspect elements were hanged in the town. Acts of sabotage have since ceased. Experience reveals: only those measures succeed which frighten the population more than the terrorism of the partisans.'[167] A constant stream of directives, orders and operational instructions prove beyond any doubt that the terrorisation of civilians was licensed and ordered by the Nazi leadership and senior generals alike. Instructions issued by 11th Army on 15 December 1941 clearly stated: 'The population must be more frightened of our reprisals than of the partisans.'[168] The message relayed from Hitler by Keitel was 'whatever succeeds is correct' and that: 'The troops must have the right and duty to use, in this fight, any means, even against women and children, provided they are conducive to success. Scruples, of any sort whatsoever, are a crime against the German people and against the front-line soldier . . . No German participating in action against bands or their associates is to be held responsible for acts of violence either from a disciplinary or a judicial point of view.'[169] Instructions to the troops on how to conduct interrogations of suspects began with the premiss that 'people here expect to be interrogated according to the methods of the NKVD, i.e. they reckon on being beaten up from the start'. This involved up to seventy-five blows with an ox-tail whip for men, or a rubber tube for women, with the victim being shot in the back of the neck after he or she had given the required information.[170]

Operating in often intractable terrain, against an enemy that was him-

(or herself) frequently barbaric, devious and indistinguishable from the civilian population, soldiers and policemen with no external disciplinary constraints slipped into routinised brutality, a sure indication that they were losing. Civilians were hanged, raped, shot and tortured and their homes destroyed. Evidence for this is not simply oral or written, since cheap cameras made this an amateur cameraman's war, despite a general prohibition on photography. Thousands of photographs, taken from dead or captured German soldiers by the Russians, or discovered among the possessions of veterans, record mass executions by hanging or shooting of putative 'partisans'. They hang sack-like from urban balconies or wayside telegraph poles, or were laid out as dead game in front of the men who killed them. The latter stare gormlessly at the camera. Why anyone should want to photograph such scenes remains unclear.[171] Judging from the way in which the majority of these pictures were composed, few of the photographers seem to have been registering revulsion or shock at what they were witnessing, albeit through the remove of a lens. That would have required less physical distance towards the faces of their subjects as is customary in modern war photoreportage. Rather, the photographs reflect a prurient desire to record something that was initially not an everyday sight, while also capturing those moments of absolute power over other human beings that the war in the east afforded. The photographs would 'tell' the tale and convey the fleeting sensation more effectively than stories.

As in subsequent (lost) irregular wars, 'success' was registered in statistical 'body counts' which did not withstand close scrutiny. Soldiers achieved meaningless kill rates, against an elusive enemy. In other words, they wanted to get out of the forests and swamps as expeditiously as possible, notching up impressive tallies of civilian victims rather than taking on the partisans in fire-fights within the sepulchral gloom of the forests or amidst the reeds of the marshes. In July 1943 an SS officer, Herf, wrote to the Head of the SS Personnel Main Office drawing his attention to the cooking of the books and the '6000/480' problem, that is, how only 480 rifles had been recovered from 6,000 dead 'partisans' in the course of the recent Operation Kottbus. The commander of the operation, SS-Obergruppenführer Curt von Gottberg had also 'liquidated' 3,709 others, and killed 2,000 local people by ordering them into minefields. Told that the 'bandits' regularly destroyed their own weapons to affect innocence, Herf commented: 'How easy it must be to suppress these guerrillas – when they destroy their own weapons.'[172] All attempts to integrate anti-partisan warfare with more conciliatory policies towards the civilian population came to nought. The war became one of illusions, that made less and less of an impact on the enemy, as the security forces blundered around while the partisans slipped away from them.

The anti-partisan war was also a convenient cover, and useful pretext, for racial-biological extermination. Reporting to his superior on 23 June 1942, Major-General Bruno Scultetus of the 281 Security Division none too dexterously rationalised the shooting of 128 Gypsies by the Secret Field Police. Partisans had been active in his region in the second half of May, although the only incident he mentioned was an attack on a lorry in which a lieutenant had been wounded. 'At the same time' Gypsies had been seen in the area. They had no fixed abode, begged rather than worked, 'and represented a burden in every respect'. Lest this seemed like an injunction to shoot the homeless, Scultetus switched his ground. 'General experience', confirmed again in Russia, taught that Gypsies often operated as spies. Moving from general to local experience, Scultetus gave a few circumstantial details: the (dead) Gypsies included many men of military age; one of those interrogated said that older Gypsies discussed the activities of partisans; Gypsies had camped near where the one attack had taken place. Moving back to the general, Scultetus remarked that 'during their interrogation, all of the Gypsies made a very unfavourable and shifty impression, and frequently contradicted themselves'. Of course there was no 'absolute proof' that Gypsies had aided and abetted partisans; none the less, the suspicion was so high, and the potential danger to the military so great, that 'their eradication seemed necessary'. Scultetus was then very careful to cover his men by detailing the precise origin of the order to kill the Gypsies, concluding with the point that since these shootings, there had been no further partisan attacks in this area. 128 people had been killed because their 'race' was slated for destruction, because they fitted an approximate enemy profile, and because a few old men had talked about the war at night.[173]

Confirmation that the anti-partisan war was used to carry out ethnic murder comes from a variety of sources. As Hitler said to his intimates on 16 July 1941, 'it [the anti-partisan war] gives us the chance of exterminating anything that opposes us'. Reflecting on these activities at Nuremberg, Bach-Zelewski confirmed that this was so, and that there was such a phenomenon as intentional chaos:

> . . . leaders at the top who are conscious of their responsibilities cannot abandon the execution of reprisals to the caprice of individual commanders. This lack of direction in responsible quarters is a cowardly devolution of responsibility on to lower echelons. But if it is obvious to everyone that lack of direction leads to a chaos of reprisals and nevertheless no clear orders are given, then the only possible conclusion is that this chaos is intended by the leaders at the top. There is no question but that reprisals both by the Wehrmacht and by SS and Police units overshot the mark by a long way. This fact was repeatedly established at conferences with generals held by Schenckendorff. Moreover the fight against partisans was gradually used as an excuse to carry out other measures, such as the extermination of Jews and Gypsies, the systematic reduction of the Slavic peoples by some 30,000,000 souls (in order to secure the supremacy of the German people), and the terrorisation of civilians by shooting and looting. The Commanders-in-Chief with whom I came in contact and with whom I collaborated (for instance Field Marshals Weichs, Küchler, Bock, and Kluge, Col-General Reinhardt and General Kitzinger) were as well aware as I of the purposes and methods of anti-partisan warfare.[174]

Bach-Zelewski was well placed to know about the convenient conflation of Jews and partisans since at a morale-boosting session held after the 1 and 2 SS-Cavalry Regiment had 'cleansed' 4,500 Jewish men, women and children in Pinsk on the flimsy pretext that a member of the town militia had been shot, he himself used the formula: 'Where there is a partisan, there is also a Jew, and where there is a Jew, there is also a partisan.' The grim reality covered by this fiction was recorded in matter-of-fact and minute detail in the war diaries of the SS units concerned. For example, in a report covering operations between noon on 3 August and noon of 6 August 1941, the 1st SS motorised Infantry Brigade gave the 'result' as being:

Jews shot	**Ostrog**	**Hrycow**	**Kuniow-Radohoszcz**
1. men	732	268	109
2. women	225	–	50
3. former Russian soldiers			
4. (partisans)	–	–	1
Total:			1385 persons[175]

With chilling regularity the detailed reports, such as one dated 8/9 August 1941 record the deaths of '232 Jews who afforded the bandits assistance'; '9 Bolshevik Jews in Mal-Goroschki'; '59 Jews shot, 8

Russians captured, search for weapons unsuccessful'; '36 Bolshevik Jews were shot in the villages' and so on.[176] Although there were Jews in the partisan units, those murdered in this way were never distinguished as such. A report on a putative anti-partisan sweep in the Pripyat swamps between 27 July and 11 August 1941 begins with the damning admission: 'impressions of combat: none'. The author of the report, SS-Sturmbannführer Franz Magill, gave a glowing account of the mainly Ukrainian rural population, who had greeted his SS-Cavalry Regiment with milk, eggs and tables covered with white cloths and laid out with the traditional bread and salt. In one place they were met by the strains of a village choir. Like an anthropologist among strange tribes, Magill noted that 'in racial terms', the stocky inhabitants made a good impression, with their fecundity reflected in the large numbers of children. They dwelled in wooden huts with thatched roofs, and possessed good school buildings. The terrain consisted of swamp, interspersed with sandy stretches. Canals and channels criss-crossed the area, with occasional clumps of birch and pine. Collectivisation had been in the process of being introduced in the countryside; and Magill returned some cows to poverty-stricken farmers. The urban artisans had been grouped in co-operatives. It seemed that Jews were being preferred as doctors. And so the Regiment rode on. The journey was free of incident; the equipment lagged behind because the tracks were a morass; a few horses were lamed, others had to be rested for long intervals; some wagons broke down; and a handful of weapons were lost.

Gradually Magill's report slipped into a different register as the tourist part of the journey gave way to the business end of the mission. 'Pacification' involved questioning village mayors about partisan activities. Partisans or suspects were identified, interrogated and shot. Magill casually remarked that 'Jewish plunderers' were also shot. What he and his regiment were actually doing was indicated by a paragraph which reads:

> Driving women and children into the swamps was not as successful as it should have been, since the swamps were not deep enough for them to sink. Because of a depth of one metre, most cases reached solid ground (probably sand) so that drowning was not possible.[177]

None of this involved partisans. They encountered no communists, merely persons suspected of communist activity. Most of the reports on the 'bands' turned out to be exaggerated. Weapon searches proved otiose. One Polish priest had been shot for propagandising a Polish national revival, in what was a predominantly Ukrainian area. Again circling around what he and his men had done, Magill noted that the Ukrainians spoke quite well of the Jews, but had none the less helped Magill herd them together. It comes as some surprise, after this evasively matter-of-fact account, to read that the total number of 'plunderers etc.' shot by this one unit came to 6,526 people, presumably including the women and children they had failed to drown in shallow swamps. The operation was deemed 'a success'. The victims had mostly been Jews. It is time to relate this one episode, albeit involving the murder of over 6,000 people, to the vaster criminal enterprise which was taking place across the length and breadth of Axis and occupied Europe, for which the racial war in the Soviet Union represented a crucial catalyst, a final lowering of the threshold of what was thought humanly possible. Before moving on to the Holocaust, however, we must trace another crucial chain of events which led to it, namely the so-called 'euthanasia' programme.

PART II

'Euthanasia'

CHAPTER FOUR

Psychiatry, German society and the Nazi 'euthanasia' programme

This chapter is concerned with the complex history of the Nazi 'euthanasia' programme. In order to get this endeavour off the ground, the references are necessarily somewhat attenuated, especially with regard to the perspective of the victims.[1] It begins by establishing the position of psychiatry after the First World War, concentrating upon the interplay between economy measures and limited reform during the Weimar Republic. Each therapeutic advance (such as occupational or somatic therapies) almost immanently involved the definition of irremediable sub-groups within the already socially marginalised psychiatric constituency. Nazi policy towards psychiatric patients during the 1930s involved further economy measures, and the introduction of negative eugenic strategies, similar in kind if not degree, to those pursued in some other countries at that time. The decision to kill the mentally ill and physically disabled was taken by Hitler in order to clear the decks for war, and was justified with the aid of crude utilitarian arguments, as well as with what limited evidence there was regarding popular attitudes on these issues. Many health professionals and psychiatrists accommodated themselves to policies which a few years later became one of the components of the 'Final Solution of the Jewish Question', i.e. Hitler's long-harboured act of vengeance against the Jewish people in circumstances of war he had envisaged much earlier.[2] This approach seems to me to have the merit of setting professionals in a broader political context, not always evident in accounts which stress the contribution of intermediate 'experts' to the solution of a putative 'social question'. One should not give a variegated and murderous 'expertocracy' greater saliency in these things than it actually merits. In the case of psychiatrists, their precise contribution was to define a pool of potential victims and then, in some cases, to participate in the business of selection and murder. The decision to carry out these policies was taken by the Nazi political elite, and was bound up (as indeed was the extermination of the Jews) with their decision to go to war. In other words, these things are not solely explicable through a medico-historical perspective, however interesting that may be in terms of explaining either the inner dynamics of specific areas of policies such as the 'euthanasia' programme or a part of the mind-set responsible for them. This chapter is thus a contribution to the political, as well as the social, history of medicine. It is widely rather than narrowly focused.

In Germany, psychiatry emerged from the First World War with its already poor image as a futile, and scientifically dubious branch of medicine, sullied yet further. Vast numbers of psychiatric patients had died during wartime from a combination of hunger, disease and neglect. Assuming an average annual peacetime mortality rate of 5.5 per cent, recent studies estimate that 71,787, or about 30 per cent of the pre-war asylum population, died between 1914 and 1919 as a result of the extreme privations of war.[3] Exhausted or 'neurotic' soldiers were medically terrorised back into conflict through crude shock therapies.[4] Revolutionaries arrested after the abortive Munich Soviet were liberally diagnosed as 'psychopaths' by forensic psychiatrists.[5] Post-war austerity contributed to a decaying physical fabric in the asylums, while economic cuts affected everything from books, drugs and heating to light-bulbs and soap.

In Wilhelmine Germany, criticism of psychiatry had often come from the Right, for example from the anti-Semitic court chaplain Adolf Stöcker, and was primarily directed against psychiatry's medicalised denial of individual liberty. In the Weimar Republic, a temporarily powerful psychiatric reform movement, including former patients' groups, went on the attack, demanding enhanced patients' rights, checks on committal procedures and an effective inspectorate.[6] Other critics saw the problem rather in terms of profligacy with scarce national resources. In 1920 the lawyer Karl Binding and the psychiatrist Alfred Hoche raised the delicate question of whether a nation faced with a dire emergency could actually afford to sustain what they dubbed 'life unworthy of life', including a putatively growing reserve army of 'mental defectives'. In a controversial tract, which was essentially a search for a post-

Christian, utilitarian ethics, Binding and Hoche deliberately conflated the issue of voluntary 'euthanasia' with the non-consensual killing of 'idiots' and the mentally ill; stressed the historical relativity of such notions as the 'sanctity of human life'; highlighted the objective futility of such emotions as 'pity' – 'where there is no suffering, there can also be no pity'; and emphasised the emotional and economic burden allegedly represented by 'entirely unproductive persons'.[7] The altruistic heroism of British Polar explorers, such as Greely or Scott, was invoked to justify chucking overboard 'dead ballast' from the 'Ship of Fools'. Two points about the tract were crucial. Firstly, it was symptomatic of how received Judaeo-Christian or humanitarian values were breaking down, with concern for narrow or wider collectivities, such as the good of a class, the economy, race or nation usurping respect for the rights and value of the individual. Secondly, it argued that in emergency wartime circumstances, where the healthy were making enormous sacrifices, one could justify the 'sacrifice' of 'not merely absolutely valueless, but negatively valued existences'.

Faced with such variegated assaults upon their activities, German psychiatrists began to think more kindly of a handful of farsighted reformers in their own midst who had hitherto been cold-shouldered. It was a question of maintaining institutional relevance through anticipatory reformist initiatives, rather than passively awaiting what unsympathetic and cost-conscious governments might do instead. Two rather remarkable men, Gustav Kolb and Hermann Simon, had long been advocating breaching the walls between asylums and the wider society, and between sickness and the world of work.[8] Their liberal recommendations found a ready response from Weimar governments obsessed with cutting costs. Patients were discharged into the arms of a new range of urban out-patient clinics or perambulatory social psychiatrists in rural areas. One can see the economic advantages of this policy: the annual overheads of an out-patient clinic established in Munich in 1924, which by 1930 was seeing over 1,000 clients, were 2,000 RM a year, whereas it cost 1,277 RM to keep one patient for a year in Munich's Eglfing-Haar asylum.[9] However, patients in asylums also were not free from the attentions of the reformers. Depressed by the effects of long-term institutionalisation in environments effectively bereft of therapy, Hermann Simon decided to use occupational therapy to engender self-satisfaction and hence repress the depressed or excitable moods which resulted from enforced idleness. Soon, asylums were humming with patient activity, with both the complexity of the work performed, and hence the degree of freedom and responsibility enjoyed, being the objective indicators of recovery. In many asylums, up to 80 per cent of patients did some form of work, which made the asylums largely self-sufficient or capable of generating modest surpluses. Judging by the flood of articles devoted to community care and occupational therapy published in the professional journals in the 1920s, psychiatry began to be a more optimistic profession.

Inevitably, there was a downside to these developments. Firstly, as psychiatrists followed their discharged patients out into the wider world, they inevitably encountered hitherto unknown ranges of 'abnormality'. What passed before them in the asylums was literally the tip of an iceberg. Being of an increasingly hereditarian cast of mind, they began to construct genealogies of the patients' families.[10] Instead of addressing themselves to questions concerning the socio-economic environment, which in fact they were powerless to affect, they opted for the control function of registering widespread deviance in primitive data banks. The sheer scale of illness they encountered engendered a certain pessimism, and hence enhanced their susceptibility to fashionable and radical eugenicist solutions. Since experience taught that people they deemed degenerate or feckless could not be counselled into voluntary low rates of reproduction, many psychiatrists began to think in terms of compulsory sterilisation. This would enable the person to return to the productive process without risk of reproductive damage ensuing to the collective biological substance of the race or nation, in itself a striking retreat from individual-centred medicine.[11]

Secondly, the widespread introduction of occupational therapy in asylums increasingly meant that patients' recoveries were measured in terms of their economic productivity. Unfortunately, not all patients were capable of rolling cigars, weaving baskets, running errands or answering the telephone. Each asylum therefore had a quantity of 'incurables' languishing in unproductive hebetude, and conditions were often parlous. The adoption of occupational therapy implicitly meant separating the able-bodied and willing from the therapy-resistant chaff. In other words, these reforms were contributing to the creation of a psychiatrically defined sub-class within a group of people already consigned to the margins of society. Long before the National Socialist government appeared on the scene, some psychiatrists advocated, or countenanced, killing this permanent reminder of the limits of their own therapeutic capacities and permanent burden upon the nation's scant resources. This included some of those responsible for running ecclesiastical charitable networks, whose slippery theological justification of such a course of action was that the artificial maintenance of such forms of life represented as much of an interference in God's dominion as the artificial acceleration of death through 'mercy killing'.[12] The Depression, with its renewed conflicts over division of the social product, again raised questions about the utility of provision in the psychiatric sector. Psychiatrists responded to the state's cost-cutting demands by advocating a two-tier system consisting of intensive therapy for acute cases, and minimal provision for the chronic, coupled with sterilisation of discharged patients to lessen the subsequent eugenic damage.[13] Thus 1933 did not mark a decisive break; most of the policies of the Nazi period were more or less apparent in the Janus-faced, and crisis-ridden, health and welfare apparatus of the Weimar Republic.

None the less, the advent of a National Socialist government had dire direct and indirect consequences for the asylum population. Asylums became freak-shows, with thousands of members of Nazi formations being given tours to illustrate the inherent uselessness of the patients. Between 1933 and 1939, 21,000 people trooped through Eglfing-Haar, including 6,000 members of the SS, some of whom came out recommending setting up machine guns at the entrance to mow down the inmates.[14] Reflecting a general brutalisation of thought and feeling, Party newspapers and journals such as the *Völkische Beobachter* or *Schwarze Korps* dilated upon the Goyaesque scenes in the asylums, and advocated killing the mentally ill, often coupling this with heroic instances of 'mercy killing' carried out by individuals.[15] A political movement which fetishised the mindless and narcissistic activism of youth almost axiomatically entailed the neglect of the elderly and frail, let alone the mentally ill or physically disabled. The young were reportedly more crass and vicious in their attitudes towards these groups than older sections of the population.[16]

With the regional health authorities increasingly in the hands of men such as Fritz Bernotat in Wiesbaden or Walter 'Bubi' Schultze in Munich who explicitly advocated killing mental patients, it is hardly surprising that conditions in the asylums soon deteriorated sharply. Specialist facilities were closed, and patients were removed from the private or religious sectors, and crammed into cheaper state institutions to save money and increase control. An asylum like Eichberg in the Rheingau had 793 patients in 1934; 1,236 by 1940. The doctor–patient ratio deteriorated from 1:162 to 1:300 between 1935 and 1938.[17] In some institutions they were as high as 1:500 which made basic care, i.e. hygiene, watering and feeding, let alone any treatment, totally impossible.[18] The meagre sums expended upon patient food were cut, for example, at Haina from 0.69 RM per day in 1932 to 0.54 RM in 1935.[19] This was against a background of general economic recovery. Enthusiastic lower-class National Socialist administrators replaced disinterested boards of upper-class philanthropists in the running of institutions such as the Idstein reformatory, gradually marginalising medical control of what went on in these institutions.[20] With trained doctors no longer necessarily in charge, the economic efficiency of 'the works' became the primary goal. Many of the psychiatrists – and it had always tended to recruit the dross of the medical profession anyway – were SS members, inherently antagonistic towards their patients. Below them, a host of thoroughly unsuitable people, armed with Party cards and Storm Trooper (SA) membership, flooded into nursing in order to escape the dole queues. Independent inspectors, some of whom deplored the fact that patients were sleeping on straw on the floor or going about virtually naked, and who objected to the brutal language used by senior health administrators such as Bernotat, were simply debarred from further visits.[21] In sum, the public presumption that a person was being entrusted to the safe-keeping of an asylum could no longer be taken as self-evident.

Apart from the on-going deterioration of general conditions, psychiatric patients were directly affected by the Law for the Prevention of Hereditarily Diseased Progeny, which sanctioned compulsory sterilisation for a range of putatively hereditary illnesses. Of course, Germany was not unique in adopting these dubious strategies, although it rapidly exceeded competitor eugenic enthusiasts in other nations in terms of numbers affected by these policies. Psychiatrists were among those statutorily responsible for initiating the procedures eventuating in a person's sterilisation, and indeed, often sat on the 220 local Hereditary Health Courts which made the final decisions. Again, this close, 'sweetheart' arrangement between those who initiated sterilisations and those who authorised them was not unique to Germany. At this time, the hereditary character of the illnesses concerned was as much a declaration of faith, as opposed to a matter of scientific certitude, as it is today.

As the later 'euthanasia' enthusiast Professor Carl Schneider put it in 1931 during the Protestant Inner Mission's conference on eugenics at Treysa, sterilisation was 'a fashion without clear foundations'.[22] This did not stop the conference from officially adopting these negative eugenic strategies. Leaving aside the fact that one genuinely hereditary illness – haemophilia – was actually omitted from the Law, the prefix 'hereditary' was dropped from schizophrenia in order to sterilise those where the cause was exogenous, while reformed drunks or people with low alcohol tolerance who imbibed relatively small quantities of drink, were sterilised as 'chronic alcoholics', on the grounds that alcoholism reflected some underlying 'asocial or psychopathic disorder', neither of which separate – and equally elastic – conditions were specified in this legislation. Nor did the courts confine themselves to the people who actually passed before them. For example, after he had ordered the sterilisation of a young woman, the Kaufbeuren psychiatrist Hermann Pfannmüller, who was also a judge in the court at Kempten, spent a week isolating twenty-one additional 'degenerates' in her family, recommending the sterilisation of ten of them as being 'highly urgent since the danger of reproduction appeared immanent'.[23] In a thoroughly pernicious development, school teachers were encouraged to set their pupils the task of constructing their own family trees, with a view to helping identify any defective members, while mayors reported single mothers, primarily to curtail the costs involved in looking after their illegitimate children.[24]

Apart from the permanent psychological damage sterilisation caused those affected, it was not uncommon for people to die on the operating table or to commit suicide before or afterwards. This was particularly true of women, in an evolving political climate which set great store upon eugenically fit, prolific, motherhood. The regime's remorseless propaganda campaign to sell these policies inevitably entailed stoking up mass resentment against the 'burden' represented by the asylum population. Propaganda films regularly disputed the human 'personality' of the mentally ill and mentally handicapped through talk of 'beings' and 'creatures'; deliberately and indiscriminately conflated dangerous criminals – notably sex offenders and murderers – with the insane; and advocated a reversion to Social-Darwinian elimination of the weak and the abandonment of a counter-selective, and eugenically deleterious, welfare apparatus. In these films, patients were degraded and stigmatised as an exponential threat to the hereditary health of the racial collective, sometimes with much stress upon the allegedly above-average proportion of Jewish psychiatric cases.[25] Being a totalitarian dictatorship, there was no possibility of alternative views being expressed, as was the case with Hollywood, which produced films actively opposed to the activities of American eugenicists.

From the mid-1930s, what had once more become a very desolate psychiatric landscape, was temporarily and partially illuminated by the arrival of a new range of somatic therapies: insulin coma, cardiazol and electro-convulsive therapy, all of which were enthusiastically adopted during the 1930s.[26] Accounts of their use often included detailed 'before and after' case histories, and the testimonies of people who felt miraculously disburdened from isolating and oppressive illnesses. For example, a young woman treated for persecution mania with a combined course of insulin and cardiazol wrote to her relatives: 'Now I can write to you as the Hilde of old! Imagine, Mummy, Saturday evening in bed, it just dawned following a conversation with the others. Naturally I am eating again, for not eating was just part of the persecution mania. You cannot imagine the feeling of being freed from every fear. One is born again so to speak. Now I look forward to Sunday and to seeing you dear Mummy. It should have clicked together before, then you would have noticed something, but none the less, we should thank our lucky stars. How are you then? I am so very happy.'[27] Notwithstanding the incidences of fractured bones, memory loss or spinal damage, a new optimism was abroad, for with these therapies, psychiatrists could argue that they actually cured people.

But paradoxically, these limited psychiatric successes with acute cases, only served once again to heighten professional embarrassment *vis-à-vis* that proportion of patients for whom they could do nothing. Acute cases could be treated (or exploited) with occupational therapy or these new somatic techniques. Any danger the person might represent to the hereditary health of the collective could be neutralised through compulsory sterilisation, or voluntary sterilisation as a condition of their release. But this still left the problem of the refractory and incurable, upon whom these therapies made no impact. Responding to a report from government auditors in November 1939, Director Hermann Pfannmüller of Eglfing-Haar commented: 'The problem of whether to maintain this patient material under the most primitive conditions or to eradicate it has now become a subject for serious discussion once more.'[28] Selective therapeutic intensity had once again pushed a certain patient constituency to the margins of an already marginal group, but this time, in a political climate where the masters of the state had no moral inhibitions about murder, and wished to clear the decks for the war they were bent on waging. Although it is difficult to reconstruct the thought processes of men who were seriously irrational, Hitler seems to have aired the view in 1935 that he would use the cover of war to kill psychiatric patients. The idea of annihilating the Jews should any war-like venture on his part escalate to the point of global conflict, and hence likely defeat, predated this.

Before turning to the 'euthanasia' programme, one final element needs to be introduced into this discussion, namely the extent to which these policies were consensual. For with this subject, matters are a little more complicated than the conventional triad of victims, bystanders and perpetrators. Most discussions of National Socialist justifications for their policies quite reasonably alight upon the influence of Binding and Hoche's utilitarian tract, without noticing that the Nazis very often refer to an author who was that tract's most passionate critic. In 1925, Ewald Meltzer, the director of the Katherinenhof asylum for backward juveniles at Grosshennersdorf in Saxony, published an extremely powerful critique of Binding and Hoche, which stressed both the joy handicapped people took in life, and the altruistic sentiments caring for them engendered in others, while condemning the inflationary and materialistic character of the arguments used by the two professors.[29]

Meltzer decided to carry out a poll of the views on 'euthanasia' held by the parents of his charges. To his obvious surprise, some 73 per cent of the 162 respondents said that they would approve 'the painless curtailment of the life of [their] child if experts had established that it is suffering from incurable idiocy'. Many of the 'yes' respondents said that they wished to offload the burden represented by an 'idiotic' child, with some of them expressing the wish that this be done surreptitiously, in a manner which anticipated later National Socialist practice. Only twenty of the forty-three 'no' respondents in fact rejected all of Meltzer's four propositions – some of the 'no' group actually consented to their child's death in the event that it was orphaned – it thus being a minority who would not sanction the death of their child under any circumstances.[30] Surveying National Socialist propaganda on these issues, it is thus not surprising that Meltzer should be as frequently cited as Binding and Hoche. The SS Security Service (SD) reports carried out later in connection with the film *Ich klage an* would also reveal that attitudes were far from clear cut on these issues, despite the fact that by that time they were less academic than they were when Meltzer conducted his survey.[31] Meltzer himself was not entirely on the side of the angels, for in 1937 he publicly acknowledged that there could be conditions of national emergency, when because of food shortages or the need for bed-space for military casualties, 'the patient too must pay his dues to the Fatherland' through some form of involuntary 'mercy killing'.[32] These circumstances arose two years later, and notionally involved the issue of 'euthanasia'.

The origins of the Nazi 'euthanasia' programme were indeed partially bound up with requests for 'mercy killing'. The reason Hitler decided to assign the task to the Chancellory of the Führer was not simply that this small prerogative agency could act secretly outside the normative channels of government, but also that the Chancellory of the Führer handled incoming petitions which included requests for 'euthanasia' from the population. These came, *inter alia*, from a woman dying of cancer, from a man blinded and severely injured after falling into a cement mixer, and from the parents of a handicapped infant called Knauer, languishing blind and without a leg and part of an arm in a Leipzig clinic.[33]

Hitler despatched Karl Brandt, the emergency accident surgeon attached to his retinue, to Leipzig to authorise the death of this child. He them commissioned Brandt and Philipp Bouhler, the head of the Chancellory of the Führer, to make similar authorisations in the future.[34] A panel of paediatric specialists – all of whom believed it was time to jettison the Judaeo-Christian ethical heritage based on the doctrine of the sanctity of human life – made the decision, with the children concerned sent 'on hold' to one of several special paediatric clinics. These promised the parents the most up-to-date treatment, with the revealing rider that this might entail serious risks.[35] Parents who had exhausted every avenue, or who were worn down by having to cope with several children, or who simply did not want some sort of eugenic 'taint' on their family pedigree, handed over their children, often in the knowledge that they would not survive the promised treatment.[36] Welfare agencies used coercive powers to compel single parents to relinquish their children.

The latter were killed by a combination of starvation and lethal medication. Some of the nurses involved may have found the work disturbing, but they also thought it right to 'release unfortunate creatures from their suffering', and appreciated the regular bonus payments. The doctors were all volunteers. That one could say 'no' is clearly illustrated by the case of Dr Friedrich Hölzel, who used the opportunity of a vacation spoiled by rain, to write to Pfannmüller declining the job of running the paediatric clinic at Eglfing. Although he approved of these policies, Hölzel felt that it was another matter to carry them out in person, a distinction which reminded him of 'the difference which exists between a judge and executioner'. He thought he was too weak, and too concerned with helping his patients, to be able to 'carry this out as a systematic policy after cold-blooded deliberation'.[37] Pfannmüller never pressed him any further on the matter. In total, as many as 6,000 children were killed in this programme, with the age range being quietly raised to encompass adolescents.

Hitler's wartime authorisation of an adult 'euthanasia' programme was conceived as an economy measure, a means of creating emergency bed-space, and hostels for ethnic German repatriates from Russia and eastern Europe, which anticipates and mirrors the linkages between 'resettlement' and murder later evident in the Holocaust.[38] These were not chimerical, futuristic or metaphorical goals merely designed to remobilise the movement's flagging dynamism, but a series of definite aims, coldly determined in advance after a great deal of co-ordination between like-minded individuals. In the eastern areas of the Reich, SS units under Eimann and Lange were sub-contracted to shoot psychiatric patients in a parallel operation. The Chancellory of the Führer established an elaborate covert bureaucracy based at Tiergartenstrasse 4 (hence the code-name 'Aktion T-4'), whose task was to organise the registration, selection, transfer and murder of a previously calculated target group of 70,000 people, including chronic schizophrenics, epileptics and long-stay patients. This apparatus was run by a group of economists, agronomists, lawyers and businessmen, with an expanded pool of academics and psychiatrists, under Werner Heyde and from 1941 Paul Nitsche, whose task was to handle the medical side of mass murder.[39]

Together, this odd assortment of highly educated, morally dulled, humanity set about registering and selecting victims; finding asylums to serve as extermination centres; establishing an effective means; and last but not least, a staff of people willing and able to commit mass murder. Both Herbert Linden, the desk officer responsible for state asylums in the Ministry of the Interior, and his regional equivalents, such as Walter

'Bubi' Schultze in Munich or Ludwig Sprauer in Stuttgart, proved co-operative since they had been advocating such policies for several years anyway. These men either identified suitable asylums, such as Grafeneck, or recommended doctors, orderlies and nurses whose track record and level of objectified ideological commitment singled them out as potential T-4 material.[40] Heyde volunteered the names of former students. The SS, which for various reasons remained at one remove from these policies, provided seasoned hard-men who could cope with the physicality of mass murder. Teams of these people were despatched to six killing centres. The doctors who monopolised killing were given perfunctory briefing sessions in Berlin, and then gradually inducted into murder, progressing from observing the procedures to carrying them out themselves. Most of them were quite young, socially insecure and hugely impressed by major academic names (de Crinis, Heyde, Carl Schneider, etc.) and grand places (the Chancellory of the Führer), that is, the usual accompaniments of petit bourgeois academic ambition. Their narrow professional training added no element of moral inhibition.[41] The nurses and orderlies were products of a professional and societal culture of obedience, and in addition, often had proven records of ideological commitment, or believed in the moral correctness of 'euthanasia' killings, especially on the grounds that monies allegedly squandered on the mentally ill in 'luxury' asylums, could be used to improve public housing.[42]

Registration forms were completed on every patient, and despatched via T-4 to assessors. Many asylum directors, who were unclear concerning the ultimate purpose of the forms, made the fatal mistake of deliberately misrepresenting a patient's capacity to work in order not to lose valuable workers as a consequence of what they took to be a survey of essential labour. Low or merely mechanical productivity, irremediable illness, or the duration of institutionalisation sufficed effectively to sign a person's death warrant. In other words, the pool of victims was drawn from the sub-class created earlier by the psychiatric reformers. The T-4 assessors, such as the ubiquitous Pfannmüller, received batches of 200 to 300 forms at a time, and were remunerated on a piecework basis. This probably accounts for the diagnostic virtuosity of such psychiatric Stakhanovites as Dr Josef Schreck, who completed 15,000 forms single-handedly in a month.[43] On the basis of these forms, groups of patients were taken from the asylums by the Community Patients Transport Service, either directly to their deaths in the gas chambers of one of six killing centres, or to proximate holding asylums, whose purpose was to confuse anxious relatives, and to stagger the burden on the crematoria. An elaborate system of deceit took care of every angle, from faking the cause of death, to lying about when and where it had occurred in order not to arouse suspicions in places where several persons happened to have been in the same asylum.

These killings inevitably meant contacts between T-4 and a host of private, state and religious asylums. Indeed half of the victims of 'Aktion T-4' came from asylums and homes run by the two main ecclesiastical welfare networks, the Protestant Inner Mission and the Roman Catholic Caritas Association. The fact that 1,911 of the 2,137 inhabitants of the Protestant Neuendettelsau asylums in Franconia were taken away and murdered comes as no surprise, given that as early as 1937 the medical director, Dr Rudolph Boeckh, said in a lecture to the local National Socialist German Workers' Party (NSDAP) group, that 'idiots' were 'a travesty of humankind' who deserved to be 'returned to the Creator'.[44] Indeed, some Inner Mission asylums, such as Scheurn in Hesse-Nassau, actually acted as intermediary holding centres for patients en route to Hadamar, while Protestant nursing sisters worked in Bernburg throughout the period when about 20,000 people were murdered there. Some asylums tried to subvert the operation by delaying completion of the forms, once they realised or heard through the grapevine of their malign purpose. The fact that one of those who went to great lengths to rewrite diagnoses in a way less harmful to the patients, Dr Karsten Jaspersen of Bethel Sarepta, was himself a Nazi 'old fighter' suggests that political affiliation was not necessarily a guide to how individuals behaved in these circumstances.[45] A few asylums tried to hide vulnerable individuals or arrange for their families to take them home with them. However, discharge depended upon the willingness of families to take them in, the response sometimes being that there was no more room in the inn.[46] In the absence of co-operation from families, most asylums contented themselves with the fact that they had haggled over the life of this or that patient, for T-4 were clever enough to countenance a degree of plea bargaining. In the case of the network of Bodelschwingh asylums at Bielefeld, the eminence of both the director and some of the patients, including Göring's brother-in-law (according to Heyde he was 'definitely a case for euthanasia'), meant that T-4 sanctioned the use of Bethel's own 'in-house' criteria for selection.[47] The fact that individual churchmen, notably Bishop Galen of Münster, protested against these policies (over a year after he was informed about them by, *inter alios*, Dr Karsten Jaspersen) has received more attention than the fact that T-4 obviously solicited a justificatory memorandum from an academic Roman Catholic theologian before they commenced operations. More damagingly, the Roman Catholic hierarchy entered into negotiations with T-4 to secure an 'opt-out clause' for Catholic asylum staff and the last sacraments for Catholic victims, negotiations which were only broken off when the Church's chief negotiator, Bishop Wienken, went so 'native' in his dealings with T-4 as seriously to embarrass his superiors.[48] One should bear in mind the fact that the Roman Catholic Church's concern with administering the last sacraments was often coupled with its priests' refusal to give Christian burial to the ashes of victims of the 'euthanasia' programme, on the grounds that they had been cremated.

In total, T-4 murdered over 70,000 people, with many of them entering a gas chamber equipped with a towel and a toothbrush. A final report translated the monthly murder rate into graphic form, while precisely enumerating how much money or which commodities, such as butter, bread, coffee or marmalade had been saved through the 'disinfection' of 70,273 persons, figures whose monetary equivalents were then extrapolated down to 1951.[49]

Following a cessation of mass gassings in August 1941, the T-4 medical assessors were turned loose on the inmates of concentration camps, where under 'Aktion 14f13' they proceeded to 'select' persons whom the SS deemed to be 'sick', or people whose race or record they disapproved of.[50] There is no evidence that the doctors involved were even conscious of having stepped across the threshold from the medical into the infernal. That same autumn, Viktor Brack, the economist who ran the T-4 operation, had an interview with Himmler, who had once employed him as a driver. Himmler allegedly said that 'Hitler had some time ago given him the order for the extermination of the Jews. He said that preparations had already been made, and I think that he used the expression that for reasons of camouflage one would have to work as quickly as possible.'[51] The T-4 staff were to become one of the separate groups involved in the various competitive, quasi-experimental pushes designed to solve the 'Jewish Question'. As experts in mass gassing, they were given the lion's share of the operation, apart from Hoess's murder factory at Auschwitz.

Some ninety-two T-4 personnel were made available by Bouhler to the Higher SS- and Police Leader in Lublin, the ex-bricklayer, Odilo Globocnik.[52] With the SS 'euthanasia' veteran Herbert Lange installed at Kulmhof, this T-4 team formed the dedicated core responsible for 'Aktion Reinhard'. A motley array of former butchers, cooks, labourers, lorry drivers and policemen, including Erich Bauer, Kurt Franz, Lorenz Hackenholt, Josef Oberhauser, Franz Stangl and Christian Wirth, moved up several social notches to preside over the murder of the Jewish masses of eastern Europe and the Jewish bourgeoisie of western Europe in Belzec, Sobibor and Treblinka. While few of them were convicted psychopaths like Hoess, these men did not become extremely violent, they began like that, indefinitely deferring and evading recognition of their own awfulness through black humour and talk of production targets. Indeed, the final statistical tally, drawn up by Globocnik in December 1943, precisely enumerated the vast sums garnered in the process, as well as nearly 2,000 wagonloads of bedding, clothing and towels, and such quotidian ephemera as sunglasses, opera glasses, powder puffs, and cigarette cases.[53] Following the dismantling of these extermination camps, the T-4 men set off once again, to operate a killing centre on the Dalmatian coast at Trieste called the Risiera, after a former rice warehouse, which they used to torture and murder Jews bottlenecked en route to Auschwitz or putative partisans. About 5,000 people died there.[54]

In the old Reich, 'euthanasia' killings continued on a more decentralised basis in an extended range of asylums. The patients were killed through starvation and lethal medication. Where religious affiliations of the nursing staff made this difficult, as at Kaufbeuren-Irsee, practised T-4 murderers, such as nurse Pauline Kneissler, were sent in with the resulting mortality rates only falling in the weeks when she went away on holiday.[55] Meetings were held in the regional health ministries to sort out the comparabilities of starvation diets, with psychiatrists exchanging 'menus' consisting of nothing more than root vegetables boiled in fluid. There were no food shortages in the asylums, since most of them continued to generate considerable surpluses, surpluses which the administrators sold off at a considerable profit.[56] There is also the well-documented fact of doctors like Friedrich Mennecke of Eichberg, whose letters reveal him gourmandising his way around the country at a time when his patients were literally starving.[57] These are recorded facts about the mentality of those involved, indicative of their unself-conscious tastelessness, if of nothing else. Both this adult programme and the killing of children continued until the last days of the war.

Death was routinely visited upon anyone deemed unproductive or whose behaviour or manner irritated the staff, with patients sometimes being co-opted into killing their fellow inmates. Escape attempts or misdemeanours resulted in lethal injections or handfuls of sedatives being forced down one's throat in the dead of night. Many of the victims were foreign forced labourers, suffering from tuberculosis, as well as from mental illnesses brought about by the inhuman conditions in which they lived or worked. Killing them on the spot was deemed cheaper than repatriation.[58] Since most of them could not communicate in German, there was no attempt to find out what was wrong with them. Indeed, in its later inflationary stages, the 'euthanasia' programme encompassed homes for geriatrics and vagrants or people driven insane by Allied bombing. 'Euthanasia' killings were supplied on demand to create bed-space for civilian casualities. SD reports recently discovered in Russia reveal widespread fear among elderly people regarding geriatric homes, sanatoria or even a routine visit to the doctor.[59]

Obviously policies, like the ones described above, which were impossible to keep secret, did nothing for the image of either asylums or psychiatry. More importantly, they were like sawing off the branch upon which one was sitting, for depopulated asylums were usually alienated for non-medical purposes. In order to counteract these unwanted tendencies, psychiatrists working for T-4 such as Paul Nitsche or Carl Schneider put forward various proposals for the 'modernisation' of psychiatry, that is using the funds saved through these killings to provide up-to-date therapies for acute cases. The more or less explicit subsidiary agenda was to build up university-based research activities, by integrating this with the neurological 'material' made available to the professors by the 'euthanasia' programme.[60] These plans were thus about reasserting professional psychiatric control over policies which were economically driven, whose effect was to put young recruits off entirely, and whose logic threatened the existence of this entire branch of medicine. They were thus a form of *ex post facto* rationalisation, a means of evading the fact that these men had in fact created conditions in the asylums which a few enlightened doctors described as a 'reversion to the psychiatry of the Middle Ages', with untended and skeletal patients lying naked in their own excrement and urine on straw sacks, and people locked alone in dark vermin-infested bunkers. Doctors bestrode the wards, not as 'modernising' idealists, but as self-styled 'soldiers' for whom the patients, particularly if they were people who spoke not a word of German, had literally become 'the enemy'.[61]

CHAPTER FIVE

The Churches, eugenics and the Nazi 'euthanasia' programme

This account of how the two major Churches responded to the Nazi 'euthanasia' programme, namely the mass murder of the mentally ill and mentally or physically deficient between 1939 and 1945, deals with the responses of their hierarchies and the stratagems adopted by the asylums which were part of their respective charitable networks. It is based upon both original archival sources and a large variety of secondary literature dealing with the two Churches and the individual asylums. Before considering how the Churches conducted themselves during the Nazi period, it is necessary to establish the broader context of their response to eugenics in general.

The Inner Mission was the principal Protestant health and welfare umbrella organisation. It disposed of several hundred institutions for the mentally or physically disabled, the mentally ill, epileptics and geriatric patients. Although many of these institutions affected the name 'Heil- und Pflegeanstalt', in practice, church-run asylums specialised in the low-cost maintenance, as opposed to the treatment, of 'incurables'. Nor was the Inner Mission impervious to international 'progressive' scientific fashions or to local anxieties regarding qualitative and quantitative demographic decline.[1] In late January 1931, the Inner Mission's Standing Conference on Eugenics convened for the first time in Treysa under the chairmanship of Hans Harmsen. Stressing the impossibility of rising social costs during a major economic crisis, Harmsen called for the introduction of differential provision for those who could be returned to the productive process and the eugenic sterilisation of the 'less valuable'. Ironically, the one dissenting voice from the general chorus advocating sterilisation was the later 'euthanasia' psychiatrist Professor Carl Schneider, who observed that sterilisation was 'a fashion without clear foundations'.[2]

Protestant theologians legitimised the abandonment of universal welfare by arguing that God had created such supra-individual entities as the family, nations or races, whose future well-being overrode the rights of individuals, which in recent times had come to be regarded as absolute.[3] Although the conference rejected both eugenic abortion and the destruction of 'life unworthy of life', it was ominous that it was necessary to observe: 'The artificial prolongation of life which is in the process of being extinguished can represent as much of an interference in God's creative will as "euthanasia" – that is the artificial curtailment of physical dissolution.'[4] These deliberations translated into support for government policy, even when that policy chose to ignore recommended qualifications and refinements. Having supported the terms of the Prussian government draft law of 2 July 1932 on voluntary sterilisation, the Protestant Church accepted the compulsory measures introduced by the National Socialists, merely arguing that force should not be employed in their own establishments and that the sterilisation of the deaf or blind remained voluntary.[5] Sterilisations of 2,399 inmates were carried out in Protestant asylums during 1934, 3,140 in the first six months of 1935.[6]

Since the authorities at the Inner Mission asylums such as Hephata repeatedly applied for permission to sterilise patients in their own facilities, to avoid the cost of sending them to university clinics or hospitals, it would be misleading to conclude that these policies were imposed on them.[7] The annual reports of asylums such as Schwäbisch Hall or Stetten were positively self-congratulatory in tone regarding how the staff had coped with the extra workload involved, or the diplomatic skill they displayed in persuading patients to 'volunteer' for sterilisation in return for enhanced privileges or premature discharge.[8] This active collusion should be viewed in the broader context of welcoming the advent of a National Socialist government. Thus, in the summer of 1933, Director Friedrich Happich of Hephata, enthused over 'the ardently hoped for turning away from a destructive parliamentarism, which had revealed itself incapable of building anything, in favour of a strong nationalist leadership of the state'.[9] Most asylums celebrated the advent of a National Socialist government as a deliverance from Bolshevism. They quickly introduced the 'Führer principle' to their establishments, regimenting the lives of their patients, and enjoined their personnel to join Nazi formations, although few emulated Pastor Johannes Wolff of the Stephansstift, who encouraged Storm Troopers (SA) on his staff to work as guards in the neighbouring Papenburg concentration camp.[10]

The Roman Catholic Church, with its parallel welfare network, the Caritas Association, was also not entirely impervious to eugenic fashions. Among prominent Roman Catholics who advocated a combination of 'positive' and 'negative' eugenic measures was the former Jesuit Hermann Muckermann, who led the section for eugenics studies at the Kaiser-Wilhelm Institute until his dismissal, notionally for having referred to the Führer as 'an idiot'.[11] There were also individual academic theologians, notably Joseph Mayer of Paderborn, who by asserting the primacy of the 'health of the body of the nation' over the rights of individuals, were prepared to countenance eugenic sterilisation. Mayer's minority opinions would play a key role during the 'euthanasia' programme. However, the 1930 papal encyclical *Casti Connubii* (On Christian Marriage) represented a major obstacle to the diffusion of such advanced views, by stressing that the right of families to have children overrode the right of the state to healthy citizens. Throughout the discussions concerning a sterilisation law, the influential *Osservatore Romano* was highly critical of the trend for governments to act as 'cattle breeders'. However, once the law was passed, in the same cabinet session which approved the Concordat with the Vatican, the tactics of the German hierarchy subtly shifted to a limited rearguard attempt to exempt the directors of Roman Catholic asylums from the duty of applying for the sterilisation of their charges. Bishops resolved the crises of conscience of individual nurses and welfare workers with sophistic distinctions between passively doing one's duty or actively soliciting another's harm.[12] Some individual Roman Catholic priests did distinguish themselves by implacably opposing these policies. The Benedictine priest Franziskus Deininger used the printing press in the monastery of Beuron to run off copies of a pamphlet severely critical of sterilisation and hence found himself before a Nazi 'Special Court'. Entire institutions, such as the home for the blind at Pfaffenhausen in Swabia, also endeavoured to protect their charges from the effects of the sterilisation law by segregating the sexes or curtailing their contact with the outside world, thus pre-empting the need for 'negative' eugenic measures.[13]

In contrast to their position on sterilisation, both Churches were unanimous in condemning calls, beginning with the arguments of Binding and Hoche in 1920, to eliminate 'life unworthy of life' either in the interests of economy or as a result of the philosophical redefinition of what constituted a 'person'.[14] In 1934, the Roman Catholic hierarchy and the Caritas Association saw off an attempt to introduce some form of legalised 'euthanasia' in the general context of a reform of criminal law. Some sections of the Inner Mission, however, conceded that the state had the right to under-provision those deemed 'life unworthy of life' in line with its restricted utilitarian ethic, while within the walls of its asylums, the Inner Mission would continue with the more expansive practice of caring for the 'poorest of the poor', thus highlighting its 'missionary' function.[15] This perverse acceptance of a dual and differential ethical system was worrying. But there were also people who were ready to concede to the state a much more proactive role in certain circumstances, as well as those working within the Inner Mission who were convinced Nazis. Two examples will suffice to illustrate each point.

In 1925, Ewald Meltzer, director of the Katherinenhof home for backward juveniles at Grosshennersdorf in Saxony, published the most systematic critique of the ideas of Binding and Hoche, marshalling an impressive array of historical, philosophical and theological arguments against the sanctioning of the 'destruction of life unworthy of life'. It was not his fault that the results of a poll he appended to the book, revealing overwhelming parental consent to the killing by the state of their 'idiot' children, became one of the main elements in National Socialist propaganda. However, his own views on the subject were far from fundamentalist. In 1934, Meltzer publicly admitted that, like the Saxon 'sterilisation apostle' Heinrich Boeters, he had also sanctioned sterilisations at a time when they were still illegal.[16] Three years later, in an address to an Inner Mission conference on 'racial hygiene', he acknowledged that there could be conditions of national emergency when, because of food shortages or the need for bed-space for military casualties, 'the patient too must pay his dues to the Fatherland' through some form of 'mercy killing'. This specifically referred to 'idiots' and hence excluded the elderly.[17]

The medical staff of some Inner Mission foundations also included vociferous advocates of the elimination of 'life unworthy of life'. In 1937, Rudolf Boeckh, the chief doctor at the Lutheran Neuendettesslau asylum in central Franconia, addressed his local National Socialist German Workers' Party (NSDAP) group on the need to eliminate such people. Pointing to the alleged explosion of welfare provision since the nineteenth century, Boeckh claimed that ordinary people were outraged that epileptics were receiving extensive dental treatment while workers went about with decaying teeth, or that 'palaces' and 'villa quarters' (he meant pavilion-style asylums) were being built to house mental patients. The 'life-affirming' National Socialist state was the first in recent times 'to regard all that is sick which cannot be restored to health as a burden'. Aware, no doubt, by virtue of the nature of his institution, of likely theological objections, Boeckh used a rather tortuous line of argument to reconcile 'euthanasia' with God's handiwork:

> Although the Creator had certainly imposed illness upon the destiny of mankind, the most severe forms of idiocy and the totally grotesque disintegration of the personality had nothing to do with the countenance of God, and the Creator had set a warning in our hearts in the form of our feeling for the affirmation of life, that we should not maintain these travesties of human form through an exaggerated, and therefore false, type of compassion, but rather we should return them to the Creator.[18]

Throughout the later 1930s, the regional health and welfare authorities, themselves dominated by Nazi 'euthanasia' enthusiasts, endeavoured to take direct control of internal affairs of church-run asylums, or failing this, to drain away their communally funded patients into state facilities where, of course, they would be more vulnerable to the consequences of radical policies. Religious who tried to prevent this happening found themselves accused of using excessive discipline or sexual abuse, with bribes sometimes being used to secure the appropriate testimony from their young charges.[19] Since the men and women who opted for a life away from the world were often ill equipped to deal with it, we should not rush to condemn them for timidity in the face of a vicious totalitarian dictatorship. This was not akin to whistle-blowing in the contemporary National Health Service. In the autumn of 1939, the Chancellory of the Führer and its various T-4 front organisations (the code came from the address of their headquarters at Tiergartenstrasse 4 in Berlin) embarked upon the 'euthanasia' programme which claimed the lives of over 70,000 people by August 1941.[20] The Churches were no longer confronted by these issues in the abstract, but with their practical and illegal implementation.

Affecting different regions in a swathe-like fashion, the first victims were thirteen patients from the Inner Mission for epileptics at Pfingstweide near Tettnang in Württemberg. In early 1940 they were 'transferred' to the former Inner Mission Samaritan Foundation home for cripples at Grafeneck which, in October 1939, T-4 had expropriated and converted into an extermination centre. Relatives who had received death certificates from Grafeneck claiming that the victims had died of 'angina', 'influenza' or 'pneumonia', found it 'funny' that the victim's religion or home address were given as 'unknown' (which would not have been the case if their medical records had accompanied them on their travels), and that they had been cremated because of the risk of 'contagious diseases', which could hardly be the case with angina. Disquieting reports such as these rang alarm bells within the Inner Mission regarding the 'practical implementation' of what had often been 'theoretically and academically contemplated'.[21] Word of what was happening at Grafeneck, where 10,000 people were killed, spread like wildfire, so that even men working on the railway line, along which trainloads of patients passed en route to the killing centre, downed tools and removed their caps out of respect for the victims.

It gradually dawned upon the staff of individual church-run asylums that they were dealing with covert prerogative organisations bent upon removing and killing their patients without any legal pretext whatsoever. The first crucial stage consisted of the arrival of registration forms which the asylum staff were obliged to complete concerning certain categories of patient. Most asylum administrators and doctors seem to have believed that these forms were part of an economy drive designed to hive off certain groups of patients into much cheaper facilities. This practice was in line with most contemporary psychiatric thinking both on differential levels of care for acute and chronic patients and on the medical advantages of separating the two categories.[22] Some doctors, such as Gebhard Ritter of Liebenau, became suspicious about questions regarding the frequency with which patients received visitors.[23] A few, notably Karsten Jaspersen, the chief psychiatrist at the Inner Mission's Sarepta asylum at Bielefeld-Bethel, made it their business to know the use these forms served and in his case not only refused to complete them but alerted his colleagues in other institutions. The fact that Jaspersen was a Nazi 'old fighter', having joined the NSDAP in 1931, suggests that an individual's political beliefs are not necessarily a reliable indicator of behaviour in these circumstances.[24]

Non-co-operation in completing these forms did not mean relief, for T-4 simply despatched roving teams of medical assessors who would carry out the work more expeditiously and capriciously. The asylum authorities at Schönbrunn accurately enough likened the arrival of such a team to the spreading of a shroud over the asylum.[25] At Bielefeld-Bethel, Jaspersen and Professor Gerhard Schorsch suggested rival strategies to deal with a visiting T-4 commission. Jaspersen recommended altering the diagnoses in the patient records, so that 'schizophrenia' became 'reactive psychosis' and 'manic-depressive illness' was metamorphosed into 'cyclothymia', through which jiggery-pokery he hoped to rescue those categories of patient most in danger. Schorsch, by contrast, met T-4 halfway by offering to categorise the 3,000 patients according to seven performance criteria ranging from 'vegetative existence' via 'mechanical work' to 'very good performance'.[26] On their departure, the T-4 team pronounced themselves 'very satisfied' with Schorsch's labours. A similar strategy seems to have been frequently used by asylums once they received lists of patients whom T-4 intended to 'transfer' elsewhere, in other words to the gas chambers. Authorities at the Inner Mission's Mariaberg asylum in Württemberg went through the lists, calculating each patient's capacity to work in percentage terms, in order to save the most valuable individuals. This merely meant introducing precision within the overall framework of T-4's own 'productionist' criteria, swapping the expendable for the non-expendable.[27] Of course, T-4 also allowed a degree of 'plea-bargaining' regarding individuals, or a given percentage of transferees, both to satisfy uneasy consciences and to secure complicity.

Further rescue strategies employed by confessional asylums to save individuals included hiding vulnerable patients, permitting them to run away, reclassifying them as private fee-paying patients or releasing them into the care of their families. Since in the last case it was risky to commit the urgency of the situation to paper, religious from the Congregation of St Josef at Ursberg preferred to discuss matters with relatives either in public places such as Augsburg railway station or in the asylum grounds.[28] Releasing patients into the care of the family naturally presupposed the latter's willingness to have them. As the director of Hephata, Adolf Nell, euphemistically observed: 'It was not always simple to deal with the parents of patients. We frequently encountered an absence of feeling regarding taking these patients home again.'[29] Pastor Ludwig Schlaich of the Inner Mission asylum at Stetten similarly noted that 'only a few [relatives] had the courage to take the patient home with them in order to rescue them, even in cases where their domestic circumstances – good will permitted – would have allowed this'.[30] To take one example from many, in 1940 the authorities at Mariaberg endeavoured to release Otto G. into the custody of his brother. Replying on 2 December, the latter explained that his wife had a weak heart; that two soldiers were billeted in his home; his son was in the army; his elderly mother-in-law was half-blind; a nephew from Cologne had come to stay with his three children; visitors from the north were imminent, in other words, that there was no room in the inn for Otto. He concluded, 'rest assured that Otto would never be forgotten', enclosing a little something for Christmas. Otto had no need of it, for he was transferred to Grafeneck on 13 December and killed on arrival.[31] Judging from statistics concerning sixty Roman Catholic asylums affected by these policies, the number of those rescued in the ways detailed above was disappointing. Whereas 1,500 patients were successfully returned to their families, fostered out, reclassified or dispersed to other institutions, 11,225 patients were 'transferred' by the T-4 authorities.[32]

In Württemberg, evidence from both lay and ecclesiastical sources regarding 'euthanasia' killings was collated by the provincial Bishop Theophil Wurm. Opting for private appeals to the better nature of individual National Socialist ministers such as Frick, Gürtner, Lammers or Kerrl, Wurm stressed their common interest in maintaining a moral-political order based upon respect for human life, albeit carefully distinguishing his 'anxieties' from any inkling of disloyalty to a regime whose recent defeat of France he had earnestly prayed for. The strategy favoured by Wurm and such Roman Catholic confrères as Archbishop Conrad Gröber of Freiburg, of appealing privately to the moral sensibilities of Nazi leaders, was by definition doomed to failure. It was also rather worrying that a bishop should write: 'Naturally, the thought has always crossed our minds of those who have seen such regrettable people: "Wouldn't it be better to put an end to such an existence?"'[33] The letters were often duplicated and circulated.

Another strategy was adopted by Pastor Gerhard Braune of the Lobetal asylum, who was commissioned by the Central Committee of the Inner Mission, of which he was vice-president, to produce a detailed memorandum, completed on 9 July 1940, setting out what had been discovered about the 'euthanasia' programme and questioning both its legality and its economic rationality. Using the numbers printed on the urns of ashes sent to relatives, Braune calculated that at Grafeneck some 2,019 people had died over a forty-three-day period in an asylum which only had 100 beds available.[34] Moving on to the deleterious general effects of these policies, Braune argued that they were destroying people's trust in the medical profession; that they were dangerously inflationary, with potential applicability to people suffering from tuberculosis or to wounded soldiers (this was indeed prophetic); and finally, that they made no difference whatsoever to the economic well-being of the nation. Braune's memorandum was handed to Lammers in mid-June 1940. He was arrested by the Gestapo that August, albeit on grounds allegedly unconnected with his memorandum, which of course concerned policies whose existence was never officially acknowledged.

An altogether more dubious approach, namely negotiations with those responsible for the killings, with the object of putting them on a legal footing, or restricting their impact to fewer categories of patient, was pursued by representatives of both Churches. Constantin Frick, President of the Central Committee of the Inner Mission, entered into discussions with both Reich Health Leader Conti and Herbert Linden, the Ministry of the Interior official with direct responsibility for asylums, and *éminence grise* of the 'euthanasia' programme. Frick accepted their spurious claims that the 'euthanasia' programme had a legal basis which, however, could not be publicly acknowledged during wartime. Frick was also prepared to tolerate the continuation of these policies, provided they were restricted to those patients who were 'no longer fit for human society'.[35]

The Roman Catholic Church may well have had some indication of the imminence of these policies before they actually commenced. In early 1939, a renegade priest and SS Security Service (SD) officer Albert Hartl approached the Paderborn moral theologian Joseph Mayer, whose ambivalent attitude towards sterilisation we have already encountered, in search of a quasi-official statement of the Roman Catholic position on 'euthanasia'. The contents of Mayer's memorandum – mental patients were 'lumps of flesh' rather than images of God – were relayed to Hitler, who then allowed word of it to be passed on to certain bishops and the apostolic nuncio Cesare Orsenigo. One of the bishops was Heinrich Wienken of Berlin, who, as the leading light of the Caritas Association, was subsequently commissioned by the Fulda episcopal synod to represent the views of the Roman Catholic

Church to the authorities. Wienken held a series of meetings with Herbert Linden and Hans Hefelmann of the T-4 apparatus, who, armed with Mayer's memorandum, were well equipped to deal with moral-theological objections. Wienken seems to have gone partially native in the sense that he gradually abandoned an absolute stance based on the fifth commandment in favour of winning limited concessions regarding the restriction of killing to 'complete idiots', access to the sacraments and the exclusion of ill Roman Catholic priests from these policies. According to Hefelmann, Wienken appeared ready to 'tolerate' these policies within more circumscribed parameters.[36] This explains the acerbic tone of a letter from Cardinal Michael Faulhaber to Wienken dated 18 November 1940, which rejected the arguments used to support these policies and dismissed Wienken's efforts to secure concessions, which focused on the fact that 'domestic national comrades are being cleared out of the way to create space for foreign national comrades', as totally unacceptable.[37] The talks between Wienken and T-4 collapsed because Hitler was not prepared to put in writing the concessions agreed upon and because, on 2 December 1940, Pius XII issued an unequivocal condemnation of the killing of so-called 'life unworthy of life'. Wienken's subsequent activities included negotiations with Eichmann in 1943 to secure the exemption of 'non-Aryan' Christians from deportation.

The final form of response to these policies was public protest. The most dramatic example was the sermon which Bishop August Clemens Graf von Galen delivered in the Lambertikirche in Münster on 3 August 1941. However, even in this case the evidence is not without ambiguities. Unlike many of his colleagues, Galen had a consistent record of opposition to National Socialism, roughly coterminous in his case with his appointment to the bishopric of Münster in 1933. He was strident in his condemnation of the neo-pagan tendencies represented by Alfred Rosenberg, objecting in 1935 to the latter's presence as a speaker at a rally in his diocese, and assiduous in his defence of the autonomy of Roman Catholic lay organisations against creeping Nazi contraventions of the terms of the Concordat. As a conservative Westphalian aristocrat, Galen was also thoroughly contemptuous of the ways in which 'foreigners' from 'Riga, Reval or Cairo and even Chile' (he meant Rosenberg, Hess and Darré) had taken it upon themselves to dictate what constituted quintessential 'German' characteristics.[38]

Galen was informed about the 'euthanasia' programme by Karsten

Jaspersen in July 1940. The latter had gone to the Roman Catholic St Rochus Hospital at Telgte where he informed the staff as to the purpose of the registration forms they had recently completed. The hospital's spiritual director then relayed a detailed memorandum from Jaspersen to Galen.[39] Regarding this as a subject of concern for the entire episcopate, Galen passed the information on to Cardinal Bertram of Breslau, who on 11 August 1940 sent a rather anodyne letter of protest to Lammers.[40] Approximately a year after he had been informed about what was happening, Galen decided to make the issue public. The immediate catalysts for this risky course of action were the imminent 'transfer' of patients from the Marienthal asylum in his diocese and the decision of the Münster Gestapo to eject both the Jesuits and the Sisters of the Immaculate Conception from property they owned in that city.[41]

On 3 August 1941 Galen delivered a powerful sermon which detailed the precise *modus operandi* employed by those responsible for 'euthanasia' killings. Articulating widespread anxieties regarding their inflationary potential Galen observed:

> If you establish and apply the principle that you can kill 'unproductive' human beings then woe betide us all when we become old and frail! If one is allowed to kill unproductive people, then woe betide the invalids who have used up, sacrificed and lost their health and strength in the productive process. If one is allowed forcibly to remove one's unproductive fellow human beings then woe betide loyal soldiers who return to the homeland seriously disabled, as cripples, as invalids . . . Woe to mankind, woe to our German nation if God's holy commandment 'Thou shalt not kill!', which God proclaimed on Mount Sinai amidst thunder and lightning, which God our Creator inscribed in the conscience of mankind from the very beginning, is not only broken, but if this transgression is actually tolerated, and permitted to go unpunished.[42]

Both the terrible circumstantiality and the widespread diffusion of the sermon (even the Royal Air Force managed to leaflet copies of it) clearly stung the Nazi leadership. Their low, gangster-like mentality quickly surfaced. Gauleiter Meyer thought the bishop should be arrested, and Martin Bormann that he should be summarily executed. Hitler's response was equally minatory, although political expediency counselled postponing an inevitable reckoning:

> I am quite sure that a man like the Bishop von Galen knows that after the war I shall extract retribution down to the last farthing. And, that if he does not succeed in the meanwhile in getting himself transferred

> to the Collegium Germanicum in Rome, he may rest assured that in the balancing of our accounts no 't' will remain uncrossed, no 'i' left undotted.[43]

It is often assumed that Galen's sermon had some direct effect upon Hitler's decision to order a 'halt' to the mass gassing of mental patients, about half of whose victims were from asylums run by the two Churches.[44] This amounts to wishful thinking. Firstly, the 'halt' order did not lead to the cessation of the parallel 'children's euthanasia' programme, nor did it 'halt' the gassing of adult concentration camp prisoners under 'Aktion 14f13' in facilities hitherto used to kill people in the 'euthanasia' programme.[45] Secondly, by August 1941, the men at T-4 had already slightly exceeded the projected target figure of 70,000 victims which they had established prior to beginning the 'euthanasia' programme.[46] Finally, the same autumn, Viktor Brack, the operational supremo of the 'euthanasia' programme, met Himmler who indicated that the extermination of the Jews was imminent.[47] Shortly afterwards, T-4 personnel were loaned to Odilo Globocnik to operate the technical side of the 'Aktion Reinhard' deathcamps. It seems that the 'euthanasia' programme was not temporarily and partially 'halted' because of some local difficulties with a bishop but because T-4's teams of practised murderers were needed to carry out yet greater enormities, where the voices of the Churches' respective hierarchies would be conspicuous by their silence.

CHAPTER SIX

The Nazi analogy and contemporary debates on euthanasia

The twelve years of National Socialist rule in Germany are often implicitly said to have special meaning and lessons for the present in a way which would not be true of, for example, the French Wars of Religion. Why else have so many books, conferences, films, journals, memorials, museums and study centres been devoted to it beyond a need to commemorate its millions of victims? The assumption seems to be that the former will have some, usually unspecified, incremental or multiplier effect, sensitising people towards intolerance, racism or signs of analogous developments in the present. This is mostly an entirely laudable endeavour, although one not without its critics.[1] Even if one is increasingly sceptical that this is the case, most historians who think about these questions probably feel obligated to the vague categorical imperative of trying to make the world a nicer place, even if they are sceptical of the sort of 'scholarship' of tenured radicals which seeks to change it.

Paradoxically, some of those most intimately acquainted with the most emblematic event of the Nazi period, namely the Holocaust, doubt what its lessons are. The eminent Israeli historian, Yehuda Bauer, seems uncertain if the Holocaust has any intrinsic meaning or serviceable lessons for posterity. Only the Nazis could invest such a lunatic enterprise with meaning or purpose; for the victims it was both incomprehensible and meaningless: 'the result of a rationally explicable outburst of irrational lust for murder which turned against them for reasons which were external to them'. This is another way of saying that the meanings are ultimately and necessarily elusive since they have no logic.

As for lessons, Bauer remarks that each generation will literally seek itself, with many of the lessons being both 'banal and self-evident', or self-servingly erroneous. When some Israeli politicians speak of the need for self-reliance and strength on Holocaust memorial day, they overlook peoples who tried to assist Jews in Nazi-dominated Europe, the dependence of modern Israel upon external alliances, and ignore the problem of whether the Holocaust was a price worth paying for the creation of Israel. As Bauer remarks, from the perspective of an ex-Israeli soldier, 'I would prefer to have six million of my people alive and no Israel.' Bauer is also sceptical of less local lessons about the nature of humanity in general. We do not need the Holocaust to know that human beings are capable of behaving murderously; for Caligula or Nero, the medieval crusaders, St Bartholomew's Night, Yagoda and Yezhov are surely quite as serviceable as Eichmann or Heydrich in this respect.[2] But this is to assume that murder is somehow especially revealing of the capacities of mankind, an assumption – so redolent of a certain type of journalism – that others are no longer prepared to make.

In his subtle and wide-ranging critique of teleological determinism in Holocaust fiction, and his salvaging of Jewish history from the event itself, Michael André Bernstein is sceptical whether anything 'about human nature or values can be learned from a situation *in extremis* except the virtual tautology that extreme pressure brings out extreme and extremely diverse behaviour'. Highly critical, on the basis of North American experience, of the pervasive cult of victimhood, noting that 'too sharp a sense of one's own victimization can easily lead to a compensatory urge to tyrannize over others', Bernstein makes the point that 'because so much of our culture is still so strongly bound to the belief that the truth lies in the extreme moments which "ordinary bourgeois life" covers over and that it is only at the (appropriately named) "cutting edge" of the unthinkable that the most valuable insights lie hidden, it has become possible, by a truly grotesque inversion, to interpret the ruthlessness of the Shoah as offering the most authentic – because most horrendous – image of the underlying reality of our world'.[3]

The ethical issues surrounding the question of euthanasia have special salience in this respect, since contemporary debate in Britain, Germany, the Netherlands and the USA is still haunted – one hesitates to say informed – by events in Nazi Germany over fifty years ago. It is assumed that Nazi experience has something to tell us, although quite what is left unexplored. As ethicists or human geneticists have often remarked, it is virtually impossible to discuss abortion, genetic engineering, in vitro fertilisation, negative or positive eugenics, euthanasia, organ transplants, psychiatry, sterilisation of the mentally incompetent or treatment of antisocial or violent individuals, without someone invoking the history of Nazi Germany to break, rather than make, a contemporary case. Entire fields of research operate under the long shadow of the swastika, notably human genetics, which as Professor Steve Jones has written, 'is marked by the fingerprints of its own history'.[4] This process seems quite arbitrary, since the discipline of economics does not suffer from analogous taints, even though – were anyone to investigate the subject systematically – one suspects that, judging from the performance of economists in Austria after the Anschluss or in occupied Poland and Russia, its record under the Nazis was equally dismal.[5]

One of the most extreme manifestations of the Nazi analogy in operation concerns the Australian Green politician, animal rights activist and utilitarian philosopher Peter Singer, whose views many young Germans identify with Nazism, notwithstanding the fact that three of his German-Jewish relatives perished in Nazi concentration camps. One might have imagined that such circles would be receptive to both his impassioned critiques of 1980s North American individualism and his 'right-on' advocacy of 'rights' for gorillas for whom he is apparently keen to establish a United Nations-recognised state of Gorillastan. But no. Every attempt by Singer to air his views in Germany has been met with demonstrations and sometimes physical violence, while Stalinistic forms of academic jiggery-pokey have been employed against the philosophers who invited him. German publishers fight shy of publishing books which are best-selling standard texts on ethics throughout the world. Hardly the first to note the fundamental emotional and psychological identity of the Nazis and people who nominally espouse diametrically opposite political sympathies, Singer wrote that the chants of 'Singer raus!' reminded him of Germany in the 1930s.[6] His problems seem to be even greater than those of scholars working under the fiery cross of political correctness across the Atlantic.

So what were these views that are so dangerous that modern Germans should not hear them, as if, notwithstanding their mature democracy, they are like children who have to be in bed by nine before the bad stuff comes on television? Put briefly, Singer claims that we have come to the end of two millennia in which most people in the West have generally subscribed to Judaeo-Christian morality. This is hardly shocking news to the nation which gave the world Nietzsche. The precise terminal date was 4 February 1993, when five British Law Lords authorised doctors to withdraw hydration and nutrition from Anthony Bland, who had been in a persistent vegetative state (PVS) since suffering severe anoxic brain damage during the Hillsborough football stadium disaster in April 1989. According to Singer, the Lords' ruling in Airedale NHS Trust v. Bland nullified the Christian belief that all human life is sacred from beginning to end. His concern, with practical morality rather than with whether morality is possible, is to develop a preference utilitarian morality in response to the question of what ethical code might guide us once belief in God and the sanctity of human life (logically if not practically entwined) have evaporated, an outcome he seems keener than most to bring about.[7] Drawing heavily upon classical utilitarianism, Singer argues that what satisfies the interests and preferences, rather than the happiness, of most people is moral.

The case of Peter Singer illustrates in extreme form, not only the parochial intolerance of some sections of the modern academy towards heterodox views, a quirk which free societies have to pay for and put up with, but how debates about bioethical issues are still charged and clouded by memories of Nazi Germany. Anyone who has discussed these issues will know that feeling of weariness when, inevitably, someone accuses their opponent of holding Nazi-like opinions on these issues, a charge which elicits an easy emotional response whether in the form of outrage or nods of eager approbation. In some circles, one simply needs to invoke Nazi Germany in order to touch base in terms of the unassailable authenticity of one's arguments. Nazi Germany is also sometimes used by commentators and historians to explicitly or implicitly denounce this or that contemporary government social policy (some of which such as 'care in the community' are the complex product of bi-partisan agreements based on patients' rights lobbies, reform psychiatry, pharmacological developments and are common to many western democracies such as Italy or parts of America), without any regard to major contextual differences.[8] Put bluntly, people who balk at comparisons between Stalin and Hitler, seem to have little difficulty in trotting out silly, jejune 'analogies' between Hitler and Baroness Thatcher. These 'analogies' are usually made by people who have never bothered to read a book on contemporary psychiatry or social policy.

A fascinating discussion of whether analogies with Nazi Germany are appropriate or legitimate took place at the Hastings Center for Bioethics in April 1976.[9] Participants included the Holocaust historian Lucy Dawidowicz, former Nuremberg prosecuting counsel Telford Taylor, Milton Himmelfarb of the American Jewish Committee, Joel Colton of the Rockefeller Foundation, Peter Steinfels the religious editor of the *New York Times* and Hastings Center staff. Part of the fascination for any historian reading the published protocol of the discussion is how people who, excepting Ms Dawidowicz, are not historians, treat the past as a practical or philosophical issue, a question historians should address more often than they usually do.

Lucy Dawidowicz began with an uncompromising rejection of any relevance of Nazi Germany to contemporary bioethical discussions: 'I am quite clear in my mind about this. I do not think we can usefully apply the Nazi analogy to gain insight or clarity to help us resolve our problems and dilemmas . . . There has been a lot of shoddy thinking and writing, making such facile comparisons.'[10] Ms Dawidowicz went on to argue that '"Euthanasia", as the Nazis used the term, is not euthanasia in our terms.' Hitler effectively used the Knauer case – where a family requested the 'mercy killing' of a severely deformed infant – to implement a programme of racially based negative eugenics designed to improve the health of the collective. Since the victims never expressed their consent, and since death was not administered to alleviate the intolerable suffering of the incurably ill, it is difficult to relate this with current debates about voluntary euthanasia for the terminally sick in our societies, debates whose central motivating premiss is compassion for individuals. Using slogans such as 'Your health does not belong to you', the Nazis were obviously not concerned with issues of personal autonomy.

By contrast, Milton Himmelfarb raised areas of possible relevance: 'Today we think of Nazism as representing a political thought which is remote from us. Yet Francis Crick, the great Nobel Prize winner in genetics, has proposed that society may have to consider seriously that no neonate should be declared legally human until it is a few days old and has passed a genetic test. Disposing of an infant which fails the test would be different from killing a human being.' The experience of Nazism, he felt, 'should complicate our thinking about such matters'.[11] One of the questions asked below will be 'should it?', and if it 'should', then can we at least narrow down areas of possible concern, freeing aspects of this ethical complex from Nazism's shadow?

The discussion gradually broadened from euthanasia to cover other areas of biomedical science, as if any work in the field of human genetics bore the potential taint of Nazism. Robert Veatch, the Hastings Center's own expert on death and dying, began by indicating how frequently conservative opponents of the legalisation of active killing of the terminally ill use the Nazi analogy, usually by reference to the 'slippery slope' argument deployed by the psychiatrist Leo Alexander during the Nuremberg Doctors' Trial:

> Whatever proportion [Nazi] crimes finally assumed, it became evident to all who investigated them that they started from small beginnings. The beginnings at first were merely a subtle shift in emphasis in the basic attitude of physicians. It started with the acceptance of the attitude, basic in the euthanasia movement, that there is such a thing as life not worthy to be lived. This attitude in its early stages concerned itself merely with the severely and chronically sick. Gradually the sphere of those to be included in this category was enlarged to encompass the socially unproductive, the ideologically unwanted, the racially unwanted and finally all non-Germans. But it is important to realize that the infinitely small wedged-in lever from which this entire trend of mind received its impetus was the attitude toward the nonrehabilitable sick.[12]

Opponents of the use of this analogy argued first that 'Americans are very different from Germans' so that 'it could not happen here', and that since the Nazi euthanasia programme was driven by racial imperatives, it had little significance for debates about the mercy killing of the terminally ill. As several participants indicated, the last concept is, of course, inherently 'slippery'. It might apply to a person's own experience of suffering, or someone else's definition of it, in terms of capacity to perform socially productive work, or indeed, a persons's failure to conform with some abstract idea of the 'race'. This last point seemed to rule out the use of the Nazi analogy in contemporary American discussions since clearly they were not informed by any comparable racial politics. Only Milton Himmelfarb raised the important issue of the extent to which Nazi policies combined questions of social utility with racial imperatives, remarking:

> In Hitler's mind these did not contradict each other at all, but analytically they are separable. You can still say it is fairly likely that a dictator, not necessarily a racist but obsessed by his notions of social utility, will use a term such as 'nonrehabilitable' to mean 'Get rid of 'em', because the cost exceeds the benefit.[13]

This crucial point muddied the waters considerably, since while no contemporary society, with the exception of communist China, is informed by crude eugenicism, questions of cost and social utility are more or less operative in all of them.[14] The discussion then reverted to the question of applying history's 'lessons'. All participants were agreed that one should actively denounce the political instrumentalisation of Nazism, as reflected in such crass phenomena as the spelling 'Amerika', a 1970s conceit that seems to have vanished in the interim. Ms Dawidowicz noted the commonplace assumption that one learns from the past, with statesmen studying the subject for guidance, with her own position being formulated as follows:

> I'm a historian and I believe that history can teach, that there are things we can learn from history that will serve us today. But I know that history is the study of particular events, that no one event is exactly like another. It is sometimes possible to make analogies and generalizations between different sets of events, but the value of those generalizations and analogies will be determined by the correct reading of the historical past, in the first place, and by a logical process of reasoning, in the second. Also, we ought to guard against using generalization in history to serve ulterior political purposes.[15]

Apropos the euthanasia debate, she stressed the faulty logic of argument which runs, the Nazis carried out 'euthanasia': the Nazis were evil: therefore euthanasia is evil, with its implicit elision of phenomena that have may have little in common. Again, Himmelfarb sounded a cautious note, pointing to an 'outlook' which when combined with technological possibilities 'could result in practices which most of us would regard as undesirable and that resemble, if not specifically Nazi, then generically totalitarian practice'.

The participants readdressed the 'slippery slope' problem. Here, Laurence McCullough addressed a key issue, namely that there might be more abstract analogies between the imperatives of a dictatorship and a democracy, in the sense that in the latter, questions of social utility or economic return might take precedence over individual freedom: 'the slippery slope then is not the precipitating act; it's the context in which the act takes place'. Peggy Steinfels added that although voluntary amniocentesis does not involve identifying defective members of any particular race, implicit within its speciesist rather than racist logic is a 'certain notion of human purity', and one could at least envisage a society in which it was mandatory. As Dan Callahan added, what begins on an ostensibly voluntaristic basis can also rapidly become subject to subtle collective pressures, with free choice mutating into 'responsible free choice', so that any responsible person over thirty-five 'would' choose amniocentesis. We can also all easily envisage a future scenario in which the cost of medical advances has soared, along with human expectations, into billions, and a younger generation questions this distribution of finite resources.[16] The warning signs of possibly dangerous discussions or developments are also far from unambiguous. Himmelfarb felt that one can detect a general coarsening of regard for life attendant on the decline of religious belief, and the ascendancy of 'a certain kind of accountant' mentality or an engineer's mentality in dealing with the questions of life', although this is rather unfair to members of either profession. The signs along 'slippery slopes' are also invariably ambiguous. In some circles, abortion is seen as representative of a coarsening of attitudes towards human life; elsewhere it reflects greater awareness and sensitivity to the needs of women. In America, the liberalisation of abortion laws was accompanied by the abolition of capital punishment, and so forth.[17] Broadly speaking then, the main conclusions of this session were that direct analogies between Nazi Germany and contemporary debates were too crude to be valuable; but that if German practice included criteria of social utility, then there were relevant overlaps with questions which affect not only modern totalitarian dictatorships such as China, but also democracies such as India or the United States of America. Health economics and social policy joined the utopian quest for engineered people as instances where Nazi Germany was deemed to have some possible relevance.

The Hasting Center returned to the subject twelve years later in a brief series of exchanges on the Nazi analogy published in its 1988 annual report.[18] The journalist Natt Hentoff began with an intemperate attack on the bioethicist Dan Callahan for advocating in his book, *Setting Limits*, a denial of expensive life-prolonging procedures, such as coronary bypass surgery, for people who have passed a certain age. This, Hentoff felt, 'is a variation . . . of the Nazis' *lebensunwertes Leben*, "life unworthy of life"'. In reply, Callahan rehearsed the actual arguments of his book, namely that medical progress and increasing numbers of elderly citizens should and would force society to rethink health care for the aged. The present bias in US Medicare should be reoriented from expensive emergency acute care to daily, home or longer-term provision, and on a less material plane, we should scale down our limitless expectations, not because the elderly are a burden, but because finite resources need to be spread evenly across the age groups. As Callahan says, 'The desire for constant progress is the real issue . . . Only in America, the land of unbounded desire, could the idea of setting limits to what is now an open-ended entitlement program shared by no other age group be seen as proto-Nazism.'[19] The lawyer and philosopher Cynthia Cohen stressed the need for precision when drawing analogies, noting that the latter will be flawed if the components are too dissimilar or if the moral principles which inform the analogies are in contradiction. The Nazis killed people because they deemed them to have no racial or social 'value'. Modern doctors who advocate withdrawing medical treatment from individuals do so for example because the person or their surrogates have chosen to do so, on account of terrible suffering (which of course is not a problem-free area), because they know their own value is bound up with their powers of choice, or because they cannot engage in first-person reflection. There is also a distinction between actively bringing about a person's death in the interests of some putative biological collective, and withdrawing medical attention thus allowing some underlying disease or illness to take its course. Cohen writes: 'Our moral responsibility for what we produce, as opposed to what we allow, is greater, even though the outcome of each may be the same.'[20] Indeed, one could make some sort of not entirely tenuous Nazi analogy against those who, because of a dogmatic adherence to the sacral value of human life, impose these views on people informed by quite contrary principles. Precision in application is everything: 'the lessons of history will be rendered meaningless if they are used indiscriminately'.

Critics of the Nazi analogy, notably Arthur Caplan, make the point that there is no worthwhile comparison to be drawn between the Nazis' covert murder of the mentally incompetent and physically handicapped for reasons of cost and racial purity, and, for example, the desire of the parents of Nancy Cruzan, who had been in a coma for seven years, to withdraw all life-saving medical treatment including food and water, a desire finally met after prolonged legal proceedings, with Nancy Cruzan's death on 26 December 1990.[21] Despite the fact that Nancy

Cruzan had indicated to friends beforehand that she would not wish to be maintained in a persistent vegetative state, and that her parents were simply respecting her wishes, the State of Missouri took the line that its interest in preserving human life overrode the family's desire to terminate it. Opponents of their freedom frequently invoked the Nazi analogy, whether in the form of condemning any discussion of the quality of life or the use of terms as 'burden' in such cases, or in terms of the alleged 'slippery slope' which allowing her death would encourage.[22] Grotesquely, as they made their way to the hospital to say goodbye to Nancy, Mr and Mrs Cruzan had to run the gauntlet of hysterical protestors screaming 'Nazi' at them.[23] This denial of human choice and the attempts to impose views on others increasingly irritates the pro-euthanasia lobby, as well it might.

Although the Nazi 'euthanasia' programme drew upon utilitarian philosophical discourse in the Weimar period, discourse which was sometimes non-racist, we should be quite clear that it was a covert policy implemented by a criminal regime, designed to save money while ridding the racial collective of allegedly defective members. Except in a few cases involving the parents of handicapped infants, even indirect consent was not in evidence, although such policies banked on widespread indifference or silent collusion among the population at large. Whatever their rhetoric, the Nazi doctors themselves were not motivated by compassion for suffering individuals, since their *modus operandi* involved making decisions on the basis of forms rather than people, while those who killed were in no way familiar with their victims.[24] To make analogies between these aberrant, ghoulish practices, and cases where individuals or their relatives express their consent to voluntary euthanasia, with doctors then reluctantly disconnecting a respirator or stopping dialysis – as opposed to enthusiastically turning on a gas tap or delivering a lethal injection – is both historically false and offensive to all concerned. The parents of Anthony Bland or Nancy Cruzan acted out of love for their children, and their doctors from compassion for these individuals who had no appreciable quality of life. Whatever arguments some people might feel inclined to deploy against them, these should not include references to a defunct totalitarian dictatorship, of no relevance to these unfortunate individuals.

Debates about the pros and cons of euthanasia can operate quite safely without any reference to Nazi Germany, for this involves introducing an emotional overload to complex personal dramas involving parents with babies devoid of possibilities for development, or individuals experiencing appalling physical pain and metaphysical distress who wish to end their own lives in a dignified fashion. What lessons does it actually teach that were not evident beforehand or which are obvious to anyone who thinks about these issues? What relevance does it have to people whose diseased bodies are so sensitive that a touch induces enormous pain, or who spend their lives intravenously feeding a child who will never know that either they, or him- or herself, are even there? One does not need to talk of Nazism to know that ethical awareness and respect for the individual patient should be built into the training of young doctors. That politicians, lawyers and journalists should zealously patrol the activities of doctors, as they have the duty and right to do in any free society. That we should be vigilant in ensuring that voluntary euthanasia – if it is legalised – remains grounded in informed consent. That we should be aware of inflationary potentialities and possibilities for misuse in any changes to the law, for which the Netherlands in the 1990s rather than Germany in the 1930s are surely a more reliable guide? These facts are well enough known to any informed person, and can be safely discussed without any reference to events in Germany fifty years ago, and indeed will be, since the more the analogy is invoked, the less effective it seems to be. In other words, the argument here is that we should probably detach arguments about euthanasia from events in Nazi Germany, even as we rightly continue to employ the analogy to condemn all collectivist forms of eugenic engineering, such as those currently being employed by Li-Peng, 'idiots breed idiots', and the bureaucrats of communist China.

PART III

Extermination

CHAPTER SEVEN

The racial state revisited

After at least four decades of preoccupation with the generic character of Fascism and Nazism, their relationship to capitalism or communist totalitarianism, or the structural determinants of the 'Final Solution', historians have once again recognised that the distinguishing characteristic of Nazi Germany was its obsession with race. This assertion does not exclude the fact that Nazism drew on pathologies and trends also common in free societies, such as Great Britain or the United States of America; or that it can be usefully compared with both Italian Fascism and that other hubristic attempt to refashion mankind, namely Bolshevik Russia's seventy-year journey along the 'road to nowhere'. In the last decade or so, historians have dramatically increased our understanding of Nazi racialism, which was until recently regarded as being effectively coterminous with racial anti-Semitism. The new cast of victims includes the so-called 'anti-social', Arab or Afro-Germans 'Rhineland bastards'), foreign forced labour, homosexuals and lesbians, the mentally and physically handicapped, Sinti and Roma ('Gypsies') and Soviet prisoners of war, none of whose horrible fates detracts from the singularity of the Nazi murder of six million European Jews, any more than the latter does vice versa. Understanding of the process of persecution now includes greater awareness of the culpable involvement of various sections of the professional intelligentsia, such as anthropologists, doctors, economists, historians, lawyers and psychiatrists, in the formation and implementation of Nazi policies, as well as some innovative studies of the interaction between the populace as a whole and the police agencies which enforced racial policy in both

Germany and Austria, by, for example, David Bankier, Robert Gellately and David J. Horwitz.

Nazi racialism had both long-term and international origins, even though its most murderous manifestation was the Nazi murder of the Jews between 1941 and 1945, an outcome that was neither entirely aleatory nor absolutely predetermined. In line with other racists elsewhere and in other times, Hitler and the National Socialists believed that intellectual and physical differences between people were indicative of their relative value in the human scale. This ideology had complex, long-term origins, frequently drawing upon extremely venerable pathologies and prejudices which must go unmentioned in this brief account. From the eighteenth century, racial anthropologists used external physical criteria, frequently the starting-point for further gross generalisations, to legitimise their claim to superiority over other peoples. Within Germany, an open, Herderian, cosmopolitan rejection of French pretensions to cultural hegemony in favour of a relativistic appreciation of all world cultures gradually degenerated into an aggressive, chauvinistic form of nativism which emphasised German cultural superiority over, for example, the Slavs, as well as the need to 'purify' the German 'race' of Jews and 'Gypsies', who were frequently elided in nineteenth-century racist discourse, as being criminous, foreign, dark-skinned, short of stature and inclined to such activities as kidnapping children.

The first comprehensive theoretical expression of racial ideology was penned by the French Restoration aristocrat Joseph Arthur Comte de Gobineau (1816–82) in his *Essai sur l'inégalité des races humaines* (Paris 1853–5). Putative inherent racial inequalities became the motor force of historical development. High cultures were the work of an '"Aryan" master race' whose decline was coeval with interbreeding with 'lesser races', whilst the French Revolution was construed as the revolt of the 'Gallic' plebs against the 'Frankish' elite, whence Gobineau, groundlessly, traced his own ancestry. Ongoing 'miscegenation' would eventuate in a Europe in which the population would 'be overcome by a dark desire to sleep, living insensitively in their nothingness, like the buffaloes ruminating in the stagnant puddles of the Pontine marshes'. In contrast to this rather marginal reactionary figure, the British naturalist Charles Darwin enjoyed enormous international prestige, with his work on natural selection appealing to diverse political constituencies, united in the belief that his findings had prescriptive applicability to the society of man. His cousin Francis Galton (1822–1911) for whom a Chair was established at University College, London (a bastion of anti-Establishment educational progressivism), coined the term 'eugenics' to denote the science of 'fine breeding'. Social-Darwinists, an unsatisfactory umbrella term covering a multitude of persuasions, shared the view that mankind should take charge of its own evolutionary process. Some believed that this should be achieved by doing nothing, so that the denizens of East End London slums would die through processes of auto-extermination. Others recommended various combinations of philoprogenitive measures, or positive eugenics, to encourage enhanced reproduction among the 'fit'; with negative procedures, such as sterilisation (either voluntary or compulsory) which would curb the fertility of the 'unfit' parts of the population. Being modern, progressive and scientific, these ideas appealed across the political spectrum, including English Fabian Socialists such as Sydney and Beatrice Webb, co-founders of the London School of Economics, or the German Socialist doctor Alfred Grotjahn, for whom they became a means of eradicating the marginal *Lumpenproletariat*. In Germany, one of their most influential exponents was the zoologist Ernst Haeckel (1834–1919), originator of a philosophy known as Monism, who, enthusing over what he probably wrongly took to be ancient Spartan practice, recommended the killing of the mentally and physically defective in the interests of strengthening the culturally and physically superior 'central type of people', whose most valuable part was the Indo-Germanic 'race'. Already in the hands of Haeckel, these questions swam into the dangerous orbit of health and emotional costs, a trend which would be accelerated by the financial exigencies occasioned by the First World War. A further aspect of these developments is most strikingly represented by the racial hygienist Alfred Ploetz (1860–1940), namely the idea that the health of society, construed as an atemporal genetic collective, should be patrolled by medical experts, who would determine who should marry or reproduce, or in other words, what type of people should be born. Scope for this interventionist power-seeking on the part of the medical profession and others was dramatically enhanced as the rather modest concerns in this area of the early nineteenth-century small state were replaced by the big government reaching into most areas of life characteristic of the twentieth century. Finally, it is important to underline the fact that the ideas discussed above not only frequently transcended political differences, but also that discontinuities and contradictions were often apparent. Not all those who advocated eugenic solutions to social problems countenanced sterilisation; some of those who thought in terms of the latter were totally opposed to the 'mercy killing' of the terminally ill, let alone the mentally or physically handicapped, and by no means all of these people would have subscribed to other forms of racism such as anti-Semitism or extreme Nordicism. These differences matter. The first country in the world to give eugenics legislative expression was the United States of America, whose eugenic enthusiasts, such as Charles Davenport or Harry Laughlin, were also engaged in a 'gene race' with their German equivalents.

Adolf Hitler, without discussion of whom any consideration of Nazi racialism is meaningless, drew upon many of the various strands of racism mentioned so far. There is not one man from whom he took his ideas; instead the process whereby his ideas were mediated was extremely complicated. Broadly speaking, Hitler – whose cardinal obsession was his hatred of the Jews – drew upon racial-anthropological and racial-hygienic discourses, including those of the elective German Englishman, Houston Stewart Chamberlain; and upon American exemplars, remarking: 'I have studied with great interest the laws of several American states concerning prevention of reproduction by people whose progeny would, in all probablility, be of no value or be injurious to the racial stock.' Hitler believed in the existence of 'higher' and 'lesser' races, the former being 'Aryans', as well as in the deleterious biological and cultural consequences of racial inter-breeding. The future völkisch state should pursue philoprogenitive policies based upon selective breeding and selective welfare benefits, coupled with the eugenic elimination of the unfit, in order to maintain racial purity and the 'victory of the better and stronger' against the logic of modern welfare whose effects he deemed counter-selective.

However, he was an inveterate conspiracy theorist, and these prescriptions paled into insignificance beside his pathological hatred of the Jews who stood behind such diverse modern phenomena as capitalism or Russian Bolshevism. The 'Jew' was a force of almost cosmic malevolence, with eschatological imagery frequently appearing in Hitler's thoughts on this subject, responsible not only for Germany's capitulation in 1918 and ensuing socio-economic immiseration, but also for the subversion of the biological substance of the German 'race', via such instrumentalities as domestic prostitution or the 'planting' of 'Black' servicemen in the occupied Rhineland. All measures to promote racial 'purity' would be rendered nugatory without a solution to the 'Jewish Question'. None of this was especially new, although the specific synthesis undoubtedly was, and implementation would obviously depend upon a variety of external contingencies such as domestic political considerations, foreign opinion and so forth. But however irrational and resentment-laden these ideas may seem, these views were held with unswerving conviction and expressed with tremendous emotional force by a man whose inner violence was poorly concealed by whatever surface he periodically adopted. They were not a nebulous ideological smoke-screen for more material interests, or simply reducible to anti-Semitism, but rather a broadly conceived vision – or 'mission statement' – which, regardless of tactical shifts, the Nazis largely realised after they achieved power.

One of the main instruments for achieving the goal of a racially 'pure' national community was legislation, most of which took the form of decrees. Jewish people bore the brunt of an incremental assault involving thousands of individual decrees and enactments. 'Aryan' clauses contained in the 7 April 1933 Law for the Restoration of the Professional Civil Service, a measure supposedly designed to 'depoliticise' the Weimar civil service, opened the way for a host of similar initiatives throughout other trades and professions. The emancipatory measures of the previous century were finally reversed by the complex known as the Nuremberg Laws of 15 September 1935 which denied Jewish people citizenship and prohibited marriage or sexual relations between Jews and 'Aryans'. Subsequent amendments and commentaries on these laws extended their scope to include Sinti and Roma and 'negroes and their bastards'. In addition to being subject to progressive formal and informal social ostracism, Jewish people were also victims of systematic attempts to deny them a livelihood (economic 'Aryanisation') whose effects were the gradual impoverishment of this part of the population. Those who remained in Germany became a stigmatised group, excluded from certain park benches, public transport, swimming baths and, in their creative endeavours, from art galleries, concert halls and the shelves of libraries. Legislation and propaganda, which had regularly and semi-pornographically insinuated that Jews 'preyed' on German women, in such racist organs as *Der Stürmer*, gradually imputed that Jews were the 'enemy within', a trend reflected in such measures as the wartime ban on their ownership of carrier-pigeons or radios. This culminated in their physical labelling as something identifiably 'other' with the introduction on 1 September 1941 of the compulsory wearing of the Star of David.

Like the Jews, the Sinti and Roma were also deemed to be racially 'alien', although as we shall see below, they were often also persecuted on the grounds of antisocial behaviour. As with anti-Semitism, discrimination against Sinti and Roma has a long history, partly stemming from the clash between sedentary and peripatetic cultures, and like anti-Semitism it a prejudice by no means local to Germany. Inheriting regional legislation whose effect was permanent harassment, the Nazis centralised the apparatus of persecution in the Reich Central Office for the Fight against the Gypsy Nuisance established in 1936. Sinti and Roma were also effectively subjected to the Nuremberg racial laws by commentaries such as those of Globke and Stuckart which prohibited marriages between racial 'aliens' and Germans. While race experts such as Robert Ritter registered Germany's Sinti and Roma, local authorities frequently took the initiative in corralling the latter in *ad hoc* camps, often as a means of shedding any obligations towards them by way of healthcare, schooling or basic utilities. These initiatives were frequently a response to popular complaints about the behaviour of Sinti and Roma. Although final formal legislative convergence regarding Jews and Sinti and Roma only took place in 1942, long before then, wagons of Sinti and Roma were regularly appended to those trains deporting Jews to Poland, while from 1941 onwards, the Einsatzgruppen, SS and police killing units in the occupied Soviet Union repeatedly referred in their reports to massacres of 'Gypsies' (as well as the mentally ill) in addition to Jewish people.

Racial-hygienic legislation commenced with the 14 July 1933 Law for the Prevention of Hereditarily Diseased Progeny which drew upon both Weimar and North American exemplars. Passed in the same Cabinet session which concluded the Concordat with the Vatican, this law sanctioned the compulsory sterilisation (by surgery or X-rays) of persons suffering from a range of supposedly hereditary illnesses including congenital feeble-mindedness, schizophrenia, manic depression, epilepsy, Huntington's chorea, blindness, deafness, severe physical deformity and chronic alcoholism. It should be noted that the hereditary character of many of these conditions was at the time a matter of faith rather than scientific certitude. Asylum psychiatrists, midwives and public health officials were obliged, and financially rewarded, for reporting cases which fell within the remit of this law. Many of the psychiatrists needed little encouragement since they had been enthusiastically advocating such measures throughout the Weimar

Republic. The decision to sterilise these people was then made by the new Hereditary Health Courts, which between 1933 and 1945 were responsible for the sterilisation of between 320,000 to 350,000 people, of whom some hundreds died as a result of surgical or post-operative complications. On 26 June 1935 the law was amended to include eugenic abortion up to the sixth month of pregnancy for hereditarily ill women. Although not all advocates of compulsory sterilisation saw the need for the 'euthanasia' killing of the mentally ill – which grew out of a rather separate discourse related to both terminal illness and questions of economic cost as well as to racial 'purity' – none the less, Nazi propaganda certainly tended that way with its constant dilation upon the costs of institutional care and its understanding for those who took the law into their own hands by killing their sick relatives. Crude graphics and progressively more sophisticated films such as *Das Erbe* or *Opfer der Vergangenheit* depicted a nation apparently menaced by hordes of mental defectives, the cost of caring for whom was haemorrhaging funds which should have been expended on public housing for the racially deserving German poor.

Being tough on crime while fetishising work and 'healthy popular morality', the Nazis also struck at those they regarded as sexual or social deviants, that is the antisocial, homosexuals and Sinti and Roma. Many of the 'antisocial' and Sinti and Roma were sterilised simply through extending the notion of feeble-mindedness from its medical meanings to encompass moral judgments about lifestyle or socio-economic effectiveness. People living on society's margins, where petty criminality was often part of their way of life, were obviously highly vulnerable to these measures. The 24 November 1933 Law against Dangerous Habitual Criminals drastically enhanced police powers of preventive detention and sanctioned castration of sexual offenders. The range of offences involving capital punishment was radically extended, from three in 1933 to twenty-five in 1939, with Hitler personally insisting on the death penalty for highway robbery on the new Autobahnen, a law given retrospective applicability to cover the case of two brothers who had recently committed this very offence. Hitler also had the habit of ordering the shooting of persons, such as bank robbers, whose sentences by the courts he considered too lenient. While the police could effectively bypass the courts, the courts became correspondingly accommodating to Nazi political and racial imperatives. In addition to the Hereditary Health Courts, the regime created an eventual total of seventy-four 'Special

Courts', and a peripatetic 'People's Court' to deal with the massively increased workload. Having once briefly rounded up beggars and vagrants without having adequate facilities in which to incarcerate them, in 1938 the SS swept into concentration camps the denizens of doss-houses, hostels and overnight shelters, in other words, the homeless. These people became part of the labour force in the second generation of SS concentration camps, those such as Flossenbürg, Mauthausen and Gross Rosen, established near stone quarries designed to supply the megalomaniac building plans of Hitler and his chief architect Albert Speer. These measures were augmented locally by various initiatives, including *ad hoc* camps with coercive features for Sinti and Roma; the demolition of slum areas with high incidences of crime in Hamburg; or the construction at Hashude near Bremen of a corrective housing project for entire antisocial families. Although the idea was certainly regularly mooted, plans for a comprehensive law against so-called 'community aliens' never went beyond the drafting stage.

For much of the nineteenth century, homophobia as we now sometimes call it, was the preserve of the political Left who used it as a tool to assail the allegedly effete upper classes, just as the German communists sometimes resorted to anti-Semitism to attack capitalism and pick up nationalist support during the Weimar Republic. Although the Nazis' political opponents sometimes drew attention to highly placed homosexuals within the movement, notably the Storm Troopers (SA) leader Ernst Röhm, and while Nazism itself undeniably reflected certain homo-erotic pathologies, none the less the Nazis could be described as virulently homophobic. Although they were not above using charges of homosexuality to discredit and destroy opponents, the primary reason for the assault on homosexuals was because the latter were self-evidently failing in their duty to contribute to the demographic expansion of the 'Aryan-Germanic race', at a time when millions of young men had perished in the First World War. Existing legislation, notably Paragraph 175 of the Reich Criminal Code, was extended to include a wider variety of homosexual behaviour and the number of prosecutions dramatically increased. While in 1934, 766 men were convicted and imprisoned, in 1936 the figure exceeded 4,000, and in 1938, 8,000. Men sentenced for homosexual offences were regularly transferred to concentration camps after they had served the statutory prison sentence. Lacking the group solidarities of, for example, professional criminals or political prisoners, and exposed to the sadism of both their guards and other inmates, many homosexual camp prisoners perished.

Running parallel with efforts to exclude and ultimately exterminate people deemed racially 'alien', unfit or criminal (which in the case of Sinti and Roma invariably involved combinations of the first and third of these categories as symbolised by their designation as 'greens' in the concentration camps) were various philoprogenitive measures designed to foster the 'Aryan-Germanic race'. Following the example set by Chancellor Brüning, the 1 June 1933 Law for the Reduction of Unemployment, part of whose agenda was to put men back to work by excluding married women from the workforce, introduced marriage loans – in the form of vouchers for consumer durables – for families in which the man alone worked. These were then amortised with every successful childbirth. Four children liquidated the debt. Racial 'aliens' and the 'hereditarily ill' were ineligible. The results of these policies were disappointing, largely because of the long-term secular drift towards two-child families, but also because they were not accompanied by any commensurate housing policy. Prolific 'Aryan' mothers were also encouraged by the awarding of decorations for outstanding service in this area, although it is important to recall that the regime distinguished sharply between families deemed to be 'rich in children' and what were disparagingly dubbed 'large families', that is fecund Lumpenproletarians. After 1935, couples who wished to marry were obliged to supply certificates of fitness to do so, certificates which involved interviews and tests with public health doctors, and which could result in an appearance before an Hereditary Health Court if any untoward facts surfaced. The 'Aryan' birthrate was also promoted by the institution of 'Lebensborn' or 'Well of Life' homes, founded in 1935, with its maternity homes in Germany and later in occupied northern Europe. Here, both married and single mothers could give birth in relative comfort, availing themselves of an adoption service if they no longer wanted their offspring. This also mirrored Himmler's aversion to conventional bourgeois morality in the sense that for racial reasons he wished to destigmatise illegitimacy, and indeed, he at least countenanced polygamy, an enthusiasm he probably derived from his time with the cranky Artamanen League during the Weimar Republic. There is no evidence that these homes contributed to an increased birthrate; on the contrary, SS officers were conspicuous in having below-average numbers of children.

Any discussion of Nazi racialism must also include the individuals and organisations which implemented these policies and some tentative observations on the responses of the German population as a whole, tentative because recently some crude and quasi-racist claims have been made about German subscription to eliminationist anti-Semitism. Of course, the legislation we have considered above did not arise in a societal vacuum. Some of it – notably the Nuremberg Laws – was undoubtedly the product of a complex dialectic involving pressure from grass-roots and Party activists to 'do something' radical on the 'Jewish Question'. Other measures, such as the Law for the Prevention of Hereditarily Diseased Progeny, clearly came about through the prompting of professional experts within and outside the Party, who had been lobbying for such measures throughout the Weimar Republic. For Nazi Germany brought boom conditions for 'scientific' experts – that strange species of modern scholar for whom mere intrinsic intellectual curiosity is not enough. Invariably providing a 'scientific' gloss for irrational and pertinacious prejudices, these men and women threw themselves in a Gadarene rush at the feet of a regime which probably despised them. The pay-off took the familiar form of enhanced research funding, facilities, new posts and promotions, as well as income supplements for writing reports on individuals for the courts, or in the case of natural scientists, a refashioned ethical climate which permitted horrible experiments on human subjects. We have already encountered Robert Ritter, who as director of the new Criminal-Biological Institute of the Security Police, was responsible for categorising all 30,000 of Germany's Sinti and Roma according to degrees of racial 'purity', a pursuit which was a life and death affair for the individuals involved. Selection on the ramps of Auschwitz completed selection on card-indexes and paper. It is important to emphasise that the pretensions of racial science recognised no limits. That no one was potentially safe from these attentions can be demonstrated by the case of Karl Astel's Landesamt für Rassewesen, which by 1938 had gathered data on a quarter of Thuringia's population, so that 'henceforth the less valuable, the asocial and criminals could more easily be excluded than before'. In Giessen, Astel's colleague Heinrich Wilhelm Kranz envisaged permanent racial selection, remarking that 'not only the hereditarily ill and asocial, but also the hereditarily healthy and the socially valuable should be continually registered, genetically investigated and put on card indexes'. No less an authority than Bishop Franz von Galen, in his sermon on 'euthanasia' in 1941, recognised the limitless inflationary potentialities in that programme when he warned his flock that soon the elderly, the terminally ill and the wounded soldiers would join the insane in the gas chambers. During the war, the ranks of these race experts were augmented by a small army of *Ostforscher*, who volunteered their expertise in the service of rearranging the ethnic composition of occupied eastern Europe. Medical scientists availed themselves of the brains of victims of the 'euthanasia' programme, or in the case of the Posen anatomist Voss, of the corpses supplied by the local Gestapo; they carried out experiments in concentration camps, involving immersion in freezing water or exposure to unbearable atmospheric pressures, tropical diseases and toxic substances; as well as carrying out both 'euthanasia' killings, and selections and gassings in extermination camps.

Control of racial policy was a congested and contested arena. The first abortive attempt to establish a central clearing house in this area was the Committee of Experts for Population and Racial Policy established by Minister of the Interior Wilhelm Frick on 28 June 1933. This came to nought, although one of its three steering groups was heavily involved in drafting the Law for the Prevention of Hereditarily Diseased Progeny. The 3 July 1934 Law for the Consolidation of the Health System opened the way for would-be *dirigistes* in the sense of introducing central control in this area. However, the role of Reich medical supremo was a contested one, with the main contenders being Arthur Gütt, Leonardo Conti, Gerhard Wagner and the accident surgeon attached to Hitler's retinue, Karl Rudolf Brandt. Nor were either the German Labour Front leader Robert Ley or the Reich SS Doctor Grawitz prepared to withdraw from this terrain without a fight. Increasingly, the implementation of racial policy was assigned to *ad hoc* teams, such as the T-4 apparatus attached to the Chancellory of the Führer, which carried out the 'euthanasia' programme beyond the control of the normative state bureaucracy.

One agency – or rather one continent-wide police empire – is correctly associated with the implementation of Nazi racial policy more than any other, namely the SS, although we should be careful in not allowing it to become a sort of alibi, laying a convenient fog over other less conspicuous lowlands of criminality. Technically subordinate to Röhm's SA, Heinrich Himmler emerged from the 'seizure of power' with the comparatively modest office of Commissary President of the Munich Police. In 1934 he became Inspector of the Prussian Secret

State Police (Gestapo), rapidly shaking off the tutelage of Göring, murdering Röhm in June 1934, and merging the Prussian Gestapo with the political police in other states. By 1936 he secured control of all police activity with the conjoint title Reichsführer-SS and Chief of the German Police. SS control of the police was personified by Himmler's henchman Reinhard Heydrich, who also commanded the SS internal and external security service or SD, which was responsible for monitoring domestic opinion, surveillance of ideological opponents, and espionage abroad. Its mood-monitoring activities were made possible by a network of approximately 30,000 'honorary' agents. Unlike the Gestapo and Kripo it had no powers of arrest, detention or interrogation. Although rivalries within the SS polycracy continued to be intense, control was nominally consolidated in 1939 with the creation of the Reich Main Security Office in Berlin. In 1939 Himmler further extended his powers with the title Reich Commissar for the Strengthening of Ethnic Germandom, with responsibilities for deportations and repatriations, while the original militarised units of the Armed or Waffen-SS became a formidable military force in their own right.

Inspired by Himmler's eccentric and ahistorical understanding of a number of elite organisations, the sole task of the SS – whose creed was mindless obedience – was to destroy the regime's opponents, understood to include those who threatened the integrity or security of the 'master race'. To that end it controlled the burgeoning concentration camp empire, which, beginning with Dachau in 1933, eventually resulted in about 10,000 core and satellite camps spread across occupied Europe. Reliable estimates suggest that following a fall to 7,500 in 1936–7, there were some 25,000 prisoners in 1939 and approximately 100,000 by early 1942. During the 1930s, increased SS involvement in racially motivated persecution was reflected in its control of Robert Ritter's Reich Central Office for the Combating of the Gypsy Nuisance and Josef Meisinger's Reich Central Office for the Combating of Abortion and Homosexuality, both located within the Reich Criminal Police headquarters. With the outbreak of war, the SS were primarily, if by no means exclusively, responsible for racial extermination, with dedicated units killing psychiatric patients, Jews, Sinti and Roma, and the elite in occupied Poland. The invasion of the Soviet Union, preconceived as a war of racial extermination, brought a gradual but massive expansion of the units involved, including the Einsatzgruppen,

SS troops attached to the Higher SS- and Police Leaders, sundry police formations, indigenous collaborators and so forth. The German military frequently colluded with these agencies, and was itself responsible for the deaths of approximately three million Soviet soldiers in captivity. Finally, many of the experts from the so-called 'euthanasia' programme, who had earlier provided mass gassing facilities for the concentration camps under 'Aktion 14f13', were now redeployed in the newly established extermination camps of Kulmhof, Belzec, Sobibor and Treblinka, themselves dwarfed by the massive complex at Auschwitz-Birkenau, the apogee of industrialised mass murder.

Summaries of these institutional forms used to implement racial policy are inadequate unless accompanied by an appreciation of the broader societal dimension. Like fish, these policemen needed a sea in which to swim. For contrary to the impression conveyed by the unreflective use of such terms as 'police state', we are actually considering what were often numerically quite small agencies. For example, the Gestapo regional headquarters based in Düsseldorf consisted of 281 agents, responsible for policing four million people. In effect, therefore, these desk-bound policemen were dependent upon denunciations and information supplied 'from below' from other agencies or the general public. Thus, of the cases of 'racial pollution' dealt with by the Gestapo in Würzburg, 57 per cent originated in denunciation by ordinary citizens, with only one case being a result of the Gestapo's own initiatives. The Saarbrücken housewife who denounced her own ex-communist husband for listening to 'enemy radio' so as to make room for her new lover, telling her son, 'Your dad will go away and you will get a much better one', was unfortunately hardly atypical, with the motives of such people being as heterogeneous and idiosyncratic as this example suggests. Similarly, the impression that Nazi racial policy was something 'done to' Germany, as if it was the first Nazi-occupied country, is further undermined by the obvious glee with which unwilling neighbours and local authorities regarded the removal of Sinti and Roma from their streets and neighbourhoods; by the obvious dependency of the Gestapo upon informants to penetrate such discreet subcultures as that of homosexuals, whose elimination was actively welcomed by wide swathes of the working class; by the ease with which people adjusted to the presence of an army of coerced foreign labour in their midst; and finally, by the all too evident willingness of some ordinary families to disburden themselves of sick members through the wartime 'euthanasia' programme. If they failed, as many did, to protest against these policies, what chance did such actively stigmatised groups as foreign forced workers, prisoners of war, the Jews or Sinti and Roma have? Regardless of the minority who actively tried to thwart these policies through acts of individual courage, the majority response ranged from 'indifference – understood as a lack of emotional concern or moral awareness rather than as self-preoccupation, through silent disapproval (mostly of the manner of persecution rather than its nominal objective, as the 1938 pogrom known as 'Reichskristallnacht' suggests), and on down to more base forms of active endorsement such as the denunciations we have considered. The variety of responses, and the fact of various degrees of resistance, naturally militates against the simple-minded view that all Germans subscribed to an eliminationist mind-set exclusively directed against Jews, a view more redolent of wartime propaganda than of serious historical scholarship.

Regardless of any inconsistencies or inefficiencies of conception or implementation, which were not apparent to its victims at the time, and which historical research sometimes exaggerates, the most salient historical characteristic of the Third Reich was the attempt to realise a singular 'racial state'. This drew upon both long-term historical pathologies and prejudices (notably towards Jews and Sinti and Roma) as well as more short-term, but equally complex, international, intellectual trends mostly generated by industrial society, and expressed in Germany as elsewhere, in the unquestioning language of scientific certitude. Germany's experiences in the wake of the First World War gave these tendencies a particularly radical political expression, resulting in the accession to power of a movement whose animating principle was the quest for 'racial purity', an atavistic aim to be achieved with all the modern technologies and administrative structures at modern man's disposal. The result was to plunge Europe into a nightmare, involving the deaths of millions of people, a nightmare from whose legacy it is only just emerging. Modern genetic science has since revealed that the animating principle was a mirage, there being no substantive genetic differences between, as opposed to within, the 'races' of people, but rather overwhelming similarity and shared characteristics.

CHAPTER EIGHT

A 'political economy of the Final Solution'? Reflections on modernity, historians and the Holocaust

INTRODUCTION

Sometimes during the 1980s it seemed as though historians of the Nazi period had exchanged the prosaic business of working in archives in favour of acrimonious 'meta-debates' which were as much about the present as the past. These included the 'Historikerstreit' (historians' debate); the related 'debate' over empathy and 'historicisation'; and various discourses about the relationship of the Holocaust to memory, rationality, science or modernity.[1] In many respects this was a salutary development, since the historiography of both Nazism and the Holocaust had become over-preoccupied with a series of increasingly technical questions, expressed in commensurately technical terms, which threatened to eclipse wider humane concerns.[2] I stress the historiography, or rather the small corner of it that is represented in historiographical evaluations, since as the final chapter below seeks to show, there is an enormous variety of creative reflection on the Holocaust, which is regrettably treated as marginal to more mainstream scholarly work in that small corner.[3]

Undistracted by these developments, an impressive number of non-professional German scholars, which is to say people not employed by universities, continued to research in archives and publish on the social history of the Nazi era. Much of this work was done by plain people keen to uncover the past of their own regions, towns, factories, schools and villages and to put human faces to anonymous victims. It would also be impossible to overestimate the contribution of lone individuals, such as the Protestant broadcaster and journalist Ernst Klee, who reconstructed the 'euthanasia' programme, availing himself of a large range of documents and a plethora of institutional studies by psychiatric reformers. Klee and others have also published some striking documentary accounts of military complicity in the Holocaust and other crimes against humanity.

A major collective contribution to our understanding of the marginalisation of Jews and 'Gypsies', sterilisation and euthanasia, the maltreatment of foreign forced labour, or the Nazi reorganisation of the European economy has also been made by the predominantly Berlin- or Hamburg-based scholars who publish in the journal *1999* or the series *Beiträge zur nationalsozialistischen Gesundheits- und Sozialpolitik*. The leading lights of this erroneously called Hamburg School are Götz Aly, Angelika Ebbinghaus, Susanne Heim and Karl-Heinz Roth.[4]

This important body of published work has some striking common characteristics. First, it rests on an impressive archival base derived from western and eastern Europe, no mean achievement for scholars without research funds – excepting the generosity of the philanthropist Jan Philipp Reemtsma – and with full-time jobs outside academia.[5] Of course, many historians of Nazi Germany utilise prodigious quantities of archival sources, without making such a song and dance about it. Secondly, their empirical approach is an implicit rejection of the overly theoretical debates which seem to preoccupy many historians of the period, and of the mystification of the Holocaust as an epistemological 'black hole' beyond not just poetry but rational understanding *per se*. Unsurprisingly, and with a certain amount of feeling for fellow outsiders, they have more time for Andreas Hillgruber and Ernst Nolte, who at least posed major questions, than for the left-liberal German academic establishment with its vulgar Weberism and ritualised handwringing over the Holocaust. In a quasi-programmatic essay, Götz Aly wrote: 'His [Andreas Hillgruber's] complete works have contributed more to an understanding of National Socialist policy and Hitler's strategy than, for example, the complete works of Eberhard Jäckel.'[6]

Thirdly, much of this work takes economists, historians and other professionals as a starting-point for discussions of the role of intermediary experts in supplying the content and forms for the vaguer ideological projects of Himmler or Hitler. This is an approach which restores human agency and intention to what Hans Mommsen and his epigones regard as the outcome of *ad hoc* processes, while retaining Mommsen's view that Nazi ideology was essentially nebulous. Unlike other 'intentionalists' however, they explicitly reject 'irrational' racial ideology as the motor force behind the Nazi extermination of the Jews and other groups of victims because they construe these policies as the translation into reality of the plans of expert 'strategists', themselves symptomatic of modern, rational, western civilisation. Finally, since these Nazi experts were mostly young people with long careers ahead of them, these alternative scholars stress intellectual and personal continuities between the social and welfare policies of Nazi Germany and the postwar Federal Republic, thus revealing a non-historical, political agenda while inviting the charges of character assassination and political partisanship. While there is nothing wrong with restoring the inhuman face of killers whose killing is too routinely depicted as the operation of a machine, the so-called Hamburg School's instrumentalisation of scholarship for political ends reflects not only what Ernst Köhler calls the conflicting desire to be a left-wing subculture and serious historians, but also ironically, an application of scholarship to ulterior ends which strangely parallels that of the Nazi academics they are bent on exposing.[7]

A 'POLITICAL ECONOMY OF THE FINAL SOLUTION'?

One theme explored by Susanne Heim and Götz Aly, either separately or in tandem in a substantial corpus of published work, has recently excited the interest of professional historians in Germany and elsewhere, and seems set to become a new debate within the historiography, a process this essay is ironically promoting. This is done less from a desire to perpetuate some pseudo-debate than to comment on the wider historical and philosophical issues. The thesis is that there was a 'political economy of the Final Solution'. This ambitious claim first made its appearance in a modest 'Perpetrator Biography' of the economist Helmut Meinhold, since 1959 the non-partisan chairman of the West German government committee on social policy.[8] The cover symbolically bears a detail of a painting by Mantegna showing an advisor whispering to Lodovico Gonzaga, beneath which young Meinhold smiles from a photograph.

During the war, Meinhold worked conjointly in the Institut für deutsche Ostarbeit and under Walter Emmerich as a general factotum in the Ministry of Economics in the Generalgouvernement in occupied Cracow. In common with many other German academics of the period, Meinhold made no secret of his desire to instrumentalise his knowledge in the service of political power, by supplying 'a moral foundation for German claims to power' in the Generalgouvernement. Meinhold's main contribution was less in the field of morality than in the economic reorganisation of this area. Specifically, he identified overpopulation (symptomised by low capital accumulation and hence industrial retardation, localised markets, low productivity, subsistence farming, resort to barter and so forth) as the source of its structural problems. Using optimal norms derived from Paul Mombert, Meinhold and his colleagues came to the conclusion that 4.5 million to 5.83 million people were surplus to economic requirements. Their solutions included using under- or unemployed 'surplus' labour in infrastructral projects; resettlement in the regions of eastern Poland about to be retrieved from the Soviets; deportation of labour to the Reich; and last but not least, the 'rationalisation' of commerce and 'exclusion' of Jews, measures which would promote the formation of an 'indigenous' middle class more disposed to collaboration with the Germans than an undifferentiated mass of helots.[9]

Aly and Heim accompanied their exposure of Meinhold's ideas with some exponentially large claims: 'The destruction of the socio-economic existence of Polish Jews did not spring from the minds of racists, but from those of respected Hanseatic economists. It was not an end in itself, but rather a vehicle for the rationalisation and at the same time dominance of the economy.'[10] We are informed that: 'This mass extermination [of the Jews] was not contrary to the Meinhold concept of industrialisation, but rather an integral part of it, while conversely those who practised extermination used just such scientific lines of argument to invest their activities with higher meaning.'[11] Acknowledging that Meinhold and others often dressed up 'hatred and meanness' in the guise of 'demographic and structure-political necessity', Aly and Heim none the less concluded: 'accepting insanity or hatred of the Jews going back to Martin Luther as grounds for the Holocaust is less disturbing than the discovery of such a coolly thought-out justification of genocide'.[12] This announced what was to become the more systematic downplaying of racist anti-Semitism as the motor force behind the Holocaust, the onset, if one will, of a sort of remorseless contemporaneity.

The unresolved tension between the cause and its intellectual rationalisation, implicit in the views quoted above, gradually vanished from subsequent elaborations of the same thesis whose heuristic ambitions spread to cover euthanasia, resettlement and 'Endlösung' in one utilitarian model. So too did the possibility of irony with regard to the precise place in the political hierarchy of young academic professionals, who now acted as one within a regime otherwise characterised by 'polycratic' chaos, and who saw the course of events as 'osmotically' determined, a conclusion achieved by the novel methodological device of leaving Hitler virtually unmentioned. Aly and Heim's extended study, 'Was there a political economy of the Final Solution?' (1987), began with an editorial critique of those historians who see the Holocaust as the result of 'automatic processes' (Hans Mommsen) – for Aly and Heim are super-intentionalists – or as a form of 'destruction for destruction's sake' beyond human comprehension (Dan Diner). They argued that instead of studying abstruse theories of Fascism or irrational racial ideologies, historians should look no further than the history of their own discipline or other social 'sciences' to discover a 'planning intelligentsia' which employed extermination as a 'means' of socio-economic modernisation.[13] Every self-respecting conspiracy theory also needs a cover-up. Thus one of the reasons why historians have apparently neglected this aspect of the subject is precisely that so many of the old oligarchs of the guild (notably the *Ostforscher* Hermann Aubin, Albert Brackmann, Werner Conze and Theodor Schieder) were all too compromised by their own enthusiastic subscription to Nazi ethnic cleansing.[14]

By now egregiously construing rationalisations as causes, Aly and Heim argued that the young planners were responsible for the 'Final Solution', in the sense that their suggestions and policy papers set the parameters for decisions made by their political masters: 'The Final Solution was gradually developed from their papers and proposals from the lower planning levels on up. It should be noted that these planners – who were not always significant in the hierarchy – did not decide, but they prepared the decisions of their superiors, who for their part attached great significance to the advice of their experts and expressly urged them to research in freedom.'[15] This thesis was in turn elaborated in a substantial book *Vordenker der Vernichtung* and related articles, and most recently in Aly's monograph *'Endlösung'. Völkerverschiebung und der Mord an den europäischen Juden.*[16] In this version, the strategists have become 'a veritable community' free to invest the 'amorphous' content of Nazi ideology with their own intellectual structures.[17] These encompassed not 'just' the murder of the mentally and physically handicapped or the killing of six million Jews, but the planned mass murder of tens of millions of people in the interests of economic modernisation on a continental scale. By derogating the Holocaust into the part of this grand design which circumstances permitted, Aly and Heim effectively diluted its terrible specificity by reference to its indisputable links with both population transfers and futuristic plans, such as the notorious 'Generalplan Ost', involving the murder of tens of millions of Slavic people throughout occupied eastern Europe. Aly is also in partial agreement with Ernst Nolte in seeing these events as part of a continuum, in this case ranging from Greco-Turkish population transfer agreements in 1923 to the post-Second World War expulsion of ethnic Germans from eastern Europe, although for Aly the deed – whether Nazi or Soviet – was not 'Asiatic' but rather inherent in modern western civilisation:

> At the centre of such political conceptions, of state-driven privileging and declassification, was always the assumption that in this fashion socio-economic structures could be revolutionised quicker, indeed even overnight. These assumptions were not just common to Stalinist and Nazi thought in those years. They could also be formulated as the 'agrarian question', as the 'refugee question', as 'the overpopulation question' and 'industrialisation question' in the normative, enlightened progressive thought of the century. The basic models behind these political ideas were popular in Europe. They also shaped the policy of the League of Nations, the International Labour Office in Geneva, and finally the peacetime conceptions of the anti-Hitler coalition.[18]

CRITICS

Although most critics are at one in praising Aly and Heim for their archival research and their exposure of the complicity in Nazi crimes of large swathes of the academic profession, their approach has few supporters. Criticism concentrated on methodological and philosophical flaws. The former could be described as proof by insinuation, omission and supposition. To begin with, there is the general problem of tracing the impact of ideas on policy, namely of proving that what '*x*' wrote actually influenced '*y*', or whether in this case, '*y*' used what '*x*' wrote to rationalise what '*y*' did. On a micro-historical level, Christopher Browning has drawn attention to the lack of unanimity among the experts involved in Jewish policy, as manifested by debates between so-called 'attritionists' and 'productionists' responsible for the fate of the inmates of the Łódź and Warsaw ghettos. Since the 'productionists', or advocates of economic self-sufficiency temporarily won, it is hard to locate the will to exterminate at this level.[19] Hermann Graml has also made the bigger point that Hitler's view of 'experts' can be read indirectly from his appointment of a 'dilettante' as Foreign Minister and a 'servile yes man' as Chief of the High Command of the Wehrmacht, and directly from the fact that he frequently ignored the best advice of 'experts' even in critical situations, notoriously during the campaign in Russia.[20]

But continuing with the theme of experts and economic modernisation, the claim that the 'Final Solution' was driven by utilitarian rather than racist criteria is undermined by a simple glance at the commensurate body of racist expertise being made available by other groups of experts, evidence which Aly and Heim systematically ignore. Why should we suppose that Himmler and his paladins listened any more closely to Meinhold or Oberländer than to, for example, the racial anthropologist Otto Reche, whose fevered racist memoranda were also demonstrably in circulation at the highest levels?[21] Given the universal tendency of academics to seek legitimation via claims to relevance, how do we know that such claims were not met by the Nazi political leadership with the same cynicism that greets them elsewhere? Of course the experts seem important if one solely studies their perspective, but what do we know of how the political consumers regarded them? Aly and Heim solve the problem of influence by extremely tenuous supposition (although the words they employ are 'capillary action' and 'osmosis') claiming that experts within the Four Year Plan apparatus first conceived of the 'Final Solution' and then delegated its implementation to the SS Reich Main Security Office.[22] The only factual link here was that on 31 July 1941 the head of the Four Year Plan, Göring, did charge Heydrich with the preparation of the 'solution of the Jewish problem by emigration and evacuation in the most suitable way'. Apart from the fact that Göring was thus effectively signing away competence over the 'Jewish Question' to Heydrich (symbolically ending the era of economic exclusion and expropriation in favour of something much worse), there is the fact that Heydrich actually drafted the text of the document, which hardly suggests he was acting as a mere delegate for the Four Year Plan, whose involvement was personal to Göring.[23] Moreover, if detailed plans and preparations based on utilitarian criteria existed, why ask Heydrich to make them? Ulrich Herbert remarks that: 'None of the papers, pamphlets, or essays cited by them [Aly and Heim] in support of their argument contains any indication – let alone evidence – that such conceptions on population policy prevalent among the so-called "planning elite" had any impact on the ultimate decision to murder Europe's Jews.' The missing link is still missing.[24] In related work, Herbert also argues that rational economic considerations lost the competition with racist ideology. Once the regime decided in 1942 to utilise Soviet labour the Jews became expendable and could be killed without reference to their labour potential.[25] Indeed, it is the obvious irrelevance of economic criteria (with the possible exception of greed) to the Holocaust which strikes other critics of the Aly and Heim thesis. What economic common denominators actually united the vastly different Jewish communities in Europe from Rome to Copenhagen or Odessa to Amsterdam? Precisely what economic logic impelled the Nazis in June 1944 to transport 2,200 Jews on Rhodes a couple of thousand miles to Auschwitz, regardless of the loss of military matériel or more pressing transport priorities?[26] What difference to the structure of the German economy was made by killing a minority consisting of less than 1 per cent of the population? If one posits Nazi exterminism as the solution of the 'social question' through destruction, then why were only a proportion of psychiatric patients killed (one in five long-term patients) with the sole exception of all Jewish patients, and why did the futuristic plans for Russia involve killing proportions of that vast population, whereas the war against the Jews allowed no exceptions?[27] Discussing high-level attitudes towards Poles and Jews in the Generalgouvernement, Martin Housden remarks: 'it was the difference between dealing with an immediate racial threat and a long-term racial burden'.[28] Such distinctions were not only matters of life and death, but also explain why anti-Semitism is qualitatively different from other forms of racism, hence we should not ignore them.

Apart from these methodological problems, the Aly and Heim thesis has been subjected to a more profound critique, which does not shy away from examining their own extra-historical agenda. Reflecting on the fact that Aly and Heim seem tantalised by the vistas of their planners, Dan Diner accuses them of a literal-minded reading of the evidence, resulting in an uncritical internalisation of the logic and perspective of the documentation which made extermination a 'solution' to a 'social question' improbably involving one 'race' of people:

> Aly and Heim fall prey to the deceptive surface of the social semantics employed in their corpus. They ascribe a bonus of special authenticity to the economic terminology there and seem to proceed in line with the quasi-magical insinuation that the more materialist a motive appears to be, the more credible its intention . . . What eludes the authors is the fact that racialist discourse can also appear in veiled, covert form of social semantics . . . Racist metaphors do not necessarily require biologizing imagery.[29]

Meinhold, Oberländer, Peter-Heinz Seraphim and the rest were using the forms of economic utilitarianism to mask gut prejudices against Jews and Poles, prejudices which could also be rationalised in terms of health or security 'threats' by other groups of experts. Moreover, we are not actually dealing with classical economics at all, conceived as an integral component of moral philosophy, but with a denatured hybrid thoroughly saturated by Nazi race ideology. This is the meaning of Diner's shrewd observation that we conceive of cannibalism as an ethical problem rather than a question of nutrition.[30] Aly and Heim also fail to consider that the reasons given for a policy could be ostensible, a sort of colouring or flavouring designed to conceal the highly unpalatable truth from both the perpetrators and other interested parties. Notions such as excuse, pretext or rationalisation do not enter into their discussion any more than ironic detachment – as distinct from sarcasm – towards their subjects. Reviewing the war against the partisans in Russia, the SS anti-partisan warfare supremo Erich von dem Bach-Zelewski said: 'The fight against partisans was gradually used as an excuse to carry out other measures, such as the extermination of Jews and Gypsies, the systematic reduction of the Slavic peoples by some 30,000,000 souls (in order to secure the supremacy of the German people), and the terrorisation of civilians by shooting and looting.'[31]

In seeking the reasons for Aly and Heim's literal-minded willingness to regard rationalisations as causes, Dan Diner turns to their extra-historical agenda: 'mass annihilation emerges as a possible, albeit extreme practice of bourgeois capitalist society. In so doing, they [Aly and Heim] reveal an element intrinsic to their method of approach: a de-temporalization of the historically specific phenonemon of National

Socialism and its "normalization", its transformation into a variant of garden-variety capitalism.'[32] Apart from the general resort to modernisation as a denatured synonym for capitalism, this part of their agenda is evident in their repeated reference to the post-war careers of many of the experts they discuss, and hence the supposed continuities of thought and practice between the Nazi period and the Federal Republic. Even were the latter to be the case, and none of the experts they cite actually seem to countenance murdering Germany's old age pensioners to diminish the 'Altenlast', the overall political context in Germany has drastically changed since 1945, with no politician being receptive to murdering people for any reason.[33] It is also apparent in the implied, subjunctive 'parallels' between other instances of population transfer (what exactly conceptually unites the expulsion of ethnic Germans after the war with the *extermination* of millions of people by the Nazis?); or in the analogies with the European Community (Union); or in the anachronistic use of such terms as 'take-off lands' or 'two-thirds society' in discussions of the Nazi period whose evils are thus implicitly elided with social problems in present-day Germany. Why else begin a discussion of Meinhold's career with a completely irrelevant digression about projected pension provision in Germany in the year 2030? In other words, the Nazi pasts of certain senior figures in German public life are being instrumentalised for wholly non-historical purposes, in this case as a crass attack on the possible privatisation of pension arrangements by the CDU government which are paralleled in many other western democracies. Like latter-day versions of the 1960s French students with their mindless chants of 'CRS:SS', Aly and Heim are implicitly asking us to believe that we are living in the sixty-second year of the Greater German Reich rather than over fifty years after its destruction.[34]

Like Dan Diner, Ulrich Herbert is also uncomfortable with Aly and Heim's attempts to sideline the allegedly 'irrational' racist causes of Nazi exterminism, which they claim would have eventuated in 'nothing more' than epiphenomenal pogrom-type violence, in favour of anything that appears to have a specious social-scientific logic or which highlights material circumstances. The main problem with this claim is that it ignores the fact that Nazi racism, regardless of whatever complex contributory streams and lability of content there may have been, also claimed to be logical and 'scientific'. It was 'a self-contained and consistent world-view, claiming to offer a cogent and all-embracing explanation for developments, contraditions, and problems in human society'.[35] However unpalatable economic-materialist historians may find it, Nazism drew on a long tradition of scientific racism whose key feature was a total, biological explanation of the past and present of human society, and which prided itself on its implacable rationality in contrast to either traditional religious anti-Semitism or resentment-driven hooliganism. While the former offered the potential escape route of conversion to Christianity and the latter, being affect-led, was not indefinitely sustainable, racial anti-Semitism permitted no exceptions and could be sustained with the ostensibly unemotional scientific logic that societies bring to epidemiology.[36] Like health and security experts, economists and population planners brought their own sectoral disciplinary 'logic' to bear upon a 'problem' which had been predetermined in terms of race. Only this fact can explain why all forms of explanation, including the one we have been considering, so very conveniently converged on Europe's Jews, quite independently in this case of the latter's myriad objective economic circumstances.

SOME REFLECTIONS ON MODERNISATION THEORIES AND THE HOLOCAUST

As Axel Schmidt and others have recently shown, the application of modernisation theories to the Third Reich has a long history, going back to Franz Borkenau's view of Italian Fascism as a developmental dictatorship, or Friedrich Meinecke's critique of the secular society.[37] In subsequent formulations, modernisation theories as applied to Germany tended to regard Nazism as a last-ditch revolt by those 'anti-modern' dysfunctional social groups – the Junkers or 'old Mittelstand' – who felt disadvantaged or threatened by modernisation, and who turned both nasty and Nazi. Once the revolt of the losers had been vanquished, normal service, so to speak, was resumed in 1945. A few scholars also went in pursuit of modernisation in the Third Reich itself, discovering it in the destructive, homogenising pressures exerted by its 'national community', or in popular perceptions of an egalitarian 'New Deal', views which have not found general favour, and which can easily be subverted by the counterfactual question 'what would Germany have been like without Nazism?'[38] These classical modernisation theories based on longer-term social consequences tended to avoid the Holocaust. As Norbert Frei has shrewdly observed, the 'come-back' of modernisation theories is related to a generational shift in and beyond academia.[39] Along with other modish fads which partially filled the vacuum left in western academia by the obvious moral and heuristic deficiencies of Marxism, modernisation theories exerted a considerable purchase, although elegant disquisition does not conceal a massive degree of conceptual confusion largely stemming from the nebulous nature of the concept.[40]

As we have seen above, the term can also be invested with political meaning, by historians whose agendas go beyond the purely academic, a pertinacious syndrome in much of the literature on National Socialism, although comment on this almost exclusively highlights the dreadful machinations of right-wing historians such as Hillgruber or Nolte. In fact, the term is employed by historians with radically different political agendas. On the German neo-Right, Rainer Zitelmann and his colleagues enthuse about the technological awareness of Adolf Hitler and argue that the social mobility allegedly fostered during the Third Reich should not be overshadowed by memory of marginal victim minorities, a novel interpretation of Martin Broszat's plea for enhanced 'historicisation'. Of course, this 'modern' Hitler can only be achieved by ignoring the regressive content of Nazi ideology or by shifting the debate from what actually happened in those twelve years to nebulous plans for the post-war period.[41] On the international political Left, the intellectual crisis of Marxism, the postmodern questioning of the foundations of Enlightenment rationality and science, and fashionable concerns with the so-called Third World, led to versions of modernisation theory which stressed the dark side of modernity.

This heady stuff opened the way for studies which traced the origins of the Holocaust to the 'spirit' of science, as an essay by Detlev Peukert is portentously called – although quite how Einstein, Crick or Rutherford fit this curiously Hegelian story is unexplored. Eschewing monocausal explanations but nevertheless offering one, Peukert claimed that having failed to transcend the mortality of individuals, 'science' switched its concern to the enduring, supra-mortal, collective gene pool, abandoning the impossible dream of mass well-being in favour of the easier goal of mass annihilation.[42] Which 'science' is this pretentious guff discussing? The sciences which explain the origins and contours of the universe, climatic changes on the sun, or which have largely eradicated cholera or malaria or which purify drinking water in Africa and Asia? What exactly does Peukert know about 'science'?

Others aligned the Holocaust within a developmental continuum encompassing Tudor enclosures, Cromwellian Ireland, the 'disappearance' of the Aboriginals or Native Americans, some of whose descendants mysteriously seem to be running multi-million dollar casinos, and rather grudgingly, Stalin's liquidation of people who owned a cow, an activity which some historians regard as not 'lacking all rationality'. Presumably it is 'rational', then, a society in which a Russian textile manufacturer felt obliged to destroy an entire run of cloth in 1938, in line with injunctions to eradicate 'concealed' images of 'enemies of the people'? For he had found, with the aid of a magnifying glass, hidden Japanese flags and swastikas in its patterns.

'Genocide', we are earnestly told by Richard Rubenstein, 'is an intrinsic expression of modern civilization as we know it.'[43] Really? It certainly does not figure in the experiences of Americans or western Europeans born after 1945, who enjoy all the freedoms of parliamentary democracies. Modern civilisation also includes not only attempts (however imperfect) to subordinate governments to more or less extensive systems of international human rights law and supranational jurisdictions but also CNN reporters armed with satellite dishes which beam images of appalling scenes in remote and not so remote places into our living rooms, making ignorance impossible and undercutting the Realpolitik of our leaders. As Jonathan Steinberg has written, we have become 'our electronic neighbour's keeper'.[44] I also fail to see what is either 'modern' or 'civilised' – in any meaningful sense of the word – about genocide in, for example Cambodia, Rwanda or Somalia, since in the first case at least, genocide seems to have come about as an attempt to obliterate 'modern' urban culture and indeed western scientific medicine, in line with dotty ideas ingested by the young Pol Pot from Marxists at the Sorbonne. To argue, as some sociologists have, that the Holocaust is inherent in 'modernity', and hence potentially repeatable, is to fail to explain why genocide occurs in these non-western societies and to exaggerate the importance of bureaucratically induced distance or the inhuman character of much of contemporary social 'science' at the expense of factors which are constantly bringing humanity into greater emotional proximity.[45] It is here – in this morally confused postmodern world – where Foucault could denigrate scientific rationality while praising the theocratic dictatorship of the Ayatollahs; where, echoing the left-wing anti-Dreyfusards, Jacques Verges could construe the crimes of Klaus Barbie as emblematic of a little local difficulty in the world-oppressing white tribe whose Resistance heroes were really torturers; where Nolte has to invoke visitors from outer space to blame Jews for the Holocaust or to compare Israel with Hitler's Germany; and where an insidious relativism so warmly embraces slippery concepts such as 'modernity' that we should locate the work of Aly and Heim on the 'political economy of the Final Solution'.[46]

CHAPTER NINE

The realm of shadows: recent writing on the Holocaust

While massacres and mass murder in former Yugoslavia and Rwanda offered grim contemporary analogies, in 1995 newspapers and television in Great Britain were haunted by images of barbarism which took place half a century ago. The year began with Steven Spielberg's *Schindler's List*. Many thought it richly deserved the plaudits heaped upon it; others that, in Ralph Fiennes's Amon Goeth, the film merely revealed Hollywood's fluency in portraying cinematic psychopaths, replete with ersatz violence, mawkish sentimentality and an atypical happy ending. The New Year, coinciding with the fiftieth anniversary of the liberation of Auschwitz, saw the return of the Holocaust as a major news event. Columnists and leader writers struggled to find contemporary parallels and universal lessons before hastening into the media blur of the next anniversary, the bombing of Dresden in February 1945, or natural disaster, with floods in northern Europe hard on the heels of the earthquake in Kobe.

Although Britain's Channel 4 offered a grim film about the Allied liberators of the western concentration camps, with US veterans providing dignified and moving testimony, BBC 2 confirmed its reputation as the last redoubt of television history by screening Holocaust-related documentaries night after night. These included Lanzmann's *Shoah*, whose problematic richness becomes more evident with every screening; workmanlike films about Pius XII or the Drancy deportation camp; and, at the lesser qualitative extreme, a vicariously distasteful piece about the children of Holocaust survivors, shown assiduously re-traumatising their own offspring with their grandparents' experiences.

Coverage of the ceremonies in Auschwitz showed bewildered survivors clad once again in those horrible, dehumanising, blue-striped uniforms, and yellow candles glowing amidst the railway tracks that once brought people to their deaths. Attempts to invest the occasion with controversy by dilating upon squabbles between Poles and Jews about degrees of suffering did not quite get off the ground. A year later, there seems no relief in sight from the Third Reich. Yet a further raft of BBC documentaries on National Socialist Germany is imminent, while Sunday quality newspapers devote pages to such curiosities – in the original sense – as an English-born, rather than immigrant, Nazi war criminal who allegedly committed atrocities while serving in the British Free Corps. In line with the solipsistic trend for journalists to write about other journalists, the personality clashes and rivalries between prominent journalist experts on the Nazi period are newsworthy, especially if they trade insults such as 'a shrivelled little prune'.[1] In some respects, Nazi Germany has become both tacky and tawdry, though no fall from grace is implied.

Although the general public could be forgiven for thinking that we have reached Holocaust saturation point, with the images themselves ceasing to appal, matters were not always so. Tony Kushner's discomfiting *Holocaust and the Liberal Imagination* is an interesting exploration of how liberalism, broadly defined, rather than overt bureaucratically entrenched anti-Semitism, limited a sense of moral obligation in the free world towards the Jews of occupied Europe, and thereafter resulted in a refusal to acknowledge the scale or specificity of the Jewish tragedy.[2] He shows the difficulties people had in accepting either the ferocious nature of Nazi anti-Semitism or how the latter functioned independently of how Jewish people 'behaved' in Germany, as exemplified in H. G. Wells's question to the heroic Polish underground emissary Jan Karski: 'why anti-Semitism emerges in every country the Jew resides in?' Kushner is of the view that 'ambivalence' rather than 'indifference' characterised public responses to the persecution of the Jews in Germany.

Not always effective in its alternation of general thesis and too specific case study, the book none the less serves to remind us that it was not only bigots in the Foreign Office or State Department who impeded the access of refugees to Britain or the United States of America. Among those who played a prominent role (although, unlike

Kushner, one does not readily associate them with either liberalism or imagination) were the trade unions, who combined campaigns on behalf of a few token political fugitives with a narrow concern for 'our people first'. Admission depended on whether refugees threatened or served entrenched interests. Thus, the Medical Practitioners Union, which had close links with the British Union of Fascists, conspired to prevent the entry of Austrian physicians. By contrast, demand on the part of middle-class women for cheap skivvies ensured the admission of 20,000 Jewish women refugees into this country. Tension frequently accompanied the latter on their journey downstairs. While one wealthy young Viennese lady used to swan down after ten in a blue crêpe-de-Chine dressing gown in search of a breakfast she should have prepared, many men and women who had been leading professionals in Germany were now treated in 'an absolutely terrible manner' by, among others, the wives of Cambridge dons. Concerned not to appear illiberal, the British were none the less equally adamant in their refusal to discriminate on behalf of the persecuted Jews, whose alleged particularism also challenged exclusivist English nationalism.

According to Kushner, the scenes from liberated Belsen or Buchenwald, in whose reporting the Jewishness of the victims was conspicuously and deliberately downplayed, paradoxically perpetuated a refusal to acknowledge the specific fate of the Jews by deflecting attention from the sites of *industrialised* mass murder in Poland. For many years, Belsen would mean more to people than Auschwitz. In Britain, consciousness of the Holocaust was restricted to survivor circles and journals such as the *Wiener Library Bulletin*. In America, the Holocaust became part of the political identity of American Jewry, and then via the television series *Holocaust* (1978), which emulated the Afro-American *Roots* (1977), part of wider popular culture. Vast sums were raised to create Holocaust memorials in Washington, New York and Los Angeles. However, Britain, apart from the laudable efforts of the Imperial War Museum to include an exhibition on Belsen in its overall depiction of the Second World War, has to date only managed a stone and a discreet garden in Hyde Park in a typically understated, and – some think – inadequate response to a crime of monumental proportions. This deficiency will soon be rectified by a major permanent exhibition at the War Museum.

Karski is the remarkable story of a self-styled 'professional hero', which apart from the hyperbolic subtitle, the journalist authors tell with sympathy and verve.[3] Jan Kozielewski (aka Witold Karski) was born in 1914 in the industrial city of Łódź. Educated by the Jesuits and at the university of L'vov, where he witnessed attacks on Jews by fellow students, and regretted his lack of intervention, Kozielewski joined the fast stream in the Polish foreign service in 1938, and graduating top of his class, seemed set to become an ambassador at an early age. The war intervened. With his horse artillery battery decimated by the Luftwaffe, Kozielewski fled eastwards, and found himself in a People's Commissariat of Internal Affairs (NKVD) prison camp in central Ukraine. Concealing his rank from Stalin's grim class warriors, Kozielewski bluffed his way back to Poland. Many of his fellow officer inmates were subsequently murdered by Stalin at Kalinin, Kharkov and Katyn. Immediately reimprisoned by Stalin's Nazi allies, Kozielewski escaped from a moving train, returning to Warsaw where his elder brother – the city police chief – gradually inducted him into the underground. Adventures that were so far tantamount to the Polish equivalent of a good war were shortly eclipsed by acts of extraordinary bravery.

Jan Kozielewski became Witold Kucharski (the name of a student contemporary conveniently marooned abroad) which, by the loss of a syllable, produced his *nom de guerre*. Karski's intelligence, languages, mnemonic skills and ability to 'wither away into the background' equipped him to act as a courier for the faction-ridden Polish underground. During briefing sessions he would listen straight-faced as the socialists relayed their fears of a post-war Fascist coup, while their nationalist allies spoke darkly of a Blum-style popular front behind which lurked Jews and freemasons, intelligence he would then store in his head as he trekked over the Tatra mountains and then half-way across Europe.

Inevitably, operations involving guides and safehouses ran the risk of betrayal. In June 1940 a Slovakian peasant turned Karski over to the Gestapo. The latter battered him with rubber truncheons, kicked out several teeth and broke a few ribs. During a period of respite from one such session, Karski extracted a razor-blade he had concealed in his boot, and sawed through his wrists in a desperate attempt at suicide. This resulted in a spell in hospital, from which his underground contacts were able to liberate him. Thirty-two people were subsequently tortured and shot for alleged or actual involvement in his escape. Underground security procedures meant that he was effectively quarantined for seven months on a country estate, where he had to take such elementary precautions as keeping his sleeves rolled down even on hot summer days, lest anyone spot the giveaway clues that scarred both of his arms.

Resuming his work as a courier, in August 1942 Karski met leaders of the Warsaw Jewish underground whose appearance enabled them to operate outside the ghetto. So agitated that their pacing shadows seemed to dance on the dimly lit walls, the Zionist and Bundist leaders were adamant that 'not a single leader of the United Nations [will] be able to say that they did not know that we were being murdered in Poland and could not be helped except from the outside', and that hence Karski would have to be smuggled into the Warsaw ghetto. After crawling through a forty-yard tunnel, Karski and a companion shuffled through the densely packed streets, past people in whom life consisted of a faint rustle beneath layers of rags, separated only by their clothing from the corpses which littered the streets. Members of the Hitler Youth amused themselves by taking pot-shots at faces incautious enough to venture near windows. In addition to returning twice to this nightmare, Karski followed the odour of evil to its operative centre. Journeying to Lublin, he disguised himself as a Ukrainian militiaman and, accompanied by a guard who had been bribed, entered a holding camp at Izbica used to regulate the flow of Jews to Belzec extermination camp. Hundreds of people were being loaded into boxcars whose floors had been covered with quicklime. They would go either directly to Belzec, or slowly expire in some railway siding en route to it. What he saw led to a nervous collapse, so apparent that it jeopardised his and his escort's lives. Afterwards he washed the experience from his body with water and temporarily from his mind with vodka.

Disguised as a French volunteer worker, Karski made his way via Berlin to Paris. A friendly dentist injected his mouth with a substance to induce tumescence, which together with the missing teeth, would plausibly offset the need to speak halting French during a long train ride. After crossing Spain, British and American secret service agents escorted him to Gibraltar and thence to an RAF base outside London. Members of the Polish government in exile arranged meetings between Karski and ever more illustrious interlocutors. It became obvious that the latter were scheming to disburden the Poles of eastern territories in order to oblige their Soviet ally. Although Karski's celebrity as a hero was used to attract the interest of senior British government figures, this strategy proved counter-productive in the sense that it allowed

British politicians to switch the subject deftly from issues of substance regarding Poland's future borders or the fate of the Jews to the courier's personal exploits, with Eden on one occasion telling him to step nearer the window because 'I want to see what an authentic hero of this war looks like.'

The same pattern was repeated in Washington. Top policy-makers were invited to dine with Karski at the Polish ambassador's residence in order to whet the appetite of a President who was fascinated with the minutiae of cloak and dagger. On one such occasion, this resulted in the curious exchange between Ambassador Ciechanowski and Supreme Court Justice Felix Frankfurter over Karski's graphic description of the fate of the Jews: 'Mr Ambassador. I did not say this young man is lying. I said I am unable to believe him. There is a difference.' Karski finally met Roosevelt. Demonstrating his unique capacity to transcend local Polish perceptions and prejudices, Karski explained the difference between Nazi policy towards the Poles and Jews: 'the Germans want to ruin the Polish state as a state; they want to rule over a Polish people deprived of its elites . . . With regard to the Jews, they want to devastate the biological substance of the Jewish nation.' Although Karski succeeded in holding the President's attention for an hour and a quarter, Roosevelt was predictably fascinated by the possibilities of equipping aircraft with skis to land in Poland; non-committal about both Poland's future borders and the plight of the Jews; and evasive on the subject of 'wily' Uncle Joe's agents' efforts to subvert the Polish underground from within. Karski left overawed, but disappointed

Since his numerous speaking engagements in America had blown his cover in occupied Europe, Karski reconciled himself to a career as a propagandist and publicist. There are a few tantalising references to wartime Manhattan, including drinking sessions with the young Leonard Bernstein. He wrote an account of his exploits, entitled *Story of a Secret State* published in 1944, although his agent persuaded him to drop a chapter on nefarious communist activities, while his publisher none too subtly indicated that he should include something on his romantic life (vulgarly defined), muttering 'Pity' on being told that these matters had a low priority in the cells of the Gestapo. Only thirty-four and somewhat adrift at the end of the war, Karski eventually resumed his studies and in 1953 joined the faculty at Georgetown. Nicknamed 'McCarthyski' by some of his students, he divided his time between teaching, buying and renovating old houses, and lecture tours in the Third World on behalf of the US Information Service. He had various on-going links with the Pentagon and CIA in their battle to make the world safe from communism. In 1978 Karski contributed his spell-binding forty-minute interview to Lanzmann's *Shoah* where the trauma of what he had seen in the Warsaw ghetto was palpable. Since the early 1980s, Karski has justifiably been feted by various Jewish communities, and in Israel where a tree bears his name in the Avenue of the Righteous. The active life peters out in the routinised world of academic Holocaust conferences. Economically written and well researched, the book does not explore in any detail why Karski risked his life on so many occasions, or what obliged him to insert the fate of Poland's Jews into the agenda of his various reports from the underground, even when this took up time that his Polish masters, who were never far from his shoulders, wanted devoted to other issues. Reading this book, we should all be grateful that the values Mr Karski embodies prevailed, and that thanks to people like him, at least in western Europe, the bullies and murderers have been confined to the margins for our lifetimes.

Paradoxically, a world that can celebrate Karski or the ambiguous Gentile Oskar Schindler, has trouble with Jews who did what they could to rescue Jews. In a meticulously researched, sane and morally sensitive study, Yehuda Bauer – one of the world's leading authorities on the Holocaust – deals with the efforts of Jews to save other Jews from persecution and mass murder through negotiation.[4] Since the time of the Kasztner affair in Israel, this subject has been highly controversial, with left-wing anti-Zionists making their own characteristically ill-informed and tasteless contribution in the form of Jim Allen's play *Perdition*. Much of the intensity of Yehuda Bauer's book will thus be lost on readers unfamiliar with, for example, debates about alleged Zionist 'Palestinocentrism' during the Nazi period or left-wing insinuations of collusive affinities between Nazis and Zionists. This does not diminish the book's importance as a commemoration of Jews who rescued Jews.

Bauer shows how, as the 'one-sided love affair' of Jews and Germans was replaced by persecution, some Jews (and one of the great merits of the book is to show just how unhomogeneous that people were) took the initiative in negotiating with the Nazis in order to remove Jewish people from Nazi clutches. Manipulating the Nazis' own exaggerated fear of an international 'Jewish' boycott of German products, the Jewish Agency established a series of financial instruments under the

Ha'avarah agreement which enabled about 20,000 German Jews with capital to order German-manufactured goods which were delivered to Palestine along with the investors, whose presence there would facilitate the emigration of poorer people. As long as Hitler thought that Jewish emigration was more important than any economic considerations the agreement held, although in a progressively attenuated form. After 1938, he seems to have been won over to the idea that one could expel the Jews without any assets, thus exporting anti-Semitism to other countries. From November 1938 he was temporarily tantalised by a multilateral agreement involving the island of Madagascar; by January 1939 he was uttering his dire semi-conditional warning that he would exterminate the Jews in the event of war. In other words, the Jews were to be removed 'so oder so', with many of these policy options being pursued simultaneously.

Negotiations between Eichmann and Jews representing either Zionist organisations or just themselves, who were determined to circumvent British restrictions on emigration to Palestine, continued after the outbreak of war. Within the broad strategy of mass murder, a few concessions to achieve tactical advantages were possible, for after all, a victorious Reich could catch up with rescued Jews in the end. Bauer illustrates this important thesis with detailed discussion of negotiations between Jewish leaders and the SS adviser on Jewish affairs Dieter Wisliceny in Slovakia. Here, the clerico-fascist Tiso state took the initiative in urging the Nazis to deport all of Slovak Jewry. Discovering that Wisliceny might be susceptible to bribery, Rabbi Michael Weissmandel and Gizi Fleischmann turned first to local sources and then to the Jewish Distribution Committee in search of funds with which the deportations could be delayed. Coming to the misleading opinion that this strategy worked, a view sedulously fostered by Wisliceny, Weissmandel conceived the bolder idea, known as the 'Europa Plan', of bribing the SS as a whole either to halt their murderous activities *tout court* or, failing that, to stop deportations of European Jews to Poland. This gambit failed because the wider Jewish community simply did not dispose of the order of money involved (two to three million dollars being the opening sum mentioned) and because it reeked of extortion on the part of men who were inherently untrustworthy.

The other question which Bauer addresses, namely what Wisliceny and his SS masters thought they were doing, is of considerable interest.

Even at the height of the Holocaust in the autumn and winter of 1942, Hitler himself was not above sanctioning opportunities to extort foreign currency in return for ransoming very rich Jews. According to Bauer, Himmler's motives for tolerating Wisliceny's activities were more complex. Precisely when he was enjoining his men to greater efforts in the extermination of the Jews, the prospect of German military defeat weighed more and more onerously upon him. Aware in a general way of the developing plot against Hitler, Himmler – who seems to have been torn between his loyalty to his Führer and an awareness that he had to be got rid of – hedged his bets by using the negotiations with the Jews as a means of opening up potential lines to the western Allies. Any promises made to the Jews could be reneged on. Unfortunately for the Jews, the Allies did not share Himmler's paranoid belief in the centrality of the Jewish 'race' to world politics: in Allied eyes they were a marginal nuisance. Thus, after Casablanca this line was virtually futile. Answering the question whether these contacts via Walter Schellenberg could have been used to save Jews, Bauer comes to the bleak conclusion that 'to save Jews in 1943, two sides had to be amenable to acting: the murderers and their Western enemies . . . Himmler might have been willing to sell, given certain conditions. There were no buyers.' Strategic considerations fused with a liberal incapacity to appreciate the Nazis' unique and murderous obsession with a minority.

After an over-long chapter on the cloak and dagger world of wartime Istanbul, no doubt of interest to OSS buffs, Bauer returns to the subject of Wisliceny in the context of negotiations to save Hungarian Jewry, whose plight became acute when the Germans occupied that country on 19 March 1944. In the absence of any other realistic alternatives Rudolf Kasztner and his fellow Transylvanian Jew Joel Brand opted for negotiation with the Nazis. A reluctant Eichmann entered into what became the so-called 'trucks for blood' deal, with Brand and a low-grade spy called Grosz despatched to Istanbul to contact the western Allies. Eichmann described the nature of the deal in characteristically inhuman terms: 'To extract necessary labor from Hungarian Jewry and sell the balance of valueless human material against valuable goods.' Grosz was sent because Himmler saw an opportunity to use the Jews as part of his bigger game of engineering a meeting between his and the enemy's intelligence officers as a preliminary to a separate peace with the western Allies. He could easily disown him. The British government (into whose hands Brand and Grosz fell) responded to these overtures by hiding behind a Soviet veto on negotiations with the Nazis and the line that the Germans were using these proposals to elicit rejection in order to 'justify' their own murderous policies. Roosevelt did not even reply to Ben-Gurion's desperate cables 'not to allow this unique and possibly last chance of saving the remains of European Jewry to be lost'. The British killed the Brand mission by leaking a version of the story to the press. Unsurprisingly, Brand later figured in the terrorist Stern Gang/'Group'. More *ad hoc* arrangements had to be used to save a proportion of the Jews of Budapest from the Nazis and Arrow Cross Fascists.

As Bauer himself repeatedly acknowledges, many of the Jews involved in these negotiations were rather unappealing individuals. They were not the sort of people one uses for the edification of schoolchildren or in whose honour parks and squares are named. Bribery and corruption, after all, are inherently unedifying activities, in all but life and death contexts. The important fact is that these people at least tried in the face of overwhelming evidence of Nazi duplicitousness and Allied indifference. A world that can celebrate Oskar Schindler can surely now recognise his non-Gentile equivalents?

Raul Hilberg's autobiography begins with a shocking account of the fate of his own family, including that of an octogenarian maternal grandmother who was hauled from her bed by the Nazis and shot in the street.[5] Growing up in pre-war Vienna, Hilberg's interest in history was aroused first by a decent atlas then by the huge swastika banners unfurled in 1938 from the roof of his apartment home. Excursions with his mother led to an abiding interest in railways. In early 1939, the family fled via France and Cuba to New York. He caught the tail-end of the war in Bavaria, before returning to the USA to resume studies in politics and history rather than chemistry. His lifelong interest in bureaucracies was stimulated by Hans Rosenberg and then Franz Neumann who, agreeing to supervise a doctoral dissertation on the 'Final Solution', remarked laconically, 'that will be your undoing'. Running out of money, Hilberg took a job on the War Documentation Project housed in a former torpedo factory in Alexandria, Virginia. The general objective was to comb captured German records for intelligence about the Soviet Union, to which end this agency had the services of sundry former Nazi officers and officials, including one who had afforded the Security Police logistical assistance in murdering 10,000 Jews in the Crimean town of Simferopol. His 'Guten Morgens' to Hilberg at the archive doors each morning were met with a glacial silence. In what are perhaps the most interesting pages in the book, Hilberg shows how he acquired his masterly skill in decoding the meaning of individual documents. After unsatisfactory temporary jobs in New York and Puerto Rico, he arrived in the place with which he would thenceforth be associated, Burlington University of Vermont.

Attempts to have his vast manuscript on the destruction of European Jews published were thwarted by the chicanery of interested parties (scholars at Yad Vashem who, keen to find European precursors of the heroic Sabra Jew, did not care for his views on the alleged absence of Jewish resistance), and by the petty-mindedness of academic publishers such as Princeton University Press which did not regard the book as an adequate 'case study' of public administration. Clearly a man never to forget a slight, Hilberg chronicles his various disputes with hostile reviewers, and his vexations with Lucy Dawidowicz and Hannah Arendt. In the latter case, one is not entirely sure whether Hilberg is more exercised by the fact that her countenance once adorned a West German stamp, than the ways in which she distorted and vulgarised his views on alleged Jewish passivity during the Holocaust through her exclusive focus on the Judenräte. Since the publication of the *Destruction*, Hilberg has occupied himself with an edition of the diary of Adam Czerniakow, and a radical rewriting of his major work to encompass the perspectives of victims and bystanders, which represents both his rejection of the political 'science' tradition he learned from Neumann, and his indebtedness to scholars who think there is more to Holocaust studies than adding up numbers of victims or following the paper trails of a lunatic bureaucracy. Hostile reviews, including one in the *New York Times*, which claimed that Hilberg's creative tide had ebbed thirty years ago, result in the author flying back to Vienna where we see him photographed, alone, outside the door to his parents' former apartment in the Wallersteinstrasse. Fascinating as an account of the tenacity and training that has made him a master of his craft, the book is diminished by the insights it affords into the rancour, paranoia and self-importance of the academic culture in which he has been privileged to work.

Michael André Bernstein's *Foregone Conclusions* is a challenging, well-written and thoughtful attack on teleological determinism in

Holocaust fiction, and one, moreover, that could be read to advantage by many historians.[6] What the author calls 'foreshadowing' consists of 'a closed universe in which all choices have already been made, in which human free will can exist only in the paradoxical sense of choosing to accept or willfully – and vainly – rebelling against what is inevitable'. By contrast, 'sideshadowing' represents 'the incommensurability of the concrete moment and refuses the tyranny of all synthetic master-schemes, it rejects the conviction that a particular code, law, or pattern exists, waiting to be uncovered beneath the heterogeneity of human existence'. Or as Philip Roth puts it without the aid of jargon: 'Life can go this way or life can go that way.' This leads Bernstein to a sustained critique of both the banal portentousness exemplified by a Kafka biography which embellishes the birth of his sister Elli with completely irrelevant intelligence on the 'antinativity' in Braunau in the same year, and works of fiction in which knowledge of the final outcome (in this case the Holocaust) is used to diminish the historical participants (in this case Austro-German Jewry in the later 1930s) for lack of prescience as to their dismal future. As Maitland reminds us, events now far in the past were once in the future.

One of the primary culprits, according to Bernstein, is the Israeli writer Aharon Appelfeld, and in particular his fable-like novella *Badenheim 1939*. Bernstein sets about Appelfeld more in sorrow than in anger, since the latter was one of the first Israeli writers to deal with the Holocaust, and does so elegiacally and sensitively at the margins of the event rather than by battering the reader's emotions *à la* William Styron with the evil that was at its dark core.

Set in an Austrian spa town, where affluent Austrian Jews gather for an annual cultural festival, *Badenheim 1939* traces its surreptitious transformation into a sealed ghetto by the sinister-sounding Sanitation Department. Badenheim's denizens refuse to see what is in store for them in Poland, billed with posters announcing 'THE AIR IS FRESHER IN POLAND', or 'THE DEVELOPMENT AREAS NEED YOU'. When the Jews are eventually shipped out in freight cars, one of the principal characters, Dr Pappenheim, observes 'if the coaches are so dirty, it must mean that we have not far to go'. Bernstein contrasts this approach with Robert Musil's *Man Without Qualities*, which satirises the conferring of retrospective teleological significance upon any given time: 'A new time had then just begun (for that is, after all, something that time is doing all the time) . . . These were stirring times, round about the end of 1913 and the beginning of 1914. But two years, or five years, earlier the times had also been stirring times.'

Bernstein's other major themes, somewhat awkwardly introduced into the book, are the political instrumentalisation of the Holocaust in both Israel and North America, and the widespread belief that extreme situations are somehow more revealing of the human condition. Bernstein shows how both sides in the 1991 Crown Heights troubles used the Holocaust or its Afro-American 'equivalent' of slavery to lend added emotional validation to their respective case. African-Americans in Brooklyn were compared with the perpetrators of Kristallnacht; Jews with the slave owners of the old South. This leads Bernstein to reflect more widely on America's ethno-cultural-sexual ghettos of perceived victimhood and 'rights' unencumbered by wider civic duties. Like Yehuda Bauer, Bernstein is also sceptical of the emblematic value of the experience for our culture as a whole, arguing 'that very little about human nature or values can be learned from a situation *in extremis* except the virtual tautology that extreme pressure brings out extreme and extremely diverse behaviour'. This view, he feels, is curiously paralleled in the atavistic and clichéd belief that war brings out man's 'true self'. By contrast, Bernstein's ideal is the non-apocalyptic, prosaic, tone of the poet Yehuda Amichai, whose 'Tourists' ends in the hope that the tourists will one day observe, not: 'you see that man over there with the baskets? A little to the right of his head is an arch from the Roman period', but rather: 'Do you see that arch over there from the Roman period? It doesn't matter, but near it, a little to the left and then down a bit, there's a man who has just bought fruit and vegetables for his family.' This is an elegant, incisive and thoughtful book that deserves a readership beyond that of university-based literary critics. It is quite simply a masterpiece.

Present fads within academia leave their mark on the first volume of Steven Katz's *The Holocaust in Historical Context*, which is largely devoted to issues of comparability with mass slaughter in ancient and pre-industrial times.[7] The footnotes often extend three-quarters of the way up the page, as everything onwards from Tiglath-Pileser III, Sargon II and Sennacherib's invasion of Judah in 734–701 BC is downloaded from the library computer. Ponderously, every term used in the book is the subject of lengthy exegesis. Thus 'phenomenological uniqueness', we are told, in the third of eight 'points' devoted to this issue, is employed in its 'generic . . . non-Husserlian, non-Schutzean, non-Schelerian, non-Heideggerian, non-Merleau-Pontyan sense'. Some sentences do little to advance what is actually a good account of the relationship – rather than just the similarity – of Christian anti-Judaism and Nazi anti-Semitism. Thus we find: 'antisemitism as an historical phenomenon, in its polymorphous concreteness, is always embodied in singular forms and unique spatiotemporal loci that directly affect its actualized character. In this sense it is always something azygos, whatever larger history the sum of its specific manifestations'. Much of the substantive argument, buried in the book, is with North American proponents of 'gynocide' (*sic*) – the absurd attempt to equate the killing of 50,000–100,000 'witches' with the Nazis' destruction of European Jewry. Does no one tell these people that these figures include male 'witches', or that dotty Himmler established an SS department to collect material on witches and heretics – whom he approved of – as evidence of a submerged pre-Christian folk religion? And related squabbles with those like the late John Boswell who were obsessed with identifying the 'historical' fate of homosexuals with that of the Jews, and sundry attempts to prove that the murder of this or that people was equal to, or worse, than that of the Jews under Nazism. In other words, rather than being an attempt to understand the reasons for the extreme radicalisation of Nazi racial policy between 1939 and 1941, which is what the Holocaust was, the book tilts at a proliferating series of 'unique' North American politico-academic windmills, of marginal significance to the study of a serious subject, but so redolent of a society where minority power is expressed through victimhood.

More mainstream scholarly writing on the Holocaust tends to revolve around a narrower set of questions than many of the books so far considered. Two themes have recently predominated, namely the origins of the 'Final Solution', and the responses of the German population to the persecution of the Jews, subject of a recent book by Daniel Jonah Goldhagen, which resulted in Foreign Minister Klaus Kinkel having to refute some of its wilder assertions before the American Jewish Congress in Washington.[8] But before considering responses, let us discuss recent accounts of the genesis of the 'Final Solution'.

Since the mid-1960s, older, linear accounts of the origins of the 'Final Solution', in which Hitler's obsessional hatred of the Jewish 'race' was simply translated into its wartime annihilation, have been challenged by various kinds of 'structure-functionalism'. The more provocative variations of this approach virtually air-brushed away both Hitler and race hatred, for neither dominant personalities nor ideas were much in fashion. They also seem to do without human volition. Although interest in these questions waned appreciably in the 1980s among younger historians, many of whom regard Nazism as a form of political epidemiology, and while it never really caught on among those few who persist in trying to pin everything on Babeuf or Lenin, perhaps with more reason than they are credited with, the intentionalist–functionalist debate still thrives in the ever larger literature dealing with the historiography of the Third Reich.

The latter, as even its practitioners shamefacedly admit, has become quasi-scholastic. Some historians argue that the 'Final Solution' was a sort of heuristic 'black hole'; others that it revealed an all too familiar rationality, for some of those who live and write freely in liberal democracies are unhappy with the 'legacy' of the Enlightenment. Others debate whether this or that was decided in March, July or September; whether the perpetrators were enraged or euphoric; whether they were ordinary, psychopathic or perhaps ordinary psychopaths. Some historians get a lot of mileage out of being literal-minded.[9] Inevitably, this vast literature is replete with its own idioms, many of a quite unselfconscious inhumanity, such as 'cumulative radicalisation' or 'conditional intentionalism'. The human victims of these policies are rarely mentioned, present only as statistical 'body counts' or in token descriptions of their shivering in Ukrainian ravines or sweating behind Baltic sand dunes. In fifty years' time, assuming the continuation of what Ernst Nolte has dubbed the super nova-like 'negative vitality' of this period in history, much of this scholarship will probably be so much scree left below Claude Lanzmann's film and half a dozen books of enduring distinction.

In view of this historiographical context, it is not surprising that Philippe Burrin's *Hitler and the Jews*, which emphatically reasserts the central role of Hitler in the 'Final Solution', should have caused a minor sensation.[10] In some senses, the book returns to the position in the historiography on the 'Final Solution' before Hans Mommsen temporarily diverted almost everyone into contemplating Hitler as the dreamer who could not realise his own vision. The first third of Burrin's book elaborates what may seem, for a lay audience, a far from contentious proposition, namely that 'Hitler occupied a key position in the Third Reich and was a fanatical antisemite.' Hitler sought to purify the

German 'race' and to encourage its propagation, with a view to conquering *Lebensraum* and ultimately, perhaps (for another 'debate' intrudes here), to world domination. By their very existence, the Jews not only subverted the first part of this agenda, but through finance capital and Marxism stood in the way of the latter. According to Burrin, Hitler learnt a crucial lesson from Germany's defeat in 1918: 'before conquering the enemies without, one must have exterminated the enemy within'. Recalling the events of November 1918, Hitler confessed that it was then that 'hate was born in me, hate for the perpetrators of these events'. Once in power, he would engineer the disenfranchisement and socio-economic exclusion of the Jews as a prelude to their deportation. However, in one potential scenario, namely a war of attrition on a global scale, Hitler countenanced far more radical measures. Accompanying the intentionalists half-way, Burrin takes the passage in *Mein Kampf* where Hitler wrote: 'If just once, at the beginning or during the course of the war, we had exposed twelve or fifteen thousand of those Hebrew corrupters of the people to the poison gas that hundreds of thousands of our best German workers . . . had to endure at the front, the sacrifice of millions of men would not have been in vain', as the basis for his thesis of 'conditional intent'. If, at some future date, Hitler's megalomaniac ambitions should face defeat, then the Jews would suffer the ultimate consequences. A homicidal potential was always present, but its implementation was conditional on the occurrence of a specific set of circumstances.

Burrin next charts the efforts of the regime to make it impossible for Jewish people to live in Germany and to force them to emigrate. Those who remained were periodically subject to 'reprisals' for alleged external and internal 'provocation'. This chapter adds very little to the fuller accounts of *inter alios* Avraham Barkai, Hermann Graml and Karl Schleunes. Burrin's hypothesis regains surer ground with Hitler's infamous speech of 30 January 1939 in which he prophesied that 'if international Jewry, in and outside Europe, once again forced the nations into a world war, the result would not be the Bolshevization of the earth and victory for the Jews, but the annihilation of the Jewish race in Europe'. Unlike the functionalists, Burrin does not insult our intelligence by dismissing this passage as being of merely metaphorical import.

While correctly observing that 'the Nazi war did not become a racist war in 1941; it had been one since 1 September 1939', Burrin none the less follows most historians of the 'Final Solution' in eliding the fact that before the war actually commenced, Hitler and his associates had planned the so-called 'euthanasia' programme, which would provide the *modus operandi* and many of the personnel for the 'Final Solution' that followed. This first exercise in mass murder had nothing to do with potential military outcomes, but rather was an attempt to 'purify' the race and to 'rationalise' hospital bed-space for a conflict which had not even started. In early 1941, as Burrin sheepishly notes, some of the spare 'capacity' of this programme was redirected to killing 'sick' concentration camp inmates, with a person's 'Jewishness' becoming a 'sickness' hitherto unknown to medical science.

In the section dealing with the early stages of the war, Burrin essentially follows the work of Christopher R. Browning and others who stress that the Jews were only one element in a grand design of population transfers, involving out-going Poles and Jews and incoming ethnic German repatriates, a theme explored with great archival detail in a recent book by Götz Aly. Those who would be most culpably involved in genocide, notably Himmler, were still dismissive of genocide as being 'un-Germanic' and 'Bolshevik'. In so far as the Nazi leaders considered a solution to the 'Jewish Question', this involved relocating Jews to a reservation in the Lublin region or to Madagascar, a generic fantasy of hardline anti-Semites in France or Poland. All this changed with the invasion of the Soviet Union, which was planned as an ideological showdown with the 'Jewish-Bolshevik' world enemy. At this point, Burrin admits that 'the historian enters the realm of shadows. There is nothing to enlighten him about conversations that took place between Hitler and Himmler, the proposals made, the initiatives taken, or the orders given.' In other words, there are virtually no sources regarding the key players (all of whom died in 1945); the written evidence is ambiguous, and may not correspond with what was ordered verbally; and post-war testimony by intermediate or low-ranking perpetrators is inherently untrustworthy.

SS task forces trailed along in the wake of the invading armies, killing an enemy which was probably initially defined as 'Jews in party and state positions', either for the benefit of their military colleagues, or because Heydrich believed in inducting his murderers gradually. Uncharacteristically reticent about the role of Hitler, Burrin notes that the forces available for these murders were drastically augmented (from an initial 3,000 to about ten times that number by Christmas) with indigenous collaborators, SS regiments and various kinds of policemen. There was a commensurate surge in the number and broadening of the kind of victim. Although he says that 'the mission of Himmler's troops had been transformed' between July and August, Burrin omits the obvious point that there was a necessary time-lag between an initial decision and its full implementation, or that in the beginning the Nazi leaders did not know how many men it would take to destroy Soviet Jewry. None of these killings was influenced by the course of the war, because the German army was carrying all before it.

Moving from the assault on Soviet Jewry to the attempt to kill every Jewish person in Europe, Burrin also plays down the letter of 31 July 1941 in which Göring charged Heydrich with the 'preparatory steps' for the realisation of 'a comprehensive solution to the Jewish Question in Germany's sphere of influence'. In the interests of relocating the origins of the 'Final Solution' to a later date than is conventional, Burrin makes much of an incident in Paris in October, when French fascists blew up a synagogue, injuring several Frenchmen and two German soldiers in the process. Since the explosives were supplied by one of Heydrich's subordinates, he assumed responsibility. Heydrich explained to the German military commandant that he had decided to sanction such 'reprisals' 'only from the moment when, at the highest level, Jewry had been forcefully designated as the culpable incendiary in Europe'. This is hardly so chronologically precise as Burrin would like us to imagine. None the less, it enables him to telescope a whole series of developments into the period between 18 September and 18 October, relating these in turn to the putative course of the war in Russia. He does not explain why, for example, the redundant 'euthanasia' personnel should have been relocated to operate death camps in Poland then rather than earlier.

Reading the moods of a man as unstable as Hitler is a difficult business. Whereas Burrin sees a steady fall into gloom and a desire for vengeance, others argue in favour of intervening periods of euphoria. Browning has argued that there was little in the strategic situation during the month Burrin regards as crucial to make Hitler anything other than confident, for Operation Typhoon hoovered up over 670,000 Soviet prisoners. Apparently there was 'unanimity over the favourableness of the situation', with Hitler 'exuding a spirit of total victory'. So far from launching the 'Final Solution' to compensate for impending checkmate or defeat, it is just as probable that Hitler embarked on these policies in a state of hubristic euphoria, taking the opportunity provided by the war in Russia to realise a hatred that was absolute and implacable rather than merely 'conditional'. Actually neither Browning nor Burrin can prove this point one way or the other. While Burrin is to be congratulated for his anti-functionalist conclusion that in 'matters of extermination Hitler had the last word; he was the prime mover', which in historiographical terms almost completes the circle, the speculative scenario he constructs does not ultimately carry much conviction.

An awareness of how other historians have construed the Holocaust is also useful to a critical appreciation of Daniel Goldhagen's provocative book, especially since rather large, and mostly unfulfilled, claims have been made on its behalf. It has become an event rather than a book, as a fresh generation of Germans again confronts the past, as their parents did with the TV series *Holocaust*. The book seems to have appealed to the desire in some quarters for a simple version of the story, and to a self-lacerating constituency in Germany worryingly impressed by the author's demagogic public performances, and hostile to a complacent historical establishment.[11] British responses have ranged between the very hostile and neutral, the only positive reviews being by Robert Harris and Elie Wiesel. Goldhagen begins by sketching in what he sees as the all-pervasiveness of eliminationist anti-Semitism in German society. Dispensing with many other gradations of anti-Semitism – and indeed construing philo-Semites as crypto anti-Semites – he asserts that it was akin to the unarticulated belief in democracy in North America, a truism which removes the need for either nuance, qualification or proof. Actually, nineteenth-century Germans thought about many subjects other than Jews, who were not an exclusive, obsessional fixation. Goldhagen also ignores such problems as why turn-of-the-century commentators regularly alighted upon France or Russia rather than Imperial Germany when they sought the source of this contagion, or why so many Jews chose to live in Germany then, and subsequently. Goldhagen takes us through the well-charted territory of how the Jews of Germany were formally and informally ostracised under the Nazis, culminating in what was tantamount to social death. Nothing whatsoever is added to what we know already, indeed much is lost in his version of the story.

Following the classic intentionalist view on the origins of the 'Final Solution', Goldhagen turns to the substantive core of his book, namely the motives of those Germans who perpetrated the Holocaust. Despite the scholarship devoted to this subject, we do not know such elementary facts as the number of perpetrators, with Goldhagen's own guesstimates ranging between 100,000 and 500,000 persons, although as he says, establishing the exact figure is a daunting task which he does not bother with. These people were deployed in a vast range of contexts, including over 10,000 camps dedicated to various squalid purposes, and in SS and police formations whose depredations were commensurate with those of the notorious Einsatzgruppen, and which have only recently been investigated.

One of these police units – Reserve Police Battalion No. 101 – is also the subject of Christopher Browning's *Ordinary Men* (echoed in Goldhagen's subtitle), and therefore one should regard Goldhagen's book as a critique of Browning's thesis. Indeed, much of the interest of the book lies in the radically different conclusions these two historians draw from the same evidence, making sweeping generalisations about human behaviour. Browning depicted these middle-aged Hamburg males as almost victims of internal group dynamics, as they busied across Poland shooting 80,000 Jews, with no apparent reason except a desire not to let each other down, and only gradually succumbing to a process of moral brutalisation. By contrast, Goldhagen restores the cruelty of thought, word and deed that accompanied their every action *ab origine*. These men could have opted out or requested transfers from sympathetic officers, but the majority did not. Nor did they and their equivalents 'just' shoot Jewish people with robotic efficiency: they taunted and tortured them, incinerating them in synagogues or burying them alive in waterlogged trenches, abusing the elderly and gripping children by the hair so as better to blow their brains out. Indeed, instances of gratuitous cruelty are intrinsic to Goldhagen's case since they prove that something more was at work than either obeying orders or simple pressures to conform. The devil, one might say, is in the excess of the detail. Again, there is nothing especially new about this line of argument, since only structuralist historians are fastidious in their avoidance of the corporeality of mass murder, finding it 'incredible' why men should lend themselves to it. Other critics have argued that such lurid accounts lend themselves to the desensitisation of readers rather than enhanced awareness.

Having correctly highlighted the limitations of Browning's monocausal explanation, Goldhagen further illustrates his thesis with a discussion of two relatively neglected forms of Nazi exterminism, namely labour camps and death marches. Here the relentless polemic relaxes into a considered and therefore more interesting discussion. In what is a refutation of those German scholars who see economic rationality operative in the 'Final Solution', Goldhagen shows that even when the Nazis belatedly decided to utilise what remained of Jewish labour potential, the ways in which they worked Jews were designed to kill them.[12] The labour force was abused, starved to the point of chronic inefficiency, and frequently occupied with utterly meaningless tasks designed to exhaust and humiliate them. The head of one camp trained a ten-year-old Jewish child, dressed in a scaled-down SS uniform, to take pot-shots at the workforce. Goldhagen's argument is that under these conditions it was impossible to 'work' at all, an effect which of course perversely confirmed Nazi stereotypes of Jewish people, even as it militated against any rational economic calculation. The Germans could not afford to expend skilled labour casually in this way, and yet in the case of the Jews they clearly did so. Likewise, any rational calculation would have told the guards who accompanied Jewish survivors on meandering marches across central Europe, that they should throw their weapons away and melt homewards. Indeed, that is what an emissary from Himmler ordered them to do – lest the marchers upset his negotiations with the western Allies – but instead, the guards chose to ignore his orders not to shoot Jews, preferring instead to abuse and murder them, beyond either clear contrary instructions or simple prudential self-interest. As Goldhagen says to damning effect: 'They were voluntaristic actors.' Both the labour camps and the death marches allegedly prove that the Jews occupied a different cognitive status in these people's minds, and that this was informed by eliminationist anti-Semitism. Actually, they are amenable to other glosses.

Finally, there is the crucial question of how representative these 'ordinary Germans' were. Reverting to his earlier impassioned indictment of German society, Goldhagen claims that the German people were the sea in which Hitler's willing executioners swam. Sweeping aside volumes of authoritative cant about the meaning of terms such as 'indifference', Goldhagen uses a commensurately slight evidential base to argue that the majority of people subscribed to Hitler's lethal racial fantasies: 'The inescapable truth is that, regarding Jews, German political culture had evolved to the point where an enormous number of ordinary, representative Germans became – and most of their fellow Germans were fit to be – Hitler's willing executioners.' In order to reach this conclusion, Goldhagen simply ignores all the available evidence to the contrary, notably SS Security Service (SD) and SPD reports which make it very clear that Nazi anti-Semitism frequently clashed with existing moral attitudes concerning law and order, the inviolability of private property, respect for religion, disapproval of pornography and, yes, common human decency towards others. Instead of treating the Germans according to age, confession or social class, where subtle differences towards anti-Semitism were obvious to most contemporaries and most modern historians, we simply get 'the Germans'. Since the only brief comparative case he makes concerns the atypical Danes and Italians, he is not in a position to consider why so many other peoples, including Austrians, Balts, Croats, Frenchmen, Hungarians, Romanians, Slovaks and Ukrainians were also involved in the Holocaust. Germanophobes will find little unsettling in his conclusions; those who seek nuance and subtlety (sometimes at the expense of the glaringly obvious) will be upset, and maybe they should be. Few readers will forget the relentless, hectoring tone, not least because it both bores and leaves one exhausted, obscuring rather than enlightening a complex subject. One wonders how a similar book about the 'Americans' would be received, if it generalised from the Ku-Klux-Klan, messianic sects and paranoid militias, or the recent spate of church burnings. But such a book is unlikely to be written.

Three further books on aspects of the 'Final Solution' represent major scholarly achievements, rather than being products of media hype. Hans Safrian already enjoys a considerable reputation on account of his *Und keiner war dabei*: a self-condemning documentary account of the anti-Semitic outrages which occurred in Vienna in the wake of the Anschluss.[13] In his cool and meticulously researched *Eichmann und seine Gehilfen*, now published in Fischer Verlag's black series (at 120 volumes, the single greatest body of scholarship on the Nazi period), Safrian traces the careers of the dedicated team of Austrian SD officers assembled by Adolf Eichmann.[14] This is an important book because although Austrians comprised 8 per cent of the population of the Greater German Reich, they supplied a third of those who worked in the SS murder apparatus. Unfortunately, the fine scholarship of Austrian historians of the Third Reich, such as Gerhard Botz or Karl

Stühlpfarrer, seems not to find its way into general accounts of the period, notwithstanding the enormous importance of the Austrian input to the radicalisation of Nazi policy.

Safrian takes us into that most sinister branch of the SS, the Sicherheitsdienst or SD, charged with domestic and external intelligence-gathering, and staffed by a more technocratic type of murderer. Eichmann's initial duties in SD department II-112 involved monitoring Zionist organisations. Despatched to Vienna in the wake of the Anschluss, he identified a career opportunity – amidst the chaos and despair which the Viennese were inflicting on their Jewish neighbours – to involve himself in the expropriation and enforced emigration of Vienna's large Jewish community. He and his subordinates, the majority fresh from the labour exchanges, moved into a former Rothschild palace, where they centralised all of the complex emigration formalities while robbing blind the Jews who passed before them. Although these men wrote essays entitled 'How I envisage the solution of the Jewish Question', and acquired a smattering of Hebrew, the designation 'desk-bound' murderers does not quite fit the bill, since in order to relieve the tedious paperwork, they frequently arose from the desks to inquire: 'What are you?' to which the only answer not eliciting a punch in the face was: 'I am a Jewish swindler, a crook.'

The success of Eichmann's agency in expediting Jewish emigration was so great that at the huge conference held in Berlin on 12 November 1938 in the wake of the pogrom, Heydrich held it up as a model that the Reich should generalise. This was not the last time that the zealous Austrians outshone the northern Germans, indeed the rest of Safrian's book is largely devoted to showing how these same men were inserted into situations the length and breadth of Europe to speed up what had become a continent-wide Jew hunt.

Beginning with a move to Prague in the summer of 1939, Eichmann and his accomplices solved such problems as how to append train cars of Berlin 'Gypsies' to those deporting Viennese Jews, or how to fiddle the latter via the 1.5 Reichsmark–Zloty exchange rate they imposed during the journey eastwards. The initial destination for these deportees, Nisko on the San, ran into a major logistical problem, namely the priority accorded the military whose next moves were in western rather than eastern Europe. Planners then briefly countenanced the Madagascar option, although the unreality and diplomatic and logistical difficulties it entailed, almost inevitably meant that other minds, including Gauleiter Greiser in the Warthegau, turned to more practicable, intermediary, solutions. Heydrich spoke of a 'territorial final solution', an interesting conflation betokening the past and the future. With high-level pressure from within the Reich to expel the Jewish populations of Berlin or Vienna, some vaguely thought in terms of deporting the Jews to the vast vistas briefly opening up in the Soviet Union, while others, such as SS-Sturmbannführer Höppner in Posen, were demonstrably thinking of killing those 'unproductive' Jews corralled in Polish ghettos 'with some quick-acting method'. Eichmann meanwhile was still solving other people's problems. In September 1941 he took a call from his Foreign Ministry friend Rademacher enquiring whether something could be done with 8,000 Serbian Jews. Eichmann recommended shooting them. An Austrian-born general carried this out before it even had time to assume the form of an order. It is highly likely that he brokered the deal struck between Himmler and Heydrich on the one side, and Greiser in the Warthegau on the other, whereby the latter would 'accommodate' Jews deported from the Reich, if the former would arrange to depopulate the existing ghettos. This meant simply redirecting the 'Sonderkommando Lange', which had been murdering psychiatric patients in East Prussia with the aid of gassing vans, to Chelmno where they would soon operate the first extermination camp. Further pressure was induced by Heydrich's insistence on deporting 88,000 Jews from the Czechoslovak 'Protektorat'. Their destination, however, was Minsk and Riga, that is into the path of Einsatzgruppen A and B, who were murdering the Jewish populations of the Baltic states and Belarus with the active assistance and connivance of indigenous collaborators and the German army. In September or October 1941, Eichmann paid a brief visit to Minsk, where he subsequently made much at his trial of having witnessed a mass execution. In fact, he was there to organise an identical reception for the Jews he was deporting, arrangements which were also made in Riga. To achieve the level of murder now envisaged, Eichmann 'agreed with' other discussions between Berlin and Riga that October, regarding the deployment in Russia of the gassing technology developed in the course of the 'euthanasia' programme. As the German advance in Russia slowed, so vague plans to deport the Jews further east were dropped altogether and deportation finally became wholesale mass murder. In December 1941 or January 1942, Eichmann visited Odilo Globocnik in Lublin and the incipient Belzec extermination camp, before setting to work deporting the entire Jewish population of central Europe to their deaths in one or other of these proliferating killing centres.

The remainder of Safrian's book follows these Austrian eager-beavers as they criss-crossed the whole of occupied Europe in search of Jews to murder, with Safrian as fluently convincing on Aegean islands as on Hungary, Serbia or France. Everywhere they went they enjoyed co-operation, or if they met obstacles, worked until they had circumvented them. The mind reels at the ingenuity and relentlessness with which they tracked down tiny Jewish populations on Crete, Corfu or Rhodes as well as murdering the Sephardim of Salonika. These men took no time off. When Josef Weiszl and his wife went for a stroll through the Schönbrünner Schlosspark in May 1942, Weiszl's wife spotted a Jewish colleague without her identifying Star of David. Weiszl insulted and threatened the woman with deportation, ordering her to report the next day. They were also without pity, as Alois Brunner's deportation of forty orphans from Izieu so clearly shows, and given to psychopathic violence, as when Anton Burger summarily shot a Corfu Jew at the dockside on Lefkadas, simply for having received a cigarette from a Greek priest. Dealing as it does with 'ordinary men', whatever that ill-defined notion is supposed to mean, Safrian's book should be both translated into English, and required reading for all those who seem to think that people become – rather than already are – deeply nasty, since there is no indication whatsoever in this book of any change of attitude, mind or morality among these men between 1938 and when they were captured or fled to Argentina or Syria. As Alois Brunner remarked: 'I regret nothing and I would do it again.'

Dieter Pohl's study of the Lublin district in the eastern part of the Polish Generalgouvernement, that is the residual territory run by Hans Frank in Cracow, and not directly incorporated into the Reich, takes us to one of the most active killing grounds of the 'Final Solution'. Belzec and Sobibor were located there, with Treblinka not far away, and one of the single largest mass shootings, Operation Harvest Festival, occurred in the Lublin district in 1943. Based on a formidable quantity of German and Polish archival and secondary materials, this is an extremely important local view of the extermination process, even though one wishes Pohl had said more about central policy, there being little authorial comment whenever Hitler makes a fleetingly strategic appearance.[15]

Pohl begins by describing the intense prejudices towards 'Ostjuden', combining as they did anti-Semitism, Polonophobia and hatred of the poor. These people were literally 'the other' in terms of language, dress, hairstyles, beards and so forth. The continuity of violence he describes is especially noteworthy. Immediately following the German invasion, German troops humiliated Jewish people – forcing them to clean lavatories, to sing or perform 'gymnastics' – or in many places simply shot them. Only a fraction of the 7,000 Jews who had been killed by the end of 1939 could be attributed to the Einsatzgruppen, from which Pohl concludes that the majority were killed by the Field Police or ordinary infantrymen. Although plans for a 'Jewish reservation' initially involved the area east of Cracow, changes to the eastern frontier taking Lublin from the Soviets, meant a switch of projected location to that area. This in turn was modified to Nisko on the San, and then finally abandoned as unworkable.

Although these plans for Lublin came to nothing, certain aspects of the German presence there are worth further comment. As is well known from the macro-histories of occupied Poland by Martin Broszat and Czeslaw Madajczyk, Hans Frank's power in the Generalgouvernement was seriously challenged and undermined by Himmler's man on the spot, the Higher SS- and Police Leader (HSSPF), who took his instructions direct from Himmler and the Reich Main Security Office, whose self-aggrandising competences included both ethnic politics and the 'Jewish Question'. While Frank imported an administrative cadre, consisting of civil servants subject to punitive transfers, chancers and Party opportunists, Himmler installed Friedrich Wilhelm Krüger as HSSPF and the Austrian Nazi Odilo Globocnik as SSPF-Lublin. It is noteworthy that both men had blots on their SS copybooks and were being afforded a second chance. Of all the Nazis one wants to know more about, Globocnik is top of the list. Born in 1904 in Trieste, the ex-bricklayer Globocnik was the illegal Nazi Gauleiter of Vienna from 1933, before being forced to flee to Bavaria, having murdered a Jewish jeweller in the course of an armed robbery. Terms like 'psychopath' are not entirely misplaced, since as Pohl points out, 'Globus' disposed of an excess of 'criminal energy', and as the record shows, had murdered someone, a background he shared with the future commandant of Auschwitz. Appointed Gauleiter of Greater Vienna, Globocnik was transferred out in the wake of a corruption scandal, before finally being appointed to the post in Lublin. Close to

Himmler, he enjoyed a considerable degree of leeway in his eastern fiefdom. He took over aspects of policy towards Jews, such as forced labour, which elsewhere in the Generalgouvernement were the remit of the civil administration. At least 1,500 Jews were shot in the Lublin region either on an individual whim or in the course of forced marches and expulsions, before any systematic instructions to murder were issued. The Jewish population of the Lublin district was spread out across the countryside, and consisted of anywhere between a quarter of a million and 400,000 people. They were subject to physical identification, economic ruination and forced labour on a series of fortified trenches on the river Bug where conditions in the labour camps were atrocious. The need to find instant accommodation for the two million troops being moved into the region for the invasion of the Soviet Union led to the expulsion of parts of the Lublin city Jewish population and the concentration of the remainder in a ghetto. Poles moved into the homes vacated by the Jews, and German troops took over the homes of the Poles. 34,000 people were packed into the Lublin ghetto. In August 1941, 100 people died of typhus, 200 in November and 300 in December. The massive racial violence being committed in Russia had an ominous backdraught in Lublin in the sense that hundreds of thousands of Soviet POWs either starved to death or were shot by the SD in camps within the district. As it was a place of recuperation for the troops from Russia, the area was awash with rumours about what was happening. Typhus and violence met when in November 1941 a decree was issued permitting the Security Police (or in Lublin the piratical Dirlewanger batallion) to shoot any Jewish person found 'wandering around' outside the ghetto or their normal place of residence.

Already distinguished by Himmler as the executor of local trial runs for the 'Generalplan Ost', Globocnik was the obvious person to turn to once it had been decided to murder the Jews. Everyone acquainted with 'Globus' acknowledged that he was an inventive, implacable man: 'That's one who creates order wherever he is deployed. A warlike man.' According to Pohl, at some point between late August and the end of October 1941, Himmler commissioned Globocnik to construct mass extermination facilities. Availing himself of diverted T-4 'euthanasia' experts, Globocnik oversaw the construction of Belzec throughout that winter. In mid-March, Ukrainians from Globocnik's training camp at Trawniki moved into the Lublin ghetto, despatching 18,000 people to their deaths in Belzec within a fortnight, and gunning down hundreds more people on the streets as they fled, or in their homes if they were infants, elderly, sick or otherwise immobile. They came back on 10 April 1942 to despatch a further 12,000 people to the camp. Word of the Lublin action spread quickly. Goebbels wrote in his diary on 27 March that procedures in Lublin were 'pretty barbaric . . . and not much remains of the Jews themselves . . . Thank god that in war we have an entire range of possibilities which were not available to us in peace. We must take advantage of them.'

In the summer of 1942, Globocnik's men were cut loose on the Warsaw ghetto, most of whose inmates were murdered in the Treblinka extermination camp, before he returned, probably via an audience with Hitler, to Lublin to slay the remaining Jewish populations there. Initially, murder coexisted uneasily with the need to exploit Jewish labour at a critical juncture in the war. This dual-track policy attracted both the SS Economic and Administrative Main Office and Globocnik who wished to relocate the defunct industries of the major ghettos such as Bialystok, Łódź and Warsaw to his own fiefdom. Any Jews deemed surplus to labour requirements were deported to Sobibor or shot en masse. Jews who had fled to the woods were murdered 'in flight' in the course of anti-partisan operations. Those Jews who survived in labour camps or labour ghettos fell victim to the radical mood which set in after the Warsaw ghetto and Treblinka and Sobibor uprisings between April and October 1943. Under the direction of Globocnik's successor Jakob Sporrenberg, zig-zag trenches were dug near the labour camps of Majdanek, Trawniki and Poniatowa. In Operation Harvest Festival on 3–4 November 1943, about 43,000 Jews were shot in one of the largest massacres of the Holocaust, probably with the agreement of Hitler, for whom they represented the largest, most easterly concentration of Jews still in German hands. The death camps were erased from the map, and a special commando unit 1005 was deployed to exhume and burn the remains of those who had died in mass shootings. 'Globus' killed himself in British detention at the end of the war.

Gordon J. Horwitz's equally low-key study of Mauthausen is a different, more reflective and stylishly written book, again on an Austrian theme.[16] Mauthausen was one of the second generation of SS concentration camps, established in the later 1930s to satisfy Hitler's (and Speer's) insatiable need for materials for grandiose construction projects. It was built near Linz in Upper Austria, hard by a granite quarry. The base camp sat atop a hill, with its walls and wire hung with red emergency lights, whose dull beams faded into the night at a ground range of 547 yards and at 109 yards from the air. Every conceivable horror was perpetrated on its inmates, whose number rose to a peak of 84,500 in March 1945. It had the harshest regime of all concentration camps, with an inmate mortality rate in 1941 of 58 per cent, compared with 36 per cent at Dachau or 19 per cent at Buchenwald. Cruelty came with a gamesome, leering face. SS men, perched 'like gargoyles on the eaves of a cathedral' around the rim of the quarry, hurled prisoners off to raucous cries of 'Attention! Parachutists!' Others encouraged prisoners to go beyond the wire to pick fruit, shooting these 'raspberry picker details' for amusement. Gradually, Mauthausen and its forty-nine satellite camps at Gusen, Melk and Redl-Zipf, became an important arms-producing centre, temporarily beyond the range of American bombers. The engines for V2 rockets were tested in deep tunnels, with the sound waves reverberating like claps of thunder around the farmhouses and venerable monasteries of the region.

However, the enormities inflicted on the inmates are not Horwitz's primary concern. Rather, he probes the communities in whose midst the camp was situated. People leased land to make room for the camp; serviced it with labour, skills and supplies; and indeed, in some cases had to pass through its physical environs en route to town. One could not avoid knowing about it, since even if one could see nothing, the area was regularly pervaded by noxious smells of burning flesh and hair. The SS also beat prisoners at the railway station, casually shot them in sight of nearby farmhouses, became garrulously drunk in pubs and bars, or chatted up local girls with such remarks as: 'Today I killed two inmates . . . I chased both of them into a pit of liquid manure, threw a crate over them, and stood on top of it until they drowned.' Apparently they rarely got the girl. Some local people were clearly sickened by this loutish conduct, including one or two individuals whose vocal disapproval landed them in concentration camps. The most people ventured in a climate of fear was to drop illicit food or to look with sympathy on people stripped of their humanity and marked with the 'Hitler cut' or a channel shaved through the middle of the hair over the scalp. But popular responses to the camp had a darker side too, including the many who averted their eyes or saw without feeling, responses of which Karl Jaspers writes: 'Blindness for the misfortune of others, lack of imagination of the heart, inner indifference toward the witnessed evil – that is moral guilt.' When in early February 1945 hundreds of prisoners broke out of the main camp, the local population exceeded the SS in the savagery with which it tracked these fugitives down, shooting and clubbing them to death. Sanctions were for those (very few) who hid escapees, not for those who did nothing to help or hinder their escape. But as a local police chief recorded: 'How brutal were our people then. At close range they shot at the poor beings kneeling before them, and then observed with satisfaction their last shudders. Yes, they boasted publicly of their deeds, heedless that their children listened to them in astonishment. In their stupidity many became murderers, and the just Judge of all things will know of it; but many fell victim to the intoxication of blood; the slumbering demon inside them broke forth and transformed them into beasts.'

Eyewitnesses and survivors provide the most graphic and unadorned forms of Holocaust writing. Calel Perechodnik was a twenty-seven-year-old French-educated engineer, from a well-to-do Jewish family, who in early 1941 made the decision to join the Jewish police in the Otwock ghetto near Warsaw in order to save the lives of his wife, small daughter and himself. In the first two cases he failed, only winning himself a temporary reprieve, for already weakened by typhus, he died in the 1944 Warsaw Uprising. In the 105 days he spent hiding in 'Polish' Warsaw, Perechodnik wrote his 'History of a Jewish Family during German Occupation', which was published in Poland in 1993 under the title *Am I A Murderer?*[17] Rescued from the oblivion of archives, and only briefly cited as a source to condemn a certain type of culpable victim, the book is a fusion of confession, chronicle and diary. Apart from being an unforgettably searing account of scenes which would have taxed the imagination of Bosch, it is an important historical document, being one of the few surviving testimonies of a widely despised group of people. Reading the full version, available for the first time, one is forced to reconsider any facile moral judgments about such individuals, who in the last analysis were forced to make choices in circumstances that most people could not even imagine in their worst nightmares.

The tone of the book, whose frequent use of Latin, Polish and Yiddish tags, accurately reflects the cultural confusions of this particular author, oscillates between anger and apathy. Anger towards the

Germans upon whom he dreams of wreaking vengeance, personally offering to kill them all in Treblinka. Drunken and thuggish, they appear relatively remotely in this account, with their horrible utterances imperfectly caught in Perechodnik's poor Yiddish renditions of their language. Anger, too, towards the Poles who rob the Jews blind and betray them in their hour of misfortune, although there are individual exceptions; and, it has to be said, anger towards the Jews who go resignedly to their deaths, a view not confirmed by recent Jewish historiography. It is almost as if, completely impotent towards the Germans and completely dependent upon the Poles, Perechodnik took out his frustrations on his own people, who no doubt regarded his own career choice with total contempt. Few people come out of this book well, including not least, the author himself.

In February 1941, Perechodnik took the decision to become a ghetto policeman because the war showed no signs of ending, and in order to avoid deportation to a forced labour camp. Adopting the passive voice, Perechodnik records that 200 sick Jews were taken from Otwock to Treblinka in January 1942: 'It was fortunate that the Jewish police did the choosing and sent out the poorest.' Those Jews who tried to flee were killed. Rumours of mass killings in Lublin reached the ghetto, but were rapidly blotted out by more local barbarities as 'a small moon can obscure a large sun'. Lacking the 'sporting instinct' to go out hunting for deportees, Perechodnik delivered bread to the ghetto command post or to the Jewish police. The Germans struck closer than Lublin, namely at the massive Warsaw ghetto. Perechodnik wrote: 'What did I do then? Nothing, and really worse than nothing.' He investigated, and then procrastinated about fostering his two-year-old daughter Aluska with a Polish family. He put off acquiring an identity card for his wife Anka, who with a few cosmetic adjustments could have passed herself off as a Christian Pole. In mid-August 1942, the Germans made preparations to deport the Jews of Otwock, three-quarters of whom sensed what was about to happen. At seven in the morning on Wednesday 19 August, truckloads of Ukrainians sped through the ghetto, indiscriminately shooting anyone who got in their way or remonstrated with them. The moment of decision approached for Perechodnik: 'I am overwhelmed by a terrible fear.' Rather than allowing his wife and child to hide, he trusted the judgment of the commander of the Jewish police who said to bring them to the main square. Along the way, Perechodnik saw a Ukrainian cut a young Jewish woman in half with a shovel since he had run out of bullets with which to shoot her. Anka realised that the police commander's wife was not in the square with the other police wives. Perechodnik wrote: 'Am I able to understand anything at this moment? There is buzzing in my head, as if a waterfall were running through it. I don't understand anything that is going on. I have lost the ability to think and act.' His wife and daughter, whom he wished he had strangled at birth, squatted with thousands of others in the scorching sun, while Germans chatted, smoked, drank beer and periodically shot into the throng. The policemen were told that their wives would be spared, if they were not already in the square. A colleague removed his armband and courageously joined his wife. Perechodnik's wife and sister Rachel requested poison, although this proved difficult to obtain without a prescription. Rachel took three Luminal tablets, spilling Anka's dose on the ground. Being fiendishly clever, the Germans ordered the policemen to take their wives to one side, and then began loading the remaining Jews onto trains. This slight chink of hope engendered eager complicity. Perechodnik again adopts the passive voice. After the trains were loaded, the Germans suddenly announce that the policemen's children were to go too. They then separated the policemen from their families, and in a rare display of physical exertion, promptly loaded both the women and children onto the train by themselves. Perechodnik saw his sister, wife and child go off in a cloud of dust, to the piercing whistle of the train as it lurched forward on the journey to Treblinka. His speculations as to their subsequent fate were all too accurate. Stumbling over corpses in the streets, Perechodnik went home, wondering whether he was a murderer or 'only a marionette of destiny, of the evil fate of Israel'. So far his home had not been looted. He slept on the sofa since he dreaded that the bed would still bear the warmth of his wife. After two hours' sleep, he went lifelessly forth to deposit corpses in pre-dug graves. Every day became a bad dream, with Friday the first day that he did not have to give his wife money for weekend shopping. Monday brought the crushing news from a Polish friend that the latter's childless sister would have been prepared to foster Aluska. He stopped believing in God. Indifferent to the looters pillaging his own apartment, Perechodnik lay apathetically in bed by day, going through the motions as a policeman at night.

Terrified of being killed, Perechodnik observed such German stratagems as leaving some neighbouring ghettos unharmed so that they would be like 'flypaper' for Jews in hiding who would credulously turn up there in the hope of surviving. While Polish housewives straightened out vacant apartments, German gendarmes and Polish police scoured the Otwock ghetto for hidden survivors who were shot into pits. Perechodnik guarded these people, most of whom had given up the desire to live. He wept and prayed alongside them: 'Why am I doing this? I asked myself. Is there anyone to pray to? Sometimes I fell into a semi-sleep, and it seemed to me that I was sitting in a movie house where some terrifying sound film was turning the blood in our veins to ice.' In the morning, he followed the condemned out to the pits where they were shot at close range.

Surviving Otwock, Perechodnik was sent to a labour camp at Piekelko to build a dyke on the Vistula. Through a complicated set of circumstances, Perechodnik was eventually hidden in the apartment of the hostile girlfriend of a friendly tram conductor. Whenever visitors arrived, he and his mother and father who had joined him would hide behind the wardrobe. The rent to the 'landlady' (who provided them with meagre food and emptied their bucket once a week) came from sales of clothes and property. Going to bed at two in the afternoon and rising at nine next morning, Perechodnik 'thought about one theme: how easy it would have been to save my wife and child. I went through thousands of combinations, one better than the other. It filled me with terrible sadness and feelings of guilt.' Relations with his parents were recriminatory and strained: his mother feared that he was going to poison her, while his father, obsessed with money and survival, did not venture a word of sympathy for his dead daughter-in-law, daughter or grandchild. Mother and father began to suffer massive boils. Every day brought some fresh demonstration of petulant feminine power by their 'landlady', who by now was walking around in Anka's old clothes. In April 1943, the Germans began the final liquidation of the Warsaw ghetto, an event Perechodnik watched through the shutters from his hiding place in the Polish part of the city. Explosions boomed and the sky lit up as the Germans systematically blew up the houses to burn or crush hiding Jews. Perechodnik's parents moved to the countryside where the father briefly succeeded in passing himself off as a devout Catholic old gentleman. They were soon back in Warsaw. In September, after thirteen months of evading the police, Perechodnik père was betrayed to the Gestapo and shot. Perechodnik and his mother, both debilitated by typhus, perished in the aftermath of the suppression of the 1944 Warsaw Uprising.

Completed on the first anniversary of his wife's death, the manuscript was partly confessional, partly a final rendering of accounts with Anka, partly 'a dead fetus into which I would breathe life', like a surrogate child. It is also an account of how Perechodnik finally overcame the fear of death which set in after the Otwock action that had claimed his wife and child, for before the action, he had just fatalistically followed the crowd. That his thoughts turned to Anka were not uninfluenced by the fact that nine months after her death he began a relationship with a woman friend; although aware of what was in store for them, neither uttered the word 'love' in three months. Sex between them seems to have been just another emotionless survival strategy like eating or keeping warm. Indescribably bleak, and in so far as it concerns others, devastatingly candid, Perechodnik's testimony is so haunting because one finishes it thinking that no one, let alone a twenty-seven-year-old, should be subjected to this kind of accelerated emotional or moral development, with ten lifetimes of betrayal, bestial savagery, extreme fear and self-lacerating guilt condensed into the space of eighteen months. No wonder, as he wrote, children looked as if they were aged 100. Historians and others who casually deal in Holocaust statistics could benefit immensely from this terrible book, not least to gain some inkling of the psychological terror these events caused in the hours, days, months and years before the victims became numbers.

The Buchenwald Report takes us back exactly fifty years to when the actuality of some of these horrors was just being revealed.[18] The *Report* was compiled at the instigation of an intelligence unit from the Psychological Warfare Division of the US Army shortly after the liberation of the camp on 11 April 1945. It was designed to provide 'in-depth analysis of the inner workings of Buchenwald and, by extension, of the entire Nazi concentration camp system'. A team under the Austrian, conservative and Catholic inmate, Eugen Kogon, drew up the analytical and descriptive Main Report, which following the suggestion of Richard Crossman, Kogon reworked and published as *Der SS-Staat* (1946, translated into English as *The Theory and Practice of Hell*). This drew upon the oral testimony of 104 prisoners interviewed while they were still in the camp. After being discovered in 1983, these testimonies, the raw material for Kogon's book, are published and translated for the first time in David Hackett's and Westview's commendably well-organised edition that will be an invaluable source for future historians of the SS concentration camp empire. Buchenwald was built by prisoner labour on a heavily wooded mountain above Weimar, housing at one point during the war nearly 90,000 people. It gradually spawned a number of eccentric facilities, such as an angora rabbit station, a zoo, a personal falconry for Hermann Göring and a vast riding hall where Ilse Koch, the commandant's wife, could prance around in front of mirrors to the tune of an SS band for half an hour twice a week. The SS guards disposed of a sculpture studio, which did a nice line in marble items for Himmler's desk, Viking longships and painted porcelain; and well-stocked cellars and larders. The 150 guard dogs had considerably better food than the inmates, who on liberation day, treated themselves to a load of dog biscuits. Corruption was endemic; sadistic abuse by SS men, including more than their share of rheumy-eyed drunks and syphilitic sexual perverts, was a fact of everyday life. Virtually every prisoner testimony bears witness to the 'hands on' nature of their approach, much of it of an extraordinary, psychopathic, savagery or else done merely to offset boredom, as when guards tossed prisoners' caps near the fencing and then ordered them to retrieve them in order to watch people being shot. The detail in the prisoner accounts is of a matter-of-fact, and frequently sickening, immediacy that leaves the mind reeling at human ingenuity in cruelty.

Hermann Langbein was an Austrian volunteer in the International Brigades in Spain, interned by the French, and then deported to Dachau, and via other camps, to Auschwitz. His book is an unadorned, insider account of how 'we knew that we would not allow ourselves to be broken, and would knowingly incur additional risks to pass muster before ourselves as active subjects'.[19] In the camps, absolute brutality reigned and prisoner solidarity was deliberately undermined. From the beginning, the SS practised divide and rule by playing off German professional criminals (or 'Greens') against those incarcerated for political reasons ('Reds'). Langbein acknowledges that matters were not as morally simple as this suggests. Some of the Green criminals were decent fellows; some of the communists (such as those in Buchenwald who engineered the transfer of the camp SPD secretary to even worse conditions in Mauthausen, or French Trotskyites to the notorious camp Dora) were clearly appalling. The prisoner population was also riven with complex national, political and inter-racial animosities which make depressing reading. Resistance took various forms: organising extra food for those weakened by starvation; swapping the files or camp numbers of prisoners the SS intended to murder with those who had been transferred or were already dead; refusal to carry out executions or beatings; corrupting guards and camp doctors, some of whom retained vestiges of humanity; sabotage; listening to clandestine radios, and sending out information on such vital subjects as the gas chambers of Auschwitz or the blueprints of V-rockets from Dora; and secreting documentary proof of Nazi crimes in hiding places for posterity. Escapes that failed resulted in torture and execution on the roll-call square; those that succeeded sometimes resulted in the escapees being handed over to the Germans by Polish peasants or murdered by anti-Semitic Polish partisans. Obviously, prisoners of war, notably Russians, were to the fore in murdering their guards with scythes or spades in order to escape, although it is equally striking how many Jewish civilians attacked the SS with bottles, knives or their bare hands up to the closure of the gas chamber doors. Major rebellions occurred among the special details who serviced the crematoria at Auschwitz and Treblinka and there was a large-scale breakout at Sobibor. In a less dramatic key, Langbein discusses such morale-boosting activities as inmate musical concerts, poetry recitals, education and the activities of priests and pastors, including Paul Schneider, whose sermons rang out during roll-call from the bunker in which he was incarcerated.

Towards the end of Lanzmann's *Shoah*, the sole survivor of the Kulmhof extermination camp is shown silently sifting earth through his fingers, as if the soil could tell of the whereabouts of over 140,000 people. The film began with him, recollecting the songs he was made to sing to the SS as a boy, and ends with him in absolute bewilderment, seeking answers in clumps of soil. It is one of the most poignant moments in cinema. In a chapter by the Dutch architect Robert-Jan van Pelt, evocatively entitled 'a site in search of a mission', which is in a remarkable collaborative history of Auschwitz that includes work by most of the leading Israeli and Polish scholars, Himmler and his friend Henns Johst are described stopping off on their drives through the Polish countryside: 'The Reichsführer-SS stopped the car, climbed over the furrowed ditches, walked into fields plowed over by grenade shells, took some dirt between his fingers, smelled it thoughtfully with his head bowed, crushed the crumbs of the field between his fingers, and looked then over the vast, vast space which was full, full to the horizon, with this good fertile earth. Thus we stood like ancient farmers, and we smiled at each other with twinkling eyes. All of this was now German soil!'[20]

The region around Auschwitz was designated for rapid industrialisation and extensive German settlement. The concentration camp, used for Polish political prisoners, was to be a huge agricultural station and source of labour for elaborate building schemes, including an artificial rubber and synthetic petrol plant run by IG Farben. In September 1941, the German army diverted 10,000 of a projected 100,000 Soviet prisoners of war to Auschwitz. By the end of January 1942, 8,000 of them were dead. Cases of cannibalism indicate the reasons why. Jewish people from the whole of occupied Europe took their place in what evolved into a vast complex of forty 'Aussen-' 'Neben-' and 'Arbeitslager' devoted to immediate, or delayed extermination through labour. The site became synonymous with human degradation and mass murder rather than with Himmler's model, mock-medieval, market town.

The illustrations, mainly from the camp archive or Moscow, include such horrors as a latrine system with a capacity of 150 persons being used each morning by 7,000 people (many of them suffering from diarrhoea or dysentery) with precisely ten minutes designated for their bodily functions, with the consequence that people were soon knee-deep in shit. There are also such surreal touches as one of the unsuccessful designs for a crematorium; the reason given to the unlucky bidder being that a marble neo-Grecian pediment was deemed to be unnecessarily ornate for the projected function. A chapter by Andrzej Strzelecki reminds us the greed and extreme utilitarianism that accompanied mass murder: human hair (in 1945, the Soviets came across 293 sackfuls from an estimated 140,000 dead people) was used to make socks for submarine crews or delayed ignition bomb mechanisms; fountain pens, safety razors and watches went to SS combat troops, Luftwaffe pilots or bombed-out Berliners. Presiding over what became a charnel house covering mile after mile was the stony-faced ex-convict Rudolf Hoess. So great was his zeal that, having been bumped upstairs to a desk job in the wake of a corruption scandal involving his magpie wife Hedwig and many SS subordinates, in 1944 Hoess arranged for the transfer of his successor at Auschwitz so that he could personally oversee the destruction of Hungarian Jewry. Evidently keen to be associated with his crimes, he code-named the operation 'Aktion Hoess'. Called as a defence witness in the Kaltenbrunner case, Hoess managed to claim credit for murdering two and a half million, rather than over one million people. The 'site' had found the 'mission' with which it will forever be associated, as the epicentre of the 'Final Solution'.

To conclude these reflections on a recent cross-section of Holocaust literature, we might look briefly at two collections of essays by Israeli scholars. Relatively few in number, Israeli historians of Germany have made an immense and valuable contribution to the study of that nation's history. One thinks of Uriel Tal and Shulamit Volkov on nineteenth-century anti-Semitism; David Bankier, Avraham Barkai and Otto Dov Kulka on the social history of the Third Reich; and from an older generation, Yehuda Bauer, Yisrael Gutman and Isaiah Trunk on the Holocaust. Omer Bartov and Steven Aschheim have published important books on the barbarisation of warfare, assimilated Jewish encounters with *Ostjuden*, and the complex reception of Friedrich Nietzsche in Germany. Unlike those scholars whose range of cultural reference seem depressingly confined to the latest article in a journal read by three people, Bartov and Aschheim know about Céline or Jünger, Finkielkraut or Lanzmann, and write accordingly. In his *Culture and Catastrophe*, Aschheim addresses the 'penetration of the barbarous within the allegedly cultured, the transgression of basic taboos within the framework of advanced civilisation, that has endowed Nazism with its distinctive status within Western sensibility', or as George Steiner put it, how 'a man can read Goethe or Rilke in the evening . . . and go to his day's work at Auschwitz in the morning'.[21] This theme is addressed implicitly rather than explicitly, with only the jacket cover having a jarring image of prisoners in the library at Dachau.

Refreshingly free of the narrow, technocratic, present-centredness characteristic of other recent collections of writings on the Holocaust, Aschheim has a sure grasp of the bigger intellectual picture and an astute awareness of the commercial exploitation, and cultural and political instrumentalisation of the Holocaust in America, Germany and Israel, as partly reflected in the cynical phrase 'no business like Shoah business'. One day, someone will write a very good book on the commercialisation and exploitation of this subject. Three essays are devoted to the longer-term aspects of the German–Jewish relationship. The claim that the emancipation of the Jews had entailed Germany's spiritual 'Judaisation', or *Verjudung*, was a persistent refrain from anti-Semites and others. It came in a Marxian version: 'the Jews have emancipated themselves in so far as the Christians have become Jews'. In its liberal version, all distasteful side-effects of the liberal embrace of capitalism were offloaded onto the Jews, while in the hands of radical anti-Semites, it became a means of construing Christianity as part of the problem rather than the solution. Following Dühring, Hitler merely turned the charge of 'Judaisation' against Marx himself, while also introducing such epidemiological fantasies as: 'Especially in the big cities, syphilis was beginning to spread more and more . . . This Jewification of our spiritual life and mammonization of our mating instincts will sooner or late destroy our entire offspring.' The essay compliments what Potsdam-based scholars such as Julius Schloeps and Joachim Schlör, are telling us about the content of anti-Semitism.

Aschheim has done more than most to trace the Nazification and de-Nazification of Nietzsche and the de-Nietzscheanisation of Nazism. The key point concerns the interpretive spaces in Nietzsche's œuvre, where 'there were clearly sufficient allusions, hints and themes to satisfy all-comers'. In this intellectual pick and mix, anti-Semites would have trouble with such lines as: 'Jews among Germans are always the higher race, more refined, spiritual, kind', while finding much to work with in: 'the Christian is the ultimate Jewish consequence'. Aschheim cites the Irish politician Conor Cruise O'Brien's characteristically shrewd comment: 'Hitler learned from Nietzsche that the traditional Christian limit on antisemitism was itself part of a Jewish trick. When the values that the Jews had reversed were destroyed, there would be no limits and no Jews.' There was also Nietzsche as diagnostician of degeneration and advocate of radical therapy and transgressive moralities. Aschheim also has an interesting and fair-minded afterword on Ernst Nolte's *Europäischer Bürgerkrieg*, which at least has the merit of addressing the question of Nazism 'as a kind of Nietzschean Great Politics', even if his methods are dubious.

The remaining essays are concerned with post-war dialogues between Germans and Jews, including Hermann Broch and Volkmar von Zuehlsdorf, or Hannah Arendt's moving correspondence with Karl Jaspers. Arendt was adamant in rejecting the 'separate path' thesis, arguing: 'Nazism owes nothing to any part of the Western tradition, be it German or not, Catholic or Protestant, Christian, Greek or Roman . . . On the contrary, Nazism is actually the breakdown of all German and European traditions, the good as well as the bad.' That is to say, nihilism activated by 'basing itself on the intoxification of destruction as an actual experience, dreaming the stupid dream of producing the void'.

The opening and concluding essays concern the politics and historiography of the Holocaust. The first is especially interesting in the sense of explaining to non-Israeli readers the extremely complex functions of the Holocaust in a society most of us know far too little about, and which is invariably the object of ill-informed clichés, especially in left-wing circles. If it comes as no surprise that Menachem Begin referred to Yasser Arafat as 'Hitler in his bunker', or that some Palestinians regard occupation as worse than the sufferings of the Jews in Treblinka and Auschwitz, it is startling to read that Sephardic rabbis refer to the Israeli Establishment as 'Aschke-Nazis', or that the Acco Theatre Group, which apparently takes Israeli audiences on a squirming roller-coaster ride, desacralises the Holocaust with the aid of an Arab guide. The final essay is a wide-ranging survey of the recent historiography of the Holocaust which, in contrast to those whose work increasingly resembles that of unimaginative technicians writing about all too horribly fertile technicians, never loses sight of the 'larger contextual and mental structures that shaped the choices made, guided action and created the atmosphere in which decisions proceeded and the machine operated', i.e. 'decisive level of explanation' rather than what motivated Sergeant Schmidt. Dismissing such ill-substantiated theses as the Holocaust as a 'side-effect' of an anti-Bolshevik crusade, or as a malign form of 'modernisation', the stock in trade of other historiographical collections, Aschheim comes back to the still unresolved paradox of 'Nazism [as] an uneasy combination of both bourgeois and anti-bourgeois elements. Embodying this dualism it managed to radically transcend middle-class morality at the same time that it paradoxically embodied it.' Concluding what constitutes one of the most challenging, thought-provoking and imaginatively wide-ranging contributions to the recent spate of essays on the Holocaust, Aschheim reminds us that in history there is no such thing as closure or a monopoly of explanation, something that the authors of self-styled and mutually uncomplimentary work on ordinary Germans as perpetrators might usefully remember when they have a quiet moment to reflect amidst the unedifying razzamatazz of their publicity campaigns.

Overlapping in concern, and as imaginative in conception, Omer Bartov's new essays are concerned with the emergence in our century of industrialised mass killing and how intellectuals, or indeed entire societies, have negotiated memories of this, in some cases by denying or ignoring it.[22] The most controversial parts of the book deal with the ways in which the Great War may have been paradigmatic for the Holocaust, an argument which flies in the face of both the traditional stereotype of the soldier as victim, or indeed recent trends which see Auschwitz as a hellish sort of racial hospital. Many of the perpetrators – including Hitler himself – were war veterans who, having survived the trenches, had few moral inhibitions about shooting millions into other trenches. Hitler did not pluck his wish to use poison gas against Jews from nowhere. The physical environment was replete with barbed wire, barracks, mud, poison gas and uniforms, but one in which one side was totally safe, and the other absolutely vulnerable. If the Holocaust was 'hell made imminent', then the brimstone had a very familiar modern smell to it. What may shock rather than surprise is the idea that the perpetrators were frustrated pacifists, who sought to evade the inescapable fact of industrialised mass killing, as established in 1914–18, by inflicting it on others in a controlled environment in which lethality was a one-way street. Actually, a lot of water had to flow beneath the bridge before Hitler, who in *Mein Kampf* retrospectively expressed the wish that 12,000 Jews had been gassed to denecessitate the war, could contemplate murdering six million people. None the less, he picked this analogy and no other. Hitler did not 'unleash the Final Solution of the Jewish Question . . . to save the world from a repetition of the industrial killing of the Great War' (an argument which shadows not only Philippe Burrin but also Ernst Nolte's notion of the Holocaust as a 'pre-emptive strike'); rather he set in motion these policies within a war he was largely responsible for unleashing. The First World War did lower the threshold of what was deemed possible, altering the moral parameters on both the domestic and fighting fronts in ways which historians have barely investigated; but a few superficially similar features do not satisfactorily explain the Holocaust, any more than arcane theories derived from Gobineau. One wishes Bartov, whose unresolved arguments are one of the book's many beguiling features, would develop these insights at greater length and with more extensive evidence.

The remainder of the book concerns cinematic representations of the Holocaust, the Second World War or war in general, and 'plastic chambers of horrors' such as the technologically elaborate Washington Holocaust Memorial. Bartov writes well about film, being pretty damning of Coppola, Syberberg and Spielberg, and sceptical of the value of museums in a world seething with violence and despair, including periodic bouts of genocide. How can artefacts, reconstructions and video films convey the horror of the experience, and what lessons are people supposed to take with them as they return to the world of CNN and O.J.? Have they been warned? Or consoled that nothing in the present could be so awful as the past they have briefly 'experienced'? How does it contribute to 'doing something' about Cambodia, Bosnia or Rwanda, or to be more parochial, the people who burn down Black churches in the southern states of America? Perhaps the developed world could emulate the simplicity of the developing world, for there is surely nothing more telling than the ossuaries marking the victims of Pol Pot's Cambodian Marxist tyranny? The subject of Bartov's researches, confronted with a singular honesty and very unacademic intensity in these essays, has clearly weighed heavily upon him. Not least, the sense of writing the 'idiot's tale' by the flickering televised light of these present genocides and outrages, or in earshot of 'slums teeming with violence and despair'. There really are no lessons, or if there are, mankind is still ill disposed to learn them. One more local lesson of these outstanding contributions to Holocaust literature is that we are still far removed from knowing the last word about it. These books all considerably advance that process.

Notes

INTRODUCTION

1 Michael Burleigh, *Prussian Society and the German Order: an Aristocratic Corporation in Crisis c. 1410–1466* (Cambridge 1984).
2 Anne Appelbaum, *Between East and West. Across the Borderlands of Europe* (London 1995).
3 Michael Burleigh, *Germany Turns Eastwards: a Study of 'Ostforschung' in the Third Reich* (Cambridge 1988).
4 Gerhard L. Weinberg, *A World at Arms: a Global History of World War II* (Cambridge 1994); Norman Davies, 'The Misunderstood War', *New York Review of Books*, 41 (1994), pp. 20–4; 'The Misunderstood Victory in Europe', *New York Review of Books*, 42 (1995), pp. 7–11; and now, Norman Davies, *Europe: a History* (Oxford 1996), pp. 897–1055.
5 Michael Burleigh, *Death and Deliverance: 'Euthanasia' in Germany c. 1900–1945* (Cambridge 1994).
6 Robert Gellately, *The Gestapo and German Society. Enforcing Racial Policy 1933–1945* (Oxford 1990).
7 Michael Burleigh and Wolfgang Wippermann, *The Racial State: Germany 1933–1945* (Cambridge 1991).
8 Anne Applebaum, 'Absent History', *Prospect*, 7 (1996), pp. 29–33.
9 My thinking has been especially influenced by Yehuda Bauer's 'The Significance of the Final Solution', in David Cesarani (ed.), *The Final Solution. Origins and Implementation* (London 1994), pp. 300–9.

1. THE KNIGHTS, NATIONALISTS AND THE HISTORIANS

1 Günter Grass, *Die Blechtrommel* (The Tin Drum), 23rd edition (Darmstadt 1984), p. 240.
2 For GDR work on the Hansa see the bibliography in K. Fritze, N. Schildhauer and W. Stark, *Die Geschichte der Hanse* (East Berlin 1974 and

West Berlin 1985), pp. 231–40; W. Küttler, 'Charakter und Entwicklungstendenzen des Deutschordensstaates in Preussen', *Zeitschrift für Geschichtswissenschaft*, 19 (1971), pp. 1504–29.

3 I. R. Mitchell, 'The Changing Image of Prussia in the German Democratic Republic', *German Life and Letters*, 37 (1983), p. 57; for Stalin and the Nevsky cult see Hans-Heinrich Nolte, '*Drang nach Osten': Sowjetische Geschichtsschreibung der deutsche Ostexpansion* (Cologne and Frankfurt am Main 1976), pp. 205–8, and W. Wippermann, *Der 'deutsche Drang nach Osten': Ideologie und Wirklichkeit eines politischen Schlagwortes* (Darmstadt 1981), p. 64.

4 Mitchell, 'The Changing Image', pp. 60–1.

5 See, for example, W. Magdefrau, 'Heinrich von Treitschke und die imperialistische "Ostforschung"', *Zeitschrift für Geschichtswissenschaft*, 11 (1963), pp. 1444ff.; F.-H. Gentzen, J. Kalisch, G. Voigt and E. Wolfgramm, 'Die "Ostforschung" – ein Stosstrupp des deutschen Imperialismus', *Zeitschrift für Geschichtswissenschaft*, 6 (1958), pp. 1193–9, and F.-H. Gentzen and E. Wolfgramm, '*Ostforscher*' – '*Ostforschung*', Taschenbuch Geschichte, 8 (East Berlin 1960). For a more recent 'differentiated' approach to the Prussian heritage in the GDR see H. Bartel's preface to, and W. Küttler's essay 'Vom Deutschen Orden zum Königreich Preussen. Die Vorgeschichte des Staatsnamens "Preussen"', in P. Bachmann and I. Knoth (eds.), *Preussen – Legende und Wirklichkeit*, 3rd edition (East Berlin 1985), pp. 5–9, 37–47.

6 S. Ekdahl, *Die Schlacht bei Tannenberg 1410, Quellenkritische Untersuchungen, Einführung und Quellenlage* (West Berlin 1982), pp. 29–30.

7 G. Rhode, 'Das Bild des Deutschen im polnischen Roman des 19. und beginnenden 20. Jahrhunderts und das polnische Nationalgefühl', *Ostdeutsche Wissenchaft*, 8 (1961), pp. 363–5; on Sienkiewicz see R.-D. Kluge, 'Darstellung und Bewertung des Deutschen Ordens in der deutschen und polnischen Literatur', *Zeitschrift für Ostforschung*, 18 (1969), pp. 45–7.

8 For contemporary Polish and German views on the subject see G. Labuda, 'Geschichte der deutschen Ostkolonisation in den neueren westdeutschen Forschungen', *Polish Western Affairs*, 2 (1961), pp. 260–83, and 'A Historiographic Analysis of the German "Drang nach Osten"', *Polish Western Affairs*, 5 (1964), pp. 221–65; W. Wippermann, *Der Ordensstaat als Ideologie. Einzelveröffentlichungen der Historischen Kommission zu Berlin*, 24, and *Publikationen zur Geschichte der deutsch-polnischen Beziehungen*, 2 (Berlin 1979); also Wippermann, 'Die Ostsiedlung in der deutschen Historiographie und Publizistik. Probleme, Methoden und Grundlinien der Entwicklung bis zum Ersten Weltkrieg', in W. Fritze (ed.), *Germania Slavica*, 1 (Berlin 1980), pp. 47–71; H. Boockmann, 'Die mittelalterliche deutsche Ostsiedlung: zum Stand ihrer Erforschung und zu ihrem Platz im allgemeinen Geschichtsbewusstsein', in H. Boockmann, K. Jürgensen and G. Stoltenbert (eds.), *Geschichte und Gegenwart: Festschrift für Karl Dietrich Erdmann* (Neumünster 1980), pp. 131–47.

9 Johann Gottfried von Herder, *Ideen zur Philosophie der Geschichte der*

Menschheit, Part 4, Book 16, in B. Suphan (ed.), *Herders Sämmtliche Werke,* XIV (Berlin 1909), pp. 269–70 for his discussion of the Finns, Letts and Prussians, and pp. 472–3 for his views on military religious orders.

10 Ibid., pp. 278–9 for Herder's famous section on the Slavs.

11 Isaiah Berlin, *Vico and Herder: Two Studies in the History of Ideas* (London 1980), p. 155.

12 K. Stavenhagen, 'Herders Geschichtsphilosophie und seine Geschichtsprophetie', *Zeitschrift für Ostforschung,* 1 (1952), pp. 19–20.

13 Berlin, Vico and Herder, p. 177.

14 M. Broszat, *Zweihundert Jahre deutsche Polenpolitik,* 2nd edition (Frankfurt am Main 1978), p. 38.

15 W. H. Hagen, *Germans, Poles and Jews: the Nationality Conflict in the Prussian East 1772–1914* (Chicago 1980), pp. 36–7.

16 Johann Friedrich Reitemeier, *Geschichte der Preussischen Staaten vor und nach ihrer Vereinigung in eine Monarchie,* I (Frankfurt-on-Oder 1801), p. x.

17 Johannes Voigt, *Geschichte Preussens von den ältesten Zeiten bis zum Untergang der Herrschaft des Deutschen Ordens,* II (Königsberg 1827–9), p. vii; for biographies of Voigt see K. Lohmeyer, *Allgemeine deutsche Biographie,* 40 (Leipzig 1896), pp. 206–10; E. Maschke, *Altpreussische Biographie,* ed. K. Forstreuter and F. Gause, II (Marburg on Lahn 1965), pp. 760–1; Max Lehnerdt, *Aus Johannes Voigts ersten Königlichen deutschen Gesellschaft zu Königsberg,* Part II (Königsberg 1929), and for a discussion of Voigt's development as a scholar see H. Boockmann, 'Johannes Voigt und Johann Nikolaus Becker', *Preussenland,* IV (1966), pp. 9ff.

18 Voigt, *Geschichte Preussens,* V, pp. 394f.

19 Ibid., II, pp. ix and 242f.

20 L. B. Namier, *1848: the Revolution of the Intellectuals* (Oxford 1944), p. 88. For an interesting comparative study of mid-nineteenth century German and Polish nationalisms see Michael G. Müller, 'Deutsche und polnische Nation im Vormärz', *Jahrbuch für die Geschichte Mittel- und Ostdeutschlands,* 30 (Berlin 1981), pp. 73ff. An earlier *Polenfreundschaft* is discussed by E. Kolb, 'Polenbild und Polenfreundschaft der deutschen Frühliberalen', *Saeculum,* 26 (1975), pp. 111ff.

21 F. Wigand (ed.), *Stenographischer Bericht über die Verhandlungen der deutschen constituierenden Nationalversammlung zu Frankfurt am Main,* II (Frankfurt am Main 1848), pp. 1149–50.

22 Andreas Dorpalen, *Heinrich von Treitschke* (New Haven 1957), p. 285.

23 Ibid., pp. 121, 130, 192; A. Dorpalen, 'Heinrich von Treitschke', in W. Laqueur and G. L. Mosse (eds.), *Historians in Politics* (London 1974), pp. 24–5.

24 P. G. Pulzer, *The Rise of Political Anti-Semitism in Germany and Austria* (New York 1964), pp. 247–50.

25 For Treitschke's audience see J. Steinberg, 'The Kaiser's Navy and German Society', *Past and Present,* 28 (1964), p. 108; Peter Winzen, 'Treitschke's Influence on the Rise of Imperialist and Anti-British Nationalism in Germany', in P. Kennedy and A. Nicholls (eds.), *Nationalist and Racialist Movements in Britain and Germany before 1914* (Oxford 1981), pp. 155–6

and 161–3. I am grateful to Professor P. Pulzer for bringing this collection of essays to my attention. For H. Class's views on the Order see his *Deutsche Geschichte von Einhart*, 8th edition (Leipzig 1919), pp. 89–91.

26 *Heinrich von Treitschke Briefe*, ed. Max Cornicelius, 2nd edition (Leipzig 1913–19), I, no. 141, p. 330. Hereafter cited as *Treitschke Briefe*.

27 Ibid., no. 155, pp. 370–1.

28 Ibid., no. 157, p. 376; no. 164, pp. 392–3.

29 Ibid., no. 175, p. 414, and II, no. 242, p. 62, for his destruction of the manuscript; for a good discussion of the projected drama see W. Bussmann, *Treitschke: sein Welt- und Geschichtsbild. Göttinger Bausteine zur Geschichtswissenschaft*, ed. H. Goetting, H. Grebing *et al.*, 2nd edition, 3/4 (Göttingen 1981), pp. 85–91.

30 *Treitschke Briefe*, II, no. 342, p. 222.

31 Ibid., no. 347, p. 230.

32 H. von Treitschke, 'Das Deutsche Ordensland Preussen', *Preussischer Jahrbücher*, 10 (1862), p. 95.

33 Ibid., p. 150.

34 For an interesting discussion of the psychopathology of these images see R. Chickering, *We Men Who Feel Most German: a Cultural Study of the Pan-German League 1886–1914* (London 1984), especially pp. 82ff. and pp. 122–30.

35 Treitschke, 'Das Deutsche Ordensland Preussen', pp. 104, 107.

36 Ibid., p. 132.

37 Ibid., pp. 147, 149.

38 Ibid., p. 148.

39 Ibid., p. 115.

40 Ibid., p. 141.

41 Ibid., p. 147.

42 Ibid., p. 112.

43 Ibid., pp. 114–15.

44 Ibid., pp. 104–5.

45 Ibid., p. 119.

46 Ibid., p. 147.

47 Ibid., p. 110.

48 Ibid., pp. 95, 151.

49 Ibid., p. 118.

50 Ibid., pp. 135–6.

51 Ibid., p. 110.

52 Bernhard Fürst von Bülow, *Denkwürdigkeiten*, I (Berlin 1930), p. 565.

53 For a contemporary description and photographs of the Kaiser's visit see H. Boockmann, *Die Marienburg im 19. Jahrhundert* (Frankfurt am Main 1982), pp. 167ff. and plate 54. For the Kaiser's views on the teaching of history see W. C. Langsam, 'Nationalism and History in the Prussian Elementary Schools under William II', in E. M. Earle (ed.), *Nationalism and Internationalism: Essays Inscribed to Carlton Hayes* (New York 1950), pp. 241ff.

54 H. Boockmann, 'Preussen, der deutsche Ritterorden und die

Wiederherstellung der Marienburg', in P. Klemens Wieser (ed.), *Acht Jahrhunderte Deutscher Orden in Einzeldarstellungen. Quellen und Studien zur Geschichte des Deutsche Ordens*, I (Bonn and Bad Godesberg 1967), pp. 556–8.

55 Ekdahl, *Die Schlacht bei Tannenberg 1410*, p. 20.

56 General Ludendorff, *My War Memoirs 1914–1918*, I (London no date), p. 57.

57 E. Maschke, 'Quellen und Darstellungen in der Geschichtsschreibung des Preussenlandes', in – edited by order of the Landeshauptmann der Provinz Ostpreussen – *Deutsche Staatenbildung und deutsche Kultur im Preusslande* (Königsberg 1931), p. 37.

58 Ibid., p. 39.

59 Käthe Schirmacher, *Unsere Ostmark, deutscher Michel, wach auf! Eine Reihe nationaler Schriften*, ed. by Oberst A. D. Immanuel, II (Leipzig 1923), p. 38; for a biography of Schirmacher see *Altpreussische Biographie*, II, p. 611.

60 Schirmacher, *Unsere Ostmark*, XI, pp. 49–50.

61 Ibid., p. 47.

62 Ibid., p. 58.

63 Michael H. Kater, 'Die Artamanen – Völkische Jugend in der Weimarer Republik', *Historische Zeitschrift*, 213 (1971), pp. 587ff.

64 Ibid., p. 603.

65 Wilhelm Kotzde, *Der Deutsche Orden im Werden und Vergehen* (Jena 1928), pp. 5 and 34.

66 Ibid., pp. 72–5.

67 A. Hitler, *Mein Kampf*, with an introduction by D. C. Watt, translated by R. Mannheim (London 1984), pp. 128–9.

68 Ekdahl, *Die Schlacht bei Tannenberg 1410*, p. 22, note 23.

69 'Erlebnis des ewigen Kampfgeistes', *Westdeutsche Beobachter* 24 April 1936 for Klotz, and 'Die NSDAP züchtet keine Mönche', *Hakenkreuzbanner* 18 July 1936 for Ley on the absence of historical models; foreign journalists thought otherwise: see *The Times* 24 April 1936, 'The National-Socialist scheme is obviously inspired by the history of the Teutonic Order'.

70 E. Hearst, 'Finishing Schools for Nazi Leaders', in *Wiener Library Bulletin*, 19 (1965), p. 15; for the *Ordensburgen* as criticism of higher education in its received form see 'Studentenführer auf Vogelsang', *National Zeitung* 10 March 1939, 'Ausrichtung für Jahrhunderte', *Westdeutsche Beobachter* 17 April 1936, and 'Die Führerauslese der NSDAP', *National Zeitung* 3 April 1937.

71 H. Scholtz, 'Die NS-Ordensburgen', *Vierteljahrsberichte für Zeitgeschichte*, 15 (1967), pp. 273–9.

72 'Führers of the Future', *Manchester Guardian*, 17 November 1937.

73 Scholtz, 'Die NS–Ordensburgen', pp. 297–8.

74 A. Rosenberg, *Gestaltung der Idee. Reden und Aufsätze von 1933–1935*, ed. Thilo von Trotha, 2nd edition (Munich 1936), II, pp. 70ff. The speech was reprinted as *Der Deutsche Ordensstaat: ein neuer Abschnitt in der Entwicklung der nationalsozialistischen Staatsgedankens* (Munich 1934) and in *Der Schulungsbriefe*, 1, 7th series (Berlin 1934), pp. 10–16.

75 Wippermann, *Der Ordensstaat als Ideologie*, pp. 266–9.
76 H. Himmler, *Die Schutzstaffel als antibolshewistische Kampforganisation*, 6th edition (Munich 1940), p. 17.
77 H. Himmler, 'Künder ewiger Grösse', *Der Schulungsbriefe*, 8 (Berlin 1941), 3rd–4th series, pp. 42–3; the piece also appeared as 'Deutsche Burgen im Osten', *SS-Leitheft*, 6 (1941), pp. 12ff.
78 There is an excellent discussion of SS manipulation of historical models in B. Wegner, *Hitlers politische Soldaten: die Waffen SS 1932–45* (Paderborn 1982), pp. 39ff.
79 Ibid., pp. 53–4, and Himmler, *Die Schutzstaffel*, pp. 27–8.
80 Wegner, *Hitlers politische Soldaten*, p. 40; Wippermann, *Der Ordensstaat*, p. 261.
81 J. Ackermann, *Heinrich Himmler als Ideologe* (Göttingen 1970), p. 205.
82 H. Buchheim, M. Broszat, H.-A. Jacobsen and H. Krausnick, *Anatomie des SS-Staates*, 2nd edition (Munich 1979), I: *Befehl und Gehorsam*, p. 247; for similar references to Herder's 'misplaced' idealism see Himmler's address to SS commanders at Hegewald (USSR) of 16 September 1942 concerning policy in the occupied east in H.-A. Jacobsen and W. Jochmann (eds.), *Ausgwählte Dokumente zur Geschichte des Nationalsozialismus 1933–1945*, IV (Bielefeld 1961), p. 3.
83 W. Wippermann '"Gen Ostland wollen wir reiten!" Ordensstaat und Ostsiedlung in der historischen Belletristik Deutschlands', in W. Fritze (ed.), *Germania Slavica*, II (Berlin 1981), pp. 231–2; see also 'Geschichte und Ideologie im historischen Roman des Dritten Reiches', in H. Denkler and K. Prümm (eds.), *Die deutsche Literatur im Dritten Reich* (Stuttgart 1976), pp. 183ff., and Ackermann, *Heinrich Himmler* pp. 64–71, for a discussion of Himmler's preoccupation with racial ancestry.
84 Wippermann, 'Geschichte und Ideologie', pp. 183ff., and Himmler, *Die Schutzstaffel*, p. 31, for a similarly rhapsodic passage on ancestors and future generations.

2. ALBERT BRACKMANN, *OSTFORSHCER*: THE YEARS OF RETIREMENT

1 Bruno Reimann, 'Die "Selbst-Gleichschaltung" der Universitäten 1933', ed. Jürg Tröger, *Hochschule und Wissenschaft im Dritten Reich* (Frankfurt am Main 1986), p. 40.
2 *Bundesarchiv Koblenz* (BA), R153 (*Publikationsstelle*)/ Nr. 1674, W. Kohte, 'Albert Brackmann und der deutsche Ostforschung', *Nordostberichte* of the PSte, 16/6/1941; for further biographical material see R153/ Nr. 1039, including Brackmann's own biographical sketch, 'Die wissenschaftlichen Entwicklung' (1941).
3 Helmut Heiber, *Walter Frank und sein Reichsinstitut für Geschichte des neuen Deutschlands* (Stuttgart 1966), pp. 851–2.
4 Ibid., p. 852; for Brackmann's support of the *Ostmarkenverein*, see Geheimes Staatsarchiv (GSA) (West Berlin), Rep. 92 *Nachlass Brackmann*/ Nr. 47, Eastern Marches Association (*Ostmarkenverein*) chairman to

Brackmann, 27/8/1926 and Nr. 57, NSDAP *Ortsgruppe* Dahlem to Brackmann, 2/3/1933.

5 Klaus Schreiner, 'Führertum, Rasse, Reich. Wissenschaft von der Geschichte nach der nationalsozialistischen Machtergreifung', in Peter Lundgreen (ed.), *Wissenschaft im Dritten Reich* (Frankfurt am Main 1985), p. 224.

6 GSA Rep. 92/ Nr. 2, Brackmann to Professor Otto Becker, 12/9/1931.

7 BA R153/ Nr. 1134, Brackmann to Dr S. Jakobson, 15/8/1933, notifying him that his grant was terminated and PSte *Bericht* 'Über die Gründe, die zur Erteilung eines Forschungsauftrages an Dr S. Jakobson im Jahre 1931 geführt haben', 20/5/1936, for a particularly unpleasant example of retrospective self-justification.

8 BA R153/ Nr. 1674 for list of telegrams received, 24/6/1941, and R153/ Nr. 1050 for Brackmann to Hitler, Frick, Göring and Ribbentrop, 27–8/6/1941, gratefully acknowledging their solicitations.

9 Albert Brackmann (ed.), *Deutschland und Polen* (Munich and Berlin 1933), IV. On the political background to the book, see M. Broszat, *Zweihundert Jahre deutsche Polenpolitik,* 2nd edition (Frankfurt am Main 1972), especially p. 245.

10 BA 153/ Nr. 216, protokol of a meeting in the Prussian Staatsministerium, 8/2/1933, at which the Foreign and Interior Ministries agreed to provide 5,000 RM each towards the costs of the book and R153/ Nr.1573 (PSte accounts) under 1933 for the financial breakdown of the book, including receipt of these subsidies.

11 BA R153/ Nr. 217, Brackmann to Professor W. Drost, 9/5/1933.

12 BA R153/ Nr. 1076, R. Drögereit to Brackmann, 21/2/1935, and Brackmann to Drögereit 27/2/1935.

13 H. Aubin, Die historisch-geographische Grundlagen der deutsche–polnischen Beziehungen', in Brackmann (ed.), *Deutschland und Polen*, p. 14.

14 H. Oncken, 'Preussen und Polen im 19. Jahrhundert', in Brackmann (ed.), *Deutschland und Polen*, p. 224. The NSDAP had certain reservations about some of the contributors, see BA R 153/ Nr. 217, Brackmann to Brandi, 26/7/1933.

15 BA R43 II (*Reichskanzlei*)/ Nr. 1480a, Brackmann to Hitler, 11/8/1933 and Regierungsrat Dr Meerwald to Brackmann, 12/8/1933 for the reply.

16 For the reviews, see BA R153/ Nr. 219, *Prawda Katolika 5* (Sandomir 1934); for the customs ban see R153/ Nr. 1220, Erich Maschke to Brackmann, 20/6/1934.

17 R153/ Nr. 1310, Brackmann to Reich and Prussian Interior Ministries, 10/1/1937, enclosing a copy of the lecture 'Polens Grenzmarkforschung und die deutsche Wissenschaft', which he delivered on 12/1/1937, see p. 9 for the abrogation of the treaty.

18 H.-U. Wehler, 'Radikaldemokratische Geschichtswissenschaft: Eckart Kehr', *Krisenherde des Kaiserreichs 1871–1918* (Göttingen 1970), p. 273.

19 GSA Rep. 92/ Nr. 82, Brackmann to Aubin, 21/6/1937 and Brackmann to Dr Klante, 21/6/1937.

20 GSA Rep. 92/ Nr. 82, Brackmann to Ministry of the Interior, 25/8/1938 and BA R153/ Nr. 627, Hans Mortensen to Brackmann on the word 'colonisation'. For my political characterisation of the Mortensens I am indebted to Mechthild Rössler, 'Die Geographie an der Universität Freiburg 1933–1945: ein Beitrag zur Wissenschaftsgeschichte des Faches im Dritten Reich' (*Zulassungsarbeit*, University of Freiburg 1983), p. 24, note 59.

21 BA R153/ Nr. 627, Hans Mortensen to Brackmann, 15/1/1938 and GSA Rep. 92/ Nr. 83, Mortensen to Ministry of the Interior, 8/9/1933, for detailed accounts of the political aims of their work.

22 BA R153/ Nr. 1263, *Deutsche Forschungsgemeinschaft* to NODFG, 10/8/1937.

23 BA R153/ Nr. 1263, NODFG (Dr W. Kohte) to *Deutsche Forschungsgemeinschaft*, 21/8/1937.

24 BA R153/ Nr. 1263, *Deutsche Forschungsgemeinschaft* to Dr Paul Wirth (and copy to NODFG), 25/8/1937.

25 BA R153/ Nr. 1233, Brackmann to Lück's 'local' patron Alfred Lattermann (Posen), 24/3/1932 and the same, 24/3/1932; for numerous subventions to Lück , see BA R153/ Nr. 1573, starting with the financial year 1933. See also Brackmann to Lattermann, 22/4/1933, for the reworking of the Schmidt book and Lattermann to Brackmann on the effects of Lück's frenetic scholarly exertions on Lück's health (both in BA R153/ Nr. 1233) and BA R153/ Nr. 1310, PSte to Foreign Office, 9/4/1937, recommending Lück's work. It is worth noting here that another patron of Lück's who survived the war, Viktor Kauder (whose *Verband Deutscher Volksbüchereien in Polen* in Kattowitz was the link between Lück and the NODFG and by extension the Foreign Office) had the temerity to reissue Lück's *Deutsche Gestalter und Ordner* as *Deutsche–polnische Nachbarschaft. Lebensbilder deutscher Helfer in Polen* for the Göttinger Arbeitskreis in 1957. On the Lück–Kauder–Brackmann chain of command, see BA R153/ Nr. 1309, NODFG to Kauder, 12/1/1934; Brackmann to Kauder, 8/2/1934; Kauder to Brackmann, 10/3/1934; Lück to Brackmann, 11/5/1934; Brackmann to Lück, 18/6/1934; Brackmann to Lück, 5/7/1934 and BA 1573, 1933 onwards for huge payments laundered through the PSte on behalf of the Interior and Foreign Ministries through the General Consulate in Kattowitz (PSte to *Devisenstelle*, 28/9/1934). On the reissue of Lück's work, see C. Klessmann, 'Osteuropaforschung und Nationalsozialismus', *Wissenschaft im Dritten Reich*, p. 381, note 66.

26 For an obituary, see BA R52 IV/ Nr. 115, Dr W. Cöblitz (Director of the Institut für deutsche Ostarbeit in Cracow). Lattermann informed Brackmann of Lück's death on 12/3/1942, see GSA Rep. 92/ Nr. 85, Lattermann to Brackmann. On Morré, see GSA Rep. 92/ Nr. 85. Brackmann to Diestelkamp, 5/2/1942 and BA R153/ Nr. 1220, Brackmann circular to members of the NODFG, 10/1/1942.

27 BA R153/ Nr. 1220, Maschke to Brackmann, 7/10/1931 and J. Papritz Aktennotiz, 11/10/1933; for the grant, see PSte (on behalf of Brackmann) to Maschke, 12/5/1932.

28 BA R153/ Nr. 1220, Maschke, *Arbeitsbericht*, June 1932, enclosed with Maschke to Papritz, 17/5/1932.
29 BA R153/ Nr. 1220, Maschke to Brackmann, 4/3/1934.
30 BA R153/ Nr. 1220, Brackmann to Maschke, 7/3/1934.
31 BA R153/ Nr. 1220, Maschke to Brackmann, 28/3/1934.
32 BA R153/ Nr. 1220, Maschke to Papritz, 10/1/1939, report on work published since June 1932, p. 5 for his political commitments.
33 BA R153/ Nr. 1220, Brackmann to Maschke, 14/3/1939.
34 BA R153/ Nr. 1220, Maschke to Papritz, report, pp. 3–4.
35 Erich Maschke, 'Hanse und Ritterorden im Zug nach Osten', *Der Schulungsbrief*, 3/4 (Berlin 1936), p. 132.
36 Ibid., p. 145. Fundamental on this subject is W. Wippermann, *Der Ordensstaat als Ideologie. Das Bild des Deutschen Ordens in der deutschen Geschichtsschreibung und Publizistik* (Berlin 1979); see also my 'The Knights, Nationalists and the Historians: Changing Images of Medieval Prussia from the Enlightenment to 1945', *European History Quarterly*, 14, (1987) p. 1.
37 GSA Rep. 92/ Nr. 83, Brackmann to Professor F. Metz, 23/9/1939.
38 Heiber, *Walter Frank*, p. 856.
39 GSA Rep. 92/ Nr. 61, Brackmann to Heinrich Himmler, 2/11/1938 and Nr. 47, RF-SS personal staff to Brackmann, 21/6/1939.
40 GSA Rep. 92/ Nr. 44, SS-Untersturmführer Dr Kaiser to Brackmann, 26/9/1939.
41 BA NS/ Nr. 444, Ahnenerbe-Stiftungs-Verlag to SS-Standartenführer Professor Dr Six, 21/11/1939.
42 Albert Brackmann, *Krisis und Aufbau in Osteuropa* (Berlin 1939), p. 13.
43 Ibid., p. 44.
44 Ibid., pp. 62–3.
45 BA NS/ Nr. 444, *Ahnenerbe Aktenvermerk*, 7/5/1940 and GSA Rep. 92/ Nr. 44, Ahnenerbe Verlag to Brackmann, 20/12/1939 and Brackmann to Kaiser, 6/1/1940.
46 BA R153/ Nr. 1197, Aubin to Brackmann, 20/4/1940, reporting on a conversation with Seyss-Inquart about IdO personnel questions. Aubin to Brackmann, 27/4/1940, enclosing a list of names he recommended to Seyss-Inquart; BA R153/ Nr. 1572, Papritz to Interior Ministry, requesting increased salaries for PSte staff on the grounds that they were being seduced away by the IdO; BA R52 IV/ Nr. 96, Brackmann to Dr W. Coblitz, agreeing to be on the 'Copernicus Prize' panel; Brackmann also hurried along to the Prussian Staatsministerium to forge a connection with Göring's rival *Reichsstiftung für deutsche Ostforschung* (Posen), see GSA Rep. 92/ Nr. 84, Brackmann to Aubin, 10/3/1941.
47 GSA Rep. 92/ Nr. 82, Brackmann to DAAD, 3/7/1937 and on the political qualifications for the job; DAAD to Brackmann, 26/6/1937.
48 BA R153/ Nr. 951, G. Sappok, 'Richtlinien für die Umbenennung von Strassennamen in den Städten des Generalgouvernements', 22/8/1940.
49 GSA Rep. 92/ Nr. 22, Brackmann to K. A. von Müller, 17/11/1939.
50 BA R153/ Nr. 1197, Brackmann to Sappok, 6/6/1940; GSA Rep. 92/

Nr. 84, Brackmann to Aubin, 23/10/1940; Nr. 85, undated memo for Brackmann, p. 405. The collection also included the Mickiewicz Museum. On the *Einsatzstab*, see R. Bollmus, *Das Amt Rosenberg und seine Gegner: Studien zur Machtkampf im nationalsozialistischen Herrschaftssystem* (Stuttgart 1970), pp. 145ff.

51 BA R153/ Nr. 1209, PSte to SS-Sonderkommando 'Gruppe-Künsberg', 29/5/1942; PSte *Aktennotiz*, 1/10/1942 and Battaillon der Waffen-SS to the library of the NODFG, 18/2/1943.

52 BA R57 DAI/ Nr. 1386, Prof. Dr W. Kuhn (Breslau) to the Chef der Sicherheitspolizei und des SD-Einwandererzentrale Nord-Ost ('Lodsch'), 22/1/1940, 'Stammesgruppen, Bodenverhältnisse, Anbaufrüchte usw. in Galizien und Wolhynien und die sich daraus für die Umsiedlung ergebenden Gesichtspunkte'.

53 BA R57 DAI/ Nr. 1386, Stellungnahme von SS-Anwärter Dr W. Gradmann. From Gradmann's comments, it is evident that Kurt Lück had also seen the manuscript of Kuhn since Gradmann quotes Lück's opinions on it.

54 BA R153/ Nr. 1250, Otto Reche to W. Kohte of the PSte, 24/5/1942 and Nr. 288, Brackmann to Reche, 22/9/1939, 28/9/1939 (also to the Interior Ministry), and 13/10/1939, 20/10/1939, 1/11/1939, 22/11/1939, reporting to Reche on his efforts on Reche's behalf. For NODFG support of Reche, see BA R153/ Nr. 1573, pp. 1935 onwards.

55 BA R153/ Nr. 1250, Reche to W. Kohte, 25/5/1942, with extensive biographical details.

56 BA R153/ Nr. 288, Reche to Brackmann, 19/9/1939 and Brackmann to Reche on the matter of lice in fur .

57 BA R153/ Nr. 1250, Reche to Kohte (PSte), 18/3/1942, on the obliteration of 'Russia' and Reche to Kohte, 24/5/1942, on his projected book.

58 BA R153/ Nr. 288, Reche to Brackmann, 19/10/1939.

59 BA R153/ Nr. 288, Brackmann to Reche, 20/10/1939.

60 BA R153/ Nr. 288, Reche to Brackmann, 26/10/1939.

61 BA R153/ Nr. 288, Brackmann to Reche, 1/11/1939.

62 BA R153/ Nr. 288, Brackmann to Reche, 1/11/1939.

63 BA R153/ Nr. 288, Reche to Brackmann, 14/11/1939.

64 BA R153/ Nr. 288, Brackmann to Regierungsrat Dr Essen, 28/9/1939; Brackmann was pleased that Reche had found the right people at last, see Brackmann to Reche, 22/11/1939.

65 BA R153/ Nr. 1456, Interior Ministry to PSte, 20/8/1942; Brackmann to Reche, 14/10/1942; Reche to Brackmann 19/10/1942 and Brackmann to Reche, 6/11/1942, noting that he had passed Reche's name to the Interior Ministry.

66 O. Reche, 'Stärke und Herkunft des Anteiles nordischer Rasse bei den West-Slawen', in H. Aubin, W. Kohte and J. Papritz (eds.), *Deutsche Ostforschung: Ergebnisse und Aufgaben seit dem ersten Weltkrieg*, I (Leipzig 1942), p. 60.

67 Reche, 'Stärke und Herkunft', p. 89.

68 BA R153/ Nr. 1050, Brackmann to Reche, 10/7/1941.

3. 'SEE YOU AGAIN IN SIBERIA': THE GERMAN–SOVIET WAR AND OTHER TRAGEDIES

1 Heinz Guderian, *Panzer Leader* (London 1987), p. 153; John Erickson, *The Road to Stalingrad* (London 1993), pp. 106–7.
2 Erickson, *Road to Stalingrad*, p. 106.
3 Amy Knight, *Beria, Stalin's First Lieutenant* (New Jersey 1993), pp. 107–8.
4 Pavel and Anatoli Sudoplatov, *Special Tasks* (Boston 1995), p. 123.
5 Edvard Radzinsky, *Stalin* (London 1996), pp. 436–7.
6 Gabriel Gorodetsky, 'Stalin und Hitlers Angriff auf die Sowjetunion', in Bernd Wegner (ed.), *Zwei Wege nach Moskau* (Munich 1991), p. 358.
7 Knight, *Beria*, pp. 107–8.
8 Stepan A. Mikoyan, 'Barbarossa and the Soviet Leadership', in John Erickson and David Dilks (eds.), *Barbarossa, the Axis and the Allies* (Edinburgh 1994), pp. 125–6.
9 Robert Conquest, *Stalin. Breaker of Nations* (London 1991), p. 234.
10 Horst Boog, 'Die Luftwaffe', in Boog *et al.* (eds.), *Der Angriff auf die Sowjetunion* (Frankfurt am Main 1991), p. 737.
11 Paul Kohl, *'Ich wundere mich, daß ich noch lebe'. Sowjetische Augenzeugen Berichten* (Gütersloh 1990), p. 68.
12 Ibid., p. 31.
13 Conquest, *Stalin*, p. 239.
14 Dmitri Volkogonov, *Stalin. Triumph and Tragedy* (London 1991), pp. 406ff.; Radzinsky, *Stalin*, pp. 454–5.
15 Manfred Menger, 'Deutschland und der finnische "Sonderkrieg" gegen die Sowjetunion', in Wegner, *Zwei Wege*, pp. 547ff.
16 Jürgen Förster, 'Die Gewinnung von Verbundeten in Südosteuropa', in Boog *et al.* (eds.), *Der Angriff auf die Sowjetunion*, pp. 396ff.
17 Ibid., p. 430.
18 Lütz Lemhöfer, 'Gegen den gottlosen Bolshevismus. Zur Stellung der Kirchen zum Krieg gegen die Sowjetunion', in Gerd R. Ueberschär and Wolfram Wette (eds.), *Der deutsche Überfall auf die Sowjetunion* (Frankfurt am Main 1991), pp. 78–9.
19 Hans-Heinrich Wilhelm, 'Motivation und "Kriegsbild" deutscher Generale und Offiziere im Krieg gegen die Sowjetunion' in Peter Jahn and Reinhard Rürup (eds.), *Erobern und Vernichtung* (Berlin 1991).
20 See Michael Burleigh, *Germany Turns Eastwards: a Study of 'Ostforschung' in the Third Reich* (Cambridge 1988); and Gabriele Camphausen, *Die wissenschaftliche historische Russlandforschung im Dritten Reich 1933–1945* (Frankfurt am Main 1990).
21 Peter Jahn, '"Russenfurcht" und Antibolshewismus: zur Entstehung und Wirkung von Feindbildern', in Jahn and Rürup (eds.) *Erobern und Vernichtung*, pp. 52–3.
22 Walter Warlimont, *Inside Hitler's Headquarters 1939–45* (London 1964), p. 140.
23 Andreas Hillgruber, 'Das Russland-Bild der führenden deutschen Militärs vor Beginn des Angriffs auf die Sowjetunion', in Wegner, *Zwei Wege*, p. 177.

24 B. Kroener, 'Der "erfrorene Blitzkrieg". Strategische Planungen der deutschen Führung gegen die Sowjetunion und die Ursachen ihres Scheiterns', in Wegner, *Zwei Wege*, p. 144.
25 Erich von Manstein, *Lost Victories* (Elstree 1987), pp. 208–9.
26 For a vivid account of the impact of winter see Alan Clark, *Barbarossa. The Russian–German Conflict* (London 1995).
27 Alexander Werth, *Russia at War 1941–1945* (London 1964), p. 163.
28 See Richard Woff, 'Rokossovsky', and other biographies of these generals, in Harold Shukman (ed.), *Stalin's Generals* (London 1993), pp. 177ff.
29 Volkogonov, *Stalin*, p. 423.
30 On events in the Ukraine see Wolodymyr Kosyk, *The Third Reich and the Ukraine* (New York 1993), p. 88; for Order No. 270 see John Barber and Mark Harrison, *The Soviet Home Front 1941–1945* (London 1991), p. 28.
31 Knight, *Beria*, p. 114.
32 Ingeborg Fleischhauer, 'Operation Barbarossa and the Deportation', in Ingeborg Fleischhauer and Benjamin Pinkus (eds.), *The Soviet Germans. Past and Present* (London 1986), pp. 78ff.
33 Warlimont, *Inside Hitler's Headquarters*, pp. 221–5.
34 H.-A. Jacobsen (ed.), *Der Weg zur Teilung der Welt. Politik und Strategie 1939–1945* (Koblenz and Bonn 1977), pp. 138–9.
35 Manstein, *Lost Victories*, pp. 280–1.
36 Guderian, *Panzer Leader*, p. 265.
37 Ibid., p. 266.
38 Manstein, *Lost Victories*, p. 281
39 Seweryn Bialer (ed.), *Stalin and his Generals. Soviet Military Memoirs of World War Two* (New York 1969), pp. 339ff.
40 Geoffrey Hosking, *A History of the Soviet Union 1917–1991* (London 1992), pp. 274–5; for a crisp description of Stalin as a war leader see also Alan Bullock, *Hitler and Stalin. Parallel Lives* (London 1991), pp. 699ff.
41 Barber and Harrison, *Soviet Home Front*, p. 127.
42 Richard J. Overy, *Why the Allies Won* (London 1995), p. 186.
43 Sudoplatov, *Special Tasks*, p. 135.
44 Werth, *Russia at War*, p. 246.
45 Hosking, *A History of the Soviet Union*, p. 236.
46 Vasily Grossmann, *Life and Fate* (London 1995), pp. 231–2.
47 Knight, *Beria*, p. 118.
48 Barber and Harrison, *Soviet Home Front*, pp. 116ff. and 170 on camp morale.
49 Warlimont, *Inside Hitler's Headquarters*, p. 252.
50 For an excellent analysis of the options, see Bernd Wegner, 'The Road to Defeat: the German Campaigns in Russia 1941–43', *Journal of Strategic Studies*, 13 (1990), pp. 114ff.
51 Wolfram Wette and Gerd Ueberschär (eds.), *Stalingrad. Mythos und Wirklichkeit einer Schlacht* (Frankfurt am Main 1993), p. 20.
52 Martin Middlebrook, 'Paulus', in Correlli Barnett (ed.), *Hitler's Generals* (London 1989), pp. 361ff.; Viktor Anfilov, 'Zhukov', in Shukman (ed.), *Stalin's Generals*, pp. 343ff.

53 Georgi K. Zhukov, *Marshal Zhukov's Greatest Battles* (London 1969), pp. 158ff. for a detailed account of the genesis of Operation Uranus.
54 Volkogonov, *Stalin*, pp. 462–3 and 475ff.
55 Bernd Böll and Hans Safrian, 'Auf dem Weg nach Stalingrad. Die 6. Armee 1941/42', in Hannes Heer and Klaus Naumann (eds.), *Vernichtungskrieg. Verbrechen der Wehrmacht 1941–1944* (Hamburg 1995), pp. 269ff.
56 Werth, *Russia at War*, p. 442.
57 Clark, *Barbarossa*, pp. 243–5.
58 Werth, *Russia at War*, p. 462.
59 Zhukov, *Marshal Zhukov's Greatest Battles*, p. 169.
60 Gerd Ueberschär, 'Stalingrad – eine Schlacht des Zweiten Weltkrieges', in Wette and Ueberschär (eds.), *Stalingrad*, pp. 18ff.
61 Wolfgang U. Eckart, 'Von der Agonie einer missbrauchten Armee. Anmerkungen zur Verwundeten- und Krankenversorgung im Kessel von Stalingrad', in Wette and Ueberschär (eds.), *Stalingrad*, pp. 109–12.
62 Landeshauptarchiv Koblenz, Bestand 700, 153 Nr. 80 cited in Wolfram Wette '"Unsere Stimmung ist auf dem Nullpunkt angekommen"', in Wette and Ueberschär (eds.), *Stalingrad*, p. 95; see also Rolf-Dieter Müller, '"Was wir an Hunger ausstehen müssen, konnt Ihr Euch gar nicht denken', in Wette and Ueberschär (eds.), *Stalingrad*, pp. 131ff.
63 Anatoly Golovchansky, Valentin Osipov, Anatoly Prokopenko, Ute Daniel and Jürgen Reulecke (eds.), *'Ich will raus aus diesem Wahnsinn.' Deutsche Briefe von der Ostfront 1941–1945 aus sowjetischen Archiven* (Hamburg 1993), p. 150.
64 Ibid., pp. 228–9.
65 Ibid., pp. 161–2.
66 Müller, 'Was wir an Hunger', p. 143.
67 David M. Glantz, *From the Don to the Dnepr. Soviet Offensive Operations December 1942–August 1943* (London 1991), pp. 215–19.
68 David M. Glantz, *Soviet Military Deception in the Second World War* (London 1989), pp. 152ff.
69 Robin Cross, *Citadel. The Battle of Kursk* (London 1993), pp. 181–2.
70 Wegner, 'The Road to Defeat: German Campaigns in Russia', *The Journal of Strategic Studies*, 13 (1990), pp. 105–27; Christian Streit, *Keine Kameraden. Die Wehrmacht und die sowjetischen Kriegsgefangenen 1941–1945* (Stuttgart 1978), and his 'Die Behandlung und Ermordung sowjetischen Kriegsgefangenen', in Klaus Meyer and Wolfgang Wippermann (eds.), *Gegen das Vergessen. Der Vernichtungskrieg gegen die Sowjetunion 1941–1945* (Frankfurt am Main 1992), pp. 91–2; Alfred Streim, *Die Behandlung sowjetischer Kriegsgefangener im 'Fall Barbarossa'. Eine Dokumentation* (Heidelberg 1981).
71 Alfred Streim, *Sowjetische Gefangene in Hitlers Vernichtungskrieg* (Heidelberg 1982), p. 22; see also Streim, 'Das völkerrecht und die Sowjetischen Kriegsgefangenen', in Wegner (ed.), *Zwei Wege*, pp. 291ff.
72 These arguments are rehearsed, and then destroyed, by Streit, *Keine Kameraden*, pp. 128–9, whose own contributions are merely modified

around the margins by the post-revisionist Theo Schulte, *The German Army and Nazi Policies in Occupied Russia* (Oxford 1989), pp. 180–4.

73 Streit, *Keine Kameraden*, p. 145.
74 Ibid., p. 152.
75 Curzio Malaparte, *Kaputt* (London 1989), pp. 208–15.
76 Streit, *Keine Kameraden*, pp. 162ff.
77 Ibid., pp. 181–2 for Reinecke's orders.
78 Ibid., pp. 57–8; see also Klaus-Jürgen Müller, 'The Brutalisation of Warfare, Nazi Crimes and the Wehrmacht', in Erickson and Dilks (eds.), *Barbarossa*, p. 233; see also, Jürgen Förster, 'The German Army and the Ideological War against the Soviet Union', in Gerhard Hirschfeld (ed.), *The Policies of Genocide. Jews and Soviet Prisoners of War in Nazi Germany* (London 1986), pp. 15–29.
79 Streit, *Keine Kameraden*, p. 31.
80 Ibid., p. 34.
81 Reprinted in Ueberschär and Wette (eds.), *Der deutsche Überfall auf die Sowjetunion*, pp. 249–50.
82 Streit, *Keine Kameraden*, pp. 33ff.
83 Jürgen Förster, 'Der Kommissar-Befehl', in Boog *et al.* (eds.), *Der Angriff auf die Sowjetunion*, pp. 520–5; on the subject of Red Army murders of German prisoners see Alfred de Zayas, *The Wehrmacht War Crimes Bureau, 1939–1945* (Lincoln, Nebraska 1989), pp. 162ff. On p. 177 de Zayas notes that individual interpretations of generalised injunctions to annihilate the invaders (which primarily meant in battle) were not comparable with orders to kill entire groups of people after they had been captured. The projection of German aggression onto the Red Army is discussed by Omer Bartov, 'Historians on the Eastern Front: Andreas Hillgruber and Germany's Tragedy', in Bartov, *Murder in Our Midst. The Holocaust, Industrial Killing, and Representation* (New York, Oxford 1996), pp. 71ff.
84 Streit, *Keine Kameraden*, p. 92.
85 'Richtlinien für das Verhalten der Truppe in Russland', in Ueberschär and Wette (eds.), *Der deutsche Überfall auf die Sowjetunion*, p. 258.
86 'Befehl des Befehlshabers der Panzergruppe 4 zur bevorstehenden Kampfführung im Osten', ibid., p. 251.
87 'Armeebefehl des Oberbefehlhabers der 6. Armee vom 10.10.1941', ibid., p. 285.
88 'Armeebefehl des Oberbefehlshaber der 17. Armee vom 17.11.1941', ibid., p. 288.
89 Schulte, *German Army and Nazi Policies*, p. 219.
90 Förster, 'The German Army and the Ideological War', pp. 22–3.
91 Streit, *Keine Kameraden*, pp. 102–3.
92 Streim, *Sowjetische Gefangene*, pp. 38–45.
93 Ibid., pp. 56ff.
94 David Hackett (ed.), *The Buchenwald Report* (Boulder 1995), pp. 238–9.
95 Streim, *Sowjetische Gefangene*, pp. 87–91.

96 Omer Bartov, *Hitler's Army. Soldiers, Nazis and War in the Third Reich* (Oxford 1991); see also his *The Eastern Front 1941–45, German Troops and the Barbarisation of Warfare* (London 1985); 'Von unten betrachtet: Überleben, Zusammenhalt und Brutalität an der Ostfront', in Wegner (ed.) *Zwei Wege*, pp. 326ff; and 'The Myths of the Wehrmacht', *History Today*, 42 (1992), pp. 30–6.
97 Theo Schulte, *The German Army and Nazi Policies in Occupied Russia* (Oxford 1989).
98 Bartov, *Hitler's Army*, pp. 38ff.
99 Ibid., pp. 95–6.
100 Schulte, *German Army and Nazi Policies*, p. 112.
101 Ilya Ehrenburg, *The War 1941–45. Men, Years – Life*, translated by Tatiana Shebunina and Yvonne Kapp (London 1964), pp. 28–9.
102 Ibid., pp. 156–60.
103 Golovchansky *et al.*, '*Ich will raus aus diesem Wahnsinn*', pp. 119–20.
104 Ibid., pp. 227–8.
105 Ibid., pp. 57–8.
106 Hannes Heer and Klaus Naumann (eds.), *Vernichtungskrieg. Verbrechen der Wehrmacht 1941–1944* (Hamburg 1995).
107 *Hitler's Table-Talk*, introduced by Hugh Trevor-Roper (Oxford 1988) (hereafter *HTT*), pp. 15, 23, 33 and so on for the India analogy.
108 *HTT*, 17 September 1941, p. 34.
109 *HTT*, 19–20 February 1942, p. 319.
110 *HTT*, 17 October 1941, p. 69.
111 *HTT*, 6 August 1942, p. 617.
112 *HTT*, 8–9 and 9–10 August 1941, p. 24.
113 Martin Bormann, 'Aktenvermerk' 16 July 1941, in Wolfgang Schumann and Ludwig Nestler (eds.) *Europa unterm Hakenkreuz. Die faschistische Okkupationspolitik in den zeitweilig besetzten Gebieten der Sowjetunion (1941–1944)* (Berlin 1991), pp. 160ff.
114 This is evident in Alexander Dallin's *German Rule in Russia 1941–1945*, 2nd edition (London 1981).
115 Timothy P. Mulligan, *The Politics of Illusion and Empire. German Occupation Policy in the Soviet Union, 1942–1943* (New York 1988), pp. 37ff.
116 Dallin, *German Rule in Russia*, pp. 46ff.
117 On the Ukraine see Bohdan Krawchenko, 'Soviet Ukraine under Nazi Occupation 1941–44', in Yury Boshyk, *Ukraine during World War II* (Edmonton 1986), pp. 15ff.; David R. Marples, *Stalinism in Ukraine in the 1940s* (London 1992), pp. 42ff.; and Mulligan, *Politics of Illusion and Empire*, pp. 61ff.
118 John Hiden and Patrick Salmon, *The Baltic Nations and Europe. Estonia, Latvia and Lithuania in the Twentieth Century* (Harlow 1991), p. 115.
119 Dr Dengel to Generalleutnant Wilhelm Schubert, 3 July 1941, in Schumann and Nestler (eds.), *Europa unterm Hakenkreuz*, pp. 155–6.
120 Mulligan, *Politics of Illusion and Empire*, pp. 126ff.
121 Herbert Backe, '12 Gebote für das Verhalten der Deutschen im Osten und

die Behandlung der Russen', 1.1.1941, in Ueberschär and Wette (eds.), *Der deutsche Überfall auf die Sowjetunion*, pp. 326–8.

122 Report from the Auslandbriefprufstelle (no date), in Schumann and Nestler (eds.), *Europa unterm Hakenkreuz*, pp. 453–4; for a general survey of the German administration see Jonathan Steinberg, 'The Third Reich Reflected: German Civil Administration in the Occupied Soviet Union', *English Historical Review* (1995), pp. 620ff.

123 Bernhard Chiari, 'Deutsche Zivilverwaltung in Weissrussland 1941–1944. Die lokale Perspektive der Besatzungsmacht', *Militärgeschichtliche Mitteilungen*, 52 (1993), p. 79.

124 Ann Sheehy and Bohdan Nahaylo, *The Crimean Tatars, Volga Germans and Meskhetians. Soviet Treatment of Some National Minorities*, Minority Rights Group Report No. 6 (London 1980), p. 7.

125 Joachim Hoffmann, *Deutsche und Kalmyken 1942 bis 1945*, 4th edition (Freiburg-im-Breisgau 1986).

126 Joachim Hoffmann, *Die Ostlegionen 1941–1943*, 3rd edition (Freiburg-im-Breisgau 1986).

127 Hoffmann, *Deutsche und Kalmyken*, pp. 120ff.

128 Samuel J. Newland, *Cossacks in the German Army* (London 1991), pp. 86.

129 See the suggestive piece by Sergei Kudryashov, 'The Hidden Dimension. Wartime Collaboration in the Soviet Union', in Erickson and Dilks (eds.), *Barbarossa*, pp. 238ff.

130 Vlasov, 'Why I Decided to Fight Bolshevism', in Catherine Andreyev (ed.), *Vlasov and the Russian Liberation Movement. Soviet Reality and Emigré Theories* (Cambridge 1987), p. 211; see also Joachim Hoffmann, *Die Geschichte der Wlassow-Armee* (Freiburg-im-Breisgau 1986).

131 Ibid., 'The Smolensk Declaration', p. 207.

132 John Erickson, 'Nazi Posters in Wartime Russia', *History Today*, 44 (1994), pp. 14–19.

133 Rosenberg, 'Neue Agrarordnung', in Schumann and Nestler (eds.), *Europa unterm Hakenkreuz*, pp. 245–8; on these reforms see also Christian Gerlach, 'Die deutsche Agrarreform und die Bevölkerungspolitik in den besetzten sowjetischen Gebieten', *Beiträge zur Geschichte der nationalsozialistischen Gesundheits- und Sozialpolitik*, (Berlin 1995), pp. 9ff.

134 'Aufzeichnungen über die Rede von Erich Koch auf der Tagung in Rowno vom 26. bis 28. August 1942', ibid., p. 322.

135 'Niederschrift einer Beratung unter dem Vorsitz von Reichsmarschall Hermann Göring am 8 November 1941 über Grundsätze bei der wirtschaftlichen Ausbeutung der okkupierten Gebiete der UdSSR', in Schumann and Nestler (eds.), *Europa unterm Hakenkreuz*, p. 217.

136 Ibid., pp. 404–5.

137 Mulligan, *Politics of Illusion and Empire*, p. 108.

138 Ibid., p. 100.

139 Lutz Schwerin von Krosigk 'Denkschrift', 4 September 1942, in Schuman and Nestler (eds.), *Europa unterm Hakenkreuz*, pp. 324–7.

140 On these plans see above all Rolf-Dieter Müller, *Hitlers Ostkrieg und die deutsche Siedlungspolitik* (Frankfurt am Main 1991); see also Mechtild Rossler, 'Konrad Meyer und der "Generalplan Ost" in der Beurteilung der Nürnberger Prozesse', in M. Rössler and S. Schleiermacher (eds.), *Der 'Generalplan Ost'. Hauptlinien der nationalsozialistischen Planungs- und Vernichtungspolitik* (Berlin 1993), pp. 356ff.; my own views on these subjects are to be found in 'A Political Economy of the Final Solution. Reflections on Modernity, Historians and the Holocaust', *Patterns of Prejudice*, 30 (London 1996), pp. 29–41.

141 Gert Gröning and Joachim Wolschke-Bulmahn (eds.), *Der Liebe zur Landschaft. Teil III: Der Drang nach Osten. Arbeiten zur sozialwissenschaftlich orientierten Freiraumplanung*, 9 (Munich 1987), p. 31.

142 Müller, *Hitlers Ostkrieg*, pp. 102–3.

143 Helmut Heiber, 'Der Generalplan Ost', *Vierteljahrshefte für Zeitgeschichte*, 6 (1958), pp. 297ff.

144 Dietrich Eichholtz, 'Der "Generalplan Ost"', *Jahrbuch für Geschichte*, 26 (1982), pp. 259ff. for Meyer's memorandum.

145 See above all Rolf-Dieter Müller, 'Das "Unternehmen Barbarossa" als wirtschaftlicher Raubkrieg', in Ueberschär and Wette (eds.), *Der deutsche Überfall auf die Sowjetunion*, pp. 125ff.

146 'Allgemeine wirtschaftspolitische Richtlinien für die Wirtschaftsorganisation Ost, Gruppe Landwirtschaft', 23.5.1941, ibid., pp. 323–5; on Backe see also Götz Aly and Susanne Heim *Vordenker der Vernichtung. Auschwitz und die deutschen Pläne für eine neue europäische Ordnung* (Hamburg 1991), pp. 365ff.

147 Extract from Halder diaries, in Ueberschär and Wette (eds.), *Der deustche Überfall auf die Sowjetunion*, pp. 278–9.

148 Werth, *Russia at War* p. 339; see also the Russian and German accounts in Ales Adamowitsch *et al.* (eds.), *Blockade Leningrad 1941–1944* (Hamburg 1992), for what follows.

149 'Aufzeichnung im Wirtschaftsstab Ost über die von Reichsmarschall Hermann Göring am 7. November 1941 gegebenen Richtlinien für den Arbeitseinsatz von Sowjetburgern', in Schumann and Nestler (eds.), *Europa unterm Hakenkreuz*, p. 214.

150 Rolf-Dieter Müller, 'Die Rekrutierung sowjetischer Zwangsarbeiter für die deutsche Kriegswirtschaft', in Ulrich Herbert (ed.), *Europa und der 'Reichseinsatz'* (Essen 1991), pp. 235–7; on Sauckel see Peter W. Becker, 'Fritz Sauckel: Plenipotentiary for the Mobilisation of Labour', in Ronald Smelser and Rainer Zitelmann (eds.), *The Nazi Elite* (London 1993), pp. 194ff.

151 See the comments reported by the Auslandsbriefprufstelle Berlin dated 11 November 1942 in Schumann and Nestler (eds.), *Europa unterm Hakenkreuz*, pp. 358ff.

152 Müller, 'Die Rekrutierung', p. 238.

153 Auslandsprufstelle Berlin report dated 11 November 1942, 'Anlage 1', in Schumann and Nestler (eds.), *Europa unterm Hakenkreuz*, pp. 359–60.

154 Notes by SS-Obersturmbannführer Erich Ehrlinger on a conference in the presence of Fritz Sauckel in Kiev on 12 August 1942, in Schumann and Nestler (eds.), *Europa unterm Hakenkreuz*, pp. 313–16.
155 Report by SS-Obersturmbannführer Erich Ehrlinger dated 20 July 1942 concerning labour recruitment raids in the Podol district of Kiev, in Schumann and Nestler (eds.), *Europa unterm Hakenkreuz*, pp. 302ff.
156 Report by Obersturmbannführer Erich Ehrlinger to SS-Gruppenführer Max Thomas dated 9 December 1942, ibid., p. 366.
157 Report from SS-Sturmbannführer Erich Ehrlinger to SS-Gruppenführer Max Thomas dated 19 December 1942, ibid., pp. 366–8.
158 Matthew Cooper, *The Phantom War. The German Struggle against Soviet Partisans 1941–1944* (London 1979), p. 12; Witalij Wilenchik, 'Die Partisanenbewegung in Weissrussland 1941–1944', *Forschungen zur Osteuropäischen Geschichte*, 34 (1984), pp. 150–1.
159 Rosenberg to Sauckel 21 December 1942, in Schumann and Nestler (eds.), *Europa unterm Hakenkreuz*, p. 147.
160 Sudoplatov, *Special Tasks*, pp. 130–3.
161 Cooper, *The Phantom War*, p. 35; on the operational space left to partisans see Center of Military History, United States Army (ed.), *Combat in Russian Forests and Swamps* (Washington DC 1986), pp. 1–4.
162 On Dirlewanger and Kaminsky see Hellmuth Auerbach, 'Die Einheit Dirlewanger', *Vierteljahrshefte fur Zeitgeschichte*, 10 (1962), pp. 250ff.; Alexander Dallin, 'The Kaminisky Brigade: a Case Study of Soviet Disaffection', in A. and J. Rabinowitch (eds.), *Revolution and Politics in Russia* (Bloomington 1973), pp. 243–80, and Hans-Peter Klausch, *Antifaschisen in SS-Uniform* (Bremen 1993).
163 Monthly report from Wirtschaftsstab Ost concerning July 1942, in Schumann and Nestler (eds.), *Europa unterm Hakenkreuz*, pp. 305ff.
164 Heinrich Himmler, 'Guidelines for the combating of bandits', September 1942, in Schumann and Nestler (eds.), *Europa unterm Hakenkreuz*, pp. 339–40.
165 Göring order concerning prevention of partisan attacks on railway lines, 16 October 1942, in Schumann and Nestler (eds.), *Europa unterm Hakenkreuz*, pp. 339–40.
166 Ibid., pp. 340–1.
167 Report from Oberkommando der 6. Armee to Army Group South dated 7 December 1941 regarding mass executions, in Schumann and Nestler (eds.), *Europa unterm Hakenkreuz*, p. 237.
168 'Memorandum on Use of Troops against Partisans', dated 15 December 1941, in Cooper, *Phantom War*, p. 181; on German strategy see also Bernd Bonwetsch, 'Die Partisanenbekämpfung und ihre Opfer im Russlandfeldzug 1941–1944', in Meyer and Wippermann (eds.), *Gegen das Vergessen*, pp. 102ff.
169 Ibid., p. 81.
170 257 Infantry Division directive dated 7 December 1941 regarding identification and interrogation of partisans, in Ernst Klee and Willi Dressen

(eds.), *'Gott mit uns'. Der deutsche Vernichtungskrieg im Osten 1939–1945* (Frankfurt am Main 1989), pp. 56–9.

171 The subject is not greatly illuminated by either Dieter Reifarth and Viktoria Schmidt-Linsendorf, 'Die Kamera der Täter' or Bernd Huppauf, 'Der entleerte Blick hinter der Kamera', in Heer and Nauman (eds.), *Vernichtungskrieg*, pp. 475ff and 504ff.

172 Cooper, *The Phantom War*, pp. 83–4.

173 Report by Generalmajor Bruno Scultetus of the 281 Sicherungsdivision to the Commanding General of Sicherungstruppen of Army Rear Area North 23 June 1942, in Schumann and Nestler (eds.), *Europa unterm Hakenkreuz*, pp. 295–7; on the mass murder of Roma in the former Soviet Union see Wolfgang Wippermann, 'Nur eine Fussnote? Die Verfolgung der sowjetischen Roma: Historiographie, Motive, Verlauf', in Meyer and Wippermann (eds.), *Gegen das Vergessen*, pp. 75ff.

174 Cooper, *The Phantom War*, pp. 56–7.

175 *Unsere Ehre heisst Treue. Kriegstagebuch des Kommandostabes Reichsführer-SS. Tätigkeitsbericht der 1. und 2. SS-Inf.Brigade, der 1. SS-Kav.-Brigade, und von Sonderkommandos der SS* (Vienna 1965), p. 108.

176 'Tätigkeitsbericht' 1. SS-Inf. Brigade (mot.), 6.8.1941–10.8.1941, ibid., pp. 111–15.

177 'Bericht über den Verlauf der Pripjet-Aktion', 12 August 1941, ibid., 227–30; see also Ruth-Bettina Birn, 'Zweierlei Wirklichkeit. Fallbeispiele zur Partisanbekämpfung im Osten', in Wegner (ed.), *Zwei Wege*, pp. 275ff.

4. PSYCHIATRY, GERMAN SOCIETY AND THE NAZI 'EUTHANASIA' PROGRAMME

1 Bibliographical surveys include the relevant sections of Christopher Beck (ed.), *Sozialdarwinismus, Rassenhygiene, Zwangssterilisation und Vernichtung 'lebensunwerten' Lebens* (Bonn 1992); and in English, Michael Burleigh '"Euthanasia" in the Third Reich: some Recent Literature', *Social History of Medicine*, 4 (1991), pp. 317–28. Also: F. W. Kersting, K. Teppe and B. Walter (eds.), *Nach Hadamar: Zum Verhältnis von Psychiatrie und Gesellschaft im 20. Jahrhundert* (Paderborn 1993). Fuller references to many of the issues explored in this paper may be found in my book *Death and Deliverance. 'Euthanasia' in Germany c. 1900–1945* (Cambridge 1994).

2 For this reading of the genesis of the 'Final Solution' see above all Philippe Burrin, *Hitler and the Jews* (London 1994), especially p. 38.

3 Hans-Ludwig Siemen, *Menschen blieben auf der Strecke* (Gütersloh 1987), p. 29. See also Heinz Faulstich, *Von der Irrenfürsorge zur 'Euthanasie'* (Freiburg im Breisgau 1993), p. 77.

4 Peter Riedesser and Axel Verderber, *Aufrüstung der Seelen* (Freiburg im Breisgau 1985), pp. 11ff.

5 Siegfried Grübitzsch, 'Revolutions- und Rätezeit 1918/19 aus der Sicht Deutscher Psychiater', *Psychologie & Gesellschaftskritik*, 9 (1985), pp. 35–8.

6 For an unsympathetic contemporary account of these various pressure

groups see Ernst Rittershaus, *Die Irrengesetzgebung in Deutschland* (Berlin 1927).

7 Karl Binding and Alfred Hoche, *Die Freigabe der Vernichtung lebensunwerten Lebens. Ihr Mass und ihre Form* (Leipzig 1920). The tract has been thoroughly analysed by *inter alios* K. H. Hafner and R. Winau, '"Die Freigabe der Vernichtung lebensunwerten Lebens", Eine Untersuchung zu der Schrift von Karl Binding und Alfred Hoche', *Medizinisches Journal*, 9 (1974), pp. 227–54.

8 For quasi-programmatic statements see Gustav Kolb, 'Reform der Irrenpflege', *Zeitschrift für die gesamte Neurologie und Psychiatrie*, 47 (1919), pp. 137–72, and Hermann Simon, 'Aktivere Kranken-behandlung in der Irrenanstalt', *Allgemeine Zeitschrift für Psychiatrie*, 87 (1927), pp. 97–145 and 90 (1929), pp. 69–121 and 245–309.

9 Bernhard Richarz, *Heilen–Pflegen–Töten. Zur Alltagsgeschichte einer Heil- und Pflegeanstalt bis zum Ende des Nationalsozialismus* (Göttingen 1987), p. 78.

10 See Karl-Heinz Roth, '"Erbbiologische Bestandsaufnahme" – ein Aspekt ausmerzender Erfassung vor der Entfesselung des Zweiten Weltkrieges', in K.-H. Roth (ed.), *Erfassung zur Vernichtung. Von der Sozialhygiene zum 'Gesetz über Sterbehilfe'* (Berlin 1984), pp. 59ff. For an alternative interpretation see P. J. Weindling, *Health, Race and German Politics between National Unification and Nazism* (Cambridge 1989), pp. 383ff.

11 See for example the Tübingen psychiatrist Robert Gaupp's address to the September 1925 meeting of the German Psychiatric Association in Cassel, 'Die Unfruchtbarmachung geistig und sittlich Minderwertiger', *Allgemeine Zeitschrift für Psychiatrie*, 83 (1926), pp. 371–90 for a lengthy version of this line of argument.

12 Sabine Schleiermacher, 'Der Centralausschuss für die Innere Mission und die Eugenik am Vorabend des Dritten Reichs', in T. Strohm and J. Thierfelder (eds.), *Diakonie im 'Dritten Reich'* (Heidelberg 1990), p. 70. I am grateful to the author for a copy of this important article.

13 See especially Hans-Ludwig Siemen, 'Reform und Radikalisierung', in N. Frei (ed.), *Medizin und Gesundheitspolitik in der NS-Zeit* (Munich 1991), pp. 197–8.

14 Gerhard Schmidt, *Selektion in der Heilanstalt 1939–1945* (Frankfurt am Main 1983), p. 26. For an interesting discussion of how psychiatrists responded to Schmidts's work, which was written shortly after the end of the war, and only published in 1965, see Dirk Blasius, 'Das Ende der Humanität', in Walter H. Pehle (ed.), *Der historische Ort des Nationalsozialismus* (Frankfurt am Main 1990), pp. 47–51.

15 For example, 'Ein mütiger Schritt', *Das Schwarze Korps*, 11 (March 1937), p. 18.

16 This worrying aspect of the Nazi youth cult was highlighted in SD reports concerning rumours of a 'euthanasia' programme for the elderly. See Götz Aly, 'SD-Berichte zu Gerüchten über "Euthanasie"-Massnahmen gegen alte Leute', *Beiträge zur nationalsozialistischen Gesundheits-und Sozialpolitik*, 11 (1993), p. 198. I am grateful to Götz Aly for a copy of this article.

17 Horst Dickel, '*Die sind doch alle unheilbar'. Zwangssterilisation und Tötung der 'Minderwertigen' im Rheingau 1934–1945* (Wiesbaden 1988), p. 84.
18 See the extracts from the report by Professor Kleist on Weilmünster reprinted in Imperial War Museum, London CIOS File no. xxviii–50, in Leo Alexander (ed.), *Public Mental Health Practice in Germany*, Appendix 6, p. 169. The accepted ratio of doctors to patients in the 1930s was about 1:180.
19 Manfred Klüppel, '*Euthanasie' und Lebensvernichtung am Beispiel der Landesheilanstalten Haina und Merxhausen* (Kassel 1985), pp. 17–18.
20 Martin Wisskirchen, 'Idiotenanstalt–Heilerziehungsanstalt–Lazarett', in C. Schrapper and D. Sengling (eds.), *Die Idee der Bildbarkeit* (Weinheim and Munich 1988), pp. 114ff.
21 This was the fate of Professor Kleist of the psychiatric clinic of the University of Frankfurt. For details of his reports see note 18 above.
22 Schleiermacher, 'Der Centralausschuss', p. 68. Given that Schneider was one of the main actors in the 'euthanasia' programme, his remarks are further illustrations of the dangers of conflating advocacy of sterilisation and 'euthanasia'.
23 Valentin Faltlhauser, 'Jahresbericht des Kreis- und Pflegeanstalt Kaufbeuren-Irsee des Jahres 1934', *Psychiatrisch-Neurologische Wochenschrift*, 37 (1935), p. 372. Pfannmüller became director of Eglfing-Haar in 1937.
24 Ibid., p. 372 for approving comments on this practice.
25 See Karl Ludwig Rost, *Sterilisation und Euthanasie im Film des 'Dritten Reiches'* (Husum 1987) for the details.
26 David Schöne and Dieter Schöne, 'Zur Entwicklung und klinischen Anwendung neuer somatischer Therapiemethoden der Psychiatrie in den 30er Jahren des 20. Jahrhunderts unter besonderer Berücksichtigung der Schocktherapien und deren Nützung in den deutschen Heil- und Pflegeanstalten', Med. Diss., University of Leipzig (1987).
27 Anton von Braunmühl, 'Die kombinierte Schock-Krampfbehandlung', *Zeitschrift für die gesamte Neurologie und Psychiatrie*, 164 (1938), pp. 72–3.
28 Staatsarchiv Munich Staatsanwaltschaften 17460/1, Trial of Hermann Pfannmüller, containing Pfannmüller's memorandum dated 1 November 1939: 'Organisations- und Wirtschaftlichkeits-prüfung bei der Heil- und Pflegeanstalt Eglfing-Haar', p. 9.
29 On Meltzer see the short piece by Jürgen Trögisch, 'Bericht über Euthanasie-Massnahmen im "Katherinenhof" Grosshennersdorf', *Fröhlich Helfen* (Berlin 1986), pp. 40ff.
30 Ewald Meltzer, *Das Problem der Abkürzung 'lebensunwerten' Lebens* (Halle 1925), pp. 87ff. for his poll.
31 Heinz Boberach (ed.), *Meldungen aus dem Reich. Die geheimen Lageberichte des Sicherheitsdienstes der SS 1938–1945* (Herrsching 1984), IX, pp. 3175–8.
32 See Ernst Klee, '*Die SA Jesu Christi'. Die Kirche im Banne Hitlers* (Frankfurt am Main 1989), p. 97.
33 Jeremy Noakes, 'Philipp Bouhler und die Kanzlei des Führers der NSDAP', in D. Rebentisch and Karl Teppe (eds.), *Verwaltung contra Menschenführung im Staat Hitlers* (Göttingen 1986), pp. 209ff.

34 Imperial War Museum, London, US. v. Karl Brandt *et al.* (1947), vol. 6, pp. 2396ff.
35 For examples of this see Klaus Bastlein, 'Die "Kinderfachabteilung" Schleswig 1941 bis 1945', ed. Arbeitskreis zur Erforschung des Nationalsozialismus in Schleswig-Holstein, *Informationen zur Schleswig-Holsteinischen Zeitgeschichte*, 20 (1993), p. 39.
36 Schmidt, *Selektion in der Heilanstalt*, p. 129. Henry Friedländer's *The Origins of Nazi Genocide* (Chapel Hill 1995) simply omits evidence that the Nazi 'euthanasia' programme was, in part, a response to requests for 'mercy killing' from distressed individuals or their relatives.
37 Imperial War Museum, London, US. v. Karl Brandt *et al.* (1947), vol. 4, p. 1549 (NO-1313), Friedrich Hölzel to Hermann Pfannmüller dated 20 August 1940.
38 Christopher Browning, 'Nazi Resettlement Policy and the Search for a Solution to the Jewish Question, 1939–1941', in his *Paths to Genocide* (Cambridge 1992), especially pp. 7ff.
39 For the details see Götz Aly (ed.), *Aktion T-4 1939–1945. Die 'Euthanasie'-Zentrale in der Tiergartenstrasse 4*, 2nd edition (Berlin 1989); for a shorter English account see Henry Friedländer, 'Euthanasia and the Final Solution', in David Cesarani (ed.), *The Final Solution* (London 1994), pp. 51ff.
40 Karl Morlok, *Wo bringt ihr uns hin?* (Stuttgart 1990), pp. 7–10 for how T-4 alighted upon Grafeneck; Zentrale Stelle des Landesjustizverwaltungen (Ludwigsburg), hereafter (ZSL), 'Euthanasie', Bra-Bz, interrogation of Viktor Brack dated 21 May 1948, p. 2 for the role of Linden in recommending doctors.
41 For an example of the outlook of these doctors, see Hessische Hauptstaatsarchiv, Wiesbaden (hereafter HHStAW), Abt. 461 Nr. 32061, Hadamar Trial, vol. 7, testimony of Bodo Gorgass dated 24 February 1947, pp. 1ff.
42 For example Paul R. (a former Hadamar orderly) in an interview with the author in September 1990: author's archive, tape transcript, p. 58.
43 Christina Vanya and Martin Vogt, 'Zu melden sind samtliche Patienten ...', in Vanya (ed.), *Euthanasie in Hadamar* (Kassel 1991), p. 29.
44 Hans Rössler, 'Die "Euthanasie" – Diskussion in Neuendettelsau 1937–1939', *Zeitschrift für bayerischen Kirchengeschichte*, 55 (1986), pp. 204ff.; Ernst Klee, *'Die SA Jesu Christi'. Die Kirche im Banne Hitlers* (Frankfurt am Main 1989), no. 40, pp. 180–1 for these details.
45 J. Thierfelder, 'Karsten Jaspersens Kampf gegen die NS-Krankenmorde', in Strohm and Thierfelder (eds.), *Diakonie im 'Dritten Reich'*, pp. 229ff.
46 Helmut Sorg, '"Euthanasie" in den evangelischen Heilanstalten in Württemberg im Dritten Reich', Magisterhausarbeit, FU (Berlin 1987), pp. 90–1.
47 Ernst Klee, *'Euthanasie' im NS-Staat* (Frankfurt am Main, 1985), especially pp. 320ff.
48 See the letter from Cardinal Faulhaber to Bishop Wienken dated 18 November 1940 reprinted in Ernst Klee (ed.), *Dokumente zur 'Euthanasie'* (Frankfurt am Main 1986), pp. 182–4. On Wienken see especially Martin

Höllen, 'Katholische Kirche und NS-"Euthanasie"', *Zeitschrift für Kirchengeschichte*, 91 (1980), pp. 53ff.

49 National Archives, Washington, T1021 Roll 18, Hartheim Statistics, p. 4.

50 See Walter Grode, *Die 'Sonderbehandlung 14f13' in den Konzentrationslagern des Dritten Reiches. Ein Beitrag zur Dynamik faschistischer Vernichtungspolitik* (Frankfurt am Main, 1987).

51 Imperial War Museum, London, US. v. Karl Brandt *et al.* (1947), vol. 16, p. 7508.

52 ZSL, 'Euthanasie', Na-Oz, interrogation of Josef Oberhauser dated 4 February 1963, pp. 6–7 for the 'loan' of T-4 personnel to Globocnik.

53 Berlin Document Centre, 0.401 Odilo Globocnik, 'Bericht über die Verwaltungsmässige Abwicklung der Aktion Reinhardt' dated December 1943.

54 Carlo Schiffrer, *La Risiera* (Trieste 1961), for one of the few accounts of this Dalmatian coast extermination centre.

55 Staatsarchiv Augsburg, Staatsanwaltschaften IKs/1949, Trial of Valentin Faltlhauser *et al.*, file containing graphs illustrating the mortality rate and Pauline Kneissler's presence or absence.

56 HHStAW Abt. 461 Nr. 32442, Eichberg Trial, vol. 2, testimony of Friedrich Mennecke dated 3 May 1946, p. 30; and Abt. 461, Nr. 31526, Idstein Trial, vol. 1, report of an inquiry into Wilhelm Grossmann dated 21 January 1945, pp. 1–6 for examples of the deliberate diversion of asylum produce.

57 For numerous examples see Peter Chroust (ed.), *Friedrich Mennecke. Innenansichten eines medizinischen Täters im Nationalsozialismus. Eine Edition seiner Briefe 1935–1945* (Hamburg 1988), vol. 1, no. 120, p. 359; no. 131, p. 407, etc.

58 Mathias Hamann, 'Die Morde an polnischen und sowjetischen Zwangsarbeitern in deutschen Anstalten', *Beiträge zur nationalsozialistischen Gesundheits- und Sozialpolitik,* 2nd edition, I (Berlin 1987), pp. 121–87.

59 Götz Aly, 'SD Berichte', pp. 196–8.

60 For a rather literal-minded discussion of these claims see Hans-Walter Schmuhl, 'Reformpsychiatrie und Massenmord', in M. Prinz and R. Zitelmann (eds.), *Nationalsozialismus und Modernisierung* (Darmstadt 1991), pp. 239ff.

61 For a description of actual conditions in the asylums during this period see HHStAW, Abt. 461, Nr. 32442, Eichberg Trial, vol. 1, testimony of Dr Elisabeth V. dated 9 August 1945, pp. 1–15. Dr V. was being rather unfair to the Middle Ages, and indeed probably to most centuries prior to the present one.

5. THE CHURCHES, EUGENICS AND THE NAZI 'EUTHANASIA' PROGRAMME

1 Kurt Nowak, 'Sterilisation, Krankenmord und Innere Mission im "Dritten Reich"' (hereafter Nowak, 'Sterilisation'), in A. Thom and G. Caregorodcev

(eds.), *Medizin unterm hakenkreuz* (Berlin 1989), p. 1688. See also Paul Weindling, *Health, Race and German Politics from National Unification to Nazism* (Cambridge 1989), pp. 388ff., for the general context.

2 Sabine Schleiermacher, 'Der Centralausschuss für die Innere Mission und die Eugenik am Vorabend des "Dritten Reichs"', in T. Strohm and J. Thierfelder (eds.), *Diakonie im 'Dritten Reich'* (Heidelberg 1990), p. 68.

3 Kurt Nowak, *'Euthanasie' und Sterilsation im Dritten Reich'. Die Konfrontation der evangelischen und katholischen Kirche mit dem 'Gesetz zur Verhütung Erbkranken Nachwuchses' und der 'Euthanasie'-Aktion,* 3rd edition (Göttingen 1984), pp. 92–5.

4 Schleiermacher, 'Der Centralausschuss', p. 70.

5 Nowak, '*Euthanasie*', p. 96.

6 Hans-Walter Schmuhl, *Rassenhygiene, Nationalsozialismus, Euthanasie. Von der Verhütung zur Vernichtung 'lebensunwerten Lebens' 1890–1945* (Göttingen 1987), p. 307.

7 Peter Göbel and Helmut Thormann (eds.), *Verlegt–vernichtet–vergessen? Leidenswege von Menschen aus Hephata im Dritten Reich* (Schwalmstadt-Treysa 1984), pp. 17ff. Published in-house at the Hephata Asylum.

8 Helmut Sorg, '"Euthanasie" in den evangelischen Heilanstalten in Württemberg im Dritten Reich', unpublished Magisterarbeit, FU (Berlin 1987), pp. 60–1.

9 Göbel and Thormann, *Verlegt–vernichtet–vergessen?*, pp. 14–15.

10 Christoph Mehl, 'Das Stephansstift im Jahr 1933', in Strohm and Thierfelder, *Diakonie*, pp. 153ff.

11 Paul Weindling, 'Weimar Eugenics: the Kaiser Wilhelm Institute for Anthropology, Human Heredity and Eugenics in Social Context', *Annals of Science*, 42 (1985), p. 316.

12 Guenther Lewy, *The Catholic Church and Nazi Germany* (London 1964), pp. 258–63; see Cornelia Hosei and Birgit Weber-Dietzmann, 'Zwangssterilisation an Hadamarer Anstaltsinsassen', in Dorothee Roer and Dieter Henkel (eds.), *Psychiatrie im Faschismus* (Bonn 1986), p. 134.

13 Gernot Römer, *Die Grauen Busse in Schwaben* (Augsburg 1986), pp. 35–7.

14 Karl Binding and Alfred Hoche, *Die Freigabe der Vernichtung lebensunwerten Lebens. Ihr Mass und Ihre Form* (Leipzig 1920).

15 Nowak, '*Euthanasie*', p. 121.

16 Ewald Meltzer, *Das Problem der Abkürzung 'lebensunwerten' Lebens* (Halle a. S. 1925).

17 Ernst Klee, *'Die SA Jesu Christi'. Die Kirche in Banne Hitlers* (Frankfurt am Main 1989), p. 97.

18 Hans Rössler, 'Die "Euthanasie"-Diskussion in Neuendettelsau 1937–1939', *Zeitschrift für bayerischen Kirchengeschichte*, 55 (1986), pp. 204ff.

19 Völker Riess, 'Auswirkungen der NS-Psychiatrie auf Einrichtungen im ehemaligen Gebiet Hessen-Darmstadt', in Landeswohlfahrtsverband Hessen (ed.), *Psychiatrie im Nationalsozialismus* (Kassel 1989), pp. 101–2; Friedrich Stöffler, 'Die "Euthanasie" im Dritten Reich', in Landeswohlfahrtsverband Hessen (ed.), *Mensch-Achte den Menschen* (Kassel 1985), pp. 57–8.

20 Götz Aly (ed.), *Aktion T-4 1939–1945* (Berlin 1987).
21 Karl Morlok, *Wo bringt ihr uns hin?* (Stuggart 1985), pp. 34–8.
22 Hessische Hauptstaatsarchiv, Wiesbaden (thereafter HHStAW) 631a/353, testimony of Dr Josef Wrede, 10/11 December 1947, p. 2.
23 HHStAW 631a/359 testimony of Dr Gebhard Ritter, May 1948, p. 1.
24 J. Thierfelder, 'Karsten Jaspersens Kampf gegen die NS-Krankenmorde', in Strohm and Thierfelder, *Diakonie*, pp. 229ff.
25 Gerhard Schmidt, *Selektion in der Heilanstalt 1939–1945* (Frankfurt am Main 1983), p. 52.
26 Ernst Klee (ed.), *Dokumente zur 'Euthanasie'* (Frankfurt am Main 1985), no. 71a for the selection criteria used by Gerhard Schorsch, pp. 188–9.
27 Sorg, '"Euthanasie"'.
28 Römer, *Die Grauen Busse*, p. 88.
29 Zentrale Stelle des Landesjustizverwaltungen, Ludwigsburg (thereafter ZSL), 'Euthanasie', Na-Oz, testimony of Adolf Nell (n.d.), p. 2.
30 Ludwig Schlaich, *Vernichtung und Neuanfang. Das Schicksal der Heil- und Plegeanstalten in Stetten i. R.* (Stuttgart 1946), p. 29. Published in-house in the Stetten Asylum.
31 Sorg, '"Euthanasie"', pp. 90–1.
32 Hans-Josef Wollasch, 'Caritas und Euthanasie im Dritten Reich', in Wollasch (ed.), *Beiträge zur Geschichte der deutschen Caritas in der Zeit der Weltkriege* (Freiburg im Breisgau 1978), p. 222.
33 Klee, *Dokumente*, no. 60, Theophil Wurm to the Reich Minister of the Interior dated 19 July 1940, p. 164. For the responses of the judicial administration to the 'euthanasia' programme, see Lothar Gruchmann, *Justiz im Dritten Reich* (Munich 1990).
34 Ibid., no. 59, memorandum by Pastor Paul Gerhard Braune dated 9 July 1940, p. 154.
35 Schmuhl, *Rassenhygiene*, p. 335.
36 ZSL, 'Euthanasie', Hefelmann, interrogation of Hans Hefelmann on 30 January 1961, pp. 11–12. On Wienken see especially Martin Höllen, 'Katholische Kirche und NS-"Euthanasie"', *Zeitschrift für Kirchengeschichte*, 91 (1980), pp. 53ff. On Mayer see Donald Dietrich, 'Joseph Mayer and the Missing Memo: a Catholic Justification for Euthanasia', *Remembering for the Future*, I (Oxford 1988), pp. 38–49.
37 Klee, *Dokumente*, no. 68, Cardinal Michael Faulhaber to Bishop Heinrich Wienken dated 18 November 1940, pp. 182–3.
38 Peter Löffler (ed.), *Clemens August Graf von Galen: Akten, Briefe, Predigten 1933–1946*, II (Mainz 1988), p. 543.
39 Thierfelder, 'Karsten Jaspersens Kampf', p. 233.
40 Klee, *Dokumente*, Cardinal Bertram to Dr Heinrich Lammers dated 11 August 1940, pp. 170–3.
41 Joachim Kurokpa (ed.), *Clemens August Graf von Galen. Sein Leben und Wirken in Bildern und Dokumenten* (Cloppenburg 1992), pp. 199–201.
42 Löffler, *Von Galen*, II, p. 878.
43 H. Trevor-Roper (ed.), *Hitler's Table Talk 1941–44* (Oxford 1988), p. 555.

44 Lewy, *Catholic Church*, p. 266.
45 ZSL, 'Euthanasie', Hefelmann, interrogation of Hans Hefelmann on 14 September 1960, p. 32; on 'Aktion 14f13' see Walter Grode, *Die Sonderbehandlung 14f13 in den Konzentrationslagern des Dritten Reiches* (Frankfurt am Main 1987).
46 F. Kaul, *Die Psychiatrie im Strudel der Euthanasie* (Frankfurt am Main 1979), pp. 63ff.
47 Imperial War Museum, London, Medical Trial, Case 1, US v. Karl Brandt *et al.* (May 1947), vol. 16, p. 7508 (May 1947).

6. THE NAZI ANALOGY AND CONTEMPORARY DEBATES ON EUTHANASIA

1 For example see Omer Bartov, 'Chambers of Horror: the Reordering of Murders Past', in Omer Bartov (ed.), *Murder in Our Midst. The Holocaust, Industrial Killing and Representation* (New York 1960), pp. 153ff.
2 Yehuda Bauer, 'The Significance of the Final Solution', in David Cesarani (ed.), *The Final Solution* (London 1994), pp. 300–9.
3 Michael Andre Bernstein, *Foregone Conclusions. Against Apocalyptic History* (Berkeley 1994), pp. 89–94.
4 Steve Jones, *The Language of the Genes* (London 1993), p. 8.
5 Michael Burleigh, *Germany Turns Eastwards: a Study of 'Ostforschung' in the Third Reich* (Cambridge 1988) deals with this subject tangentially.
6 Peter Singer, 'On Being Silenced in Germany', *The New York Review of Books*, 38 (1991), pp. 34ff. See also his 'Bioethics and Academic Freedom', *Bioethics*, 4 (1990), pp. 33–44. It is worth noting that in Britain, Singer has been feted as one of the thinkers whose work will have a major influence on our futures, as indeed the legalisation of voluntary euthanasia in the Northern Territories of Australia seems to bear out.
7 Bryan Appleyard, 'A moral life in this godless world', Thinkers of the Nineties, *The Independent* 13 November 1995, p. 19; Peter Singer, *Practical Ethics* (Cambridge 1979).
8 Michael Donnelly, *The Politics of Mental Health in Italy* (London 1992), p. 71 shows that the Italian Communist Party (PCI) was one the most enthusiastic promoters of psychiatric reform as advocated by Psichiatria Democratica. The negative effects of law 180 are as evident in Italy as they are in Britain.
9 *Biomedical Ethics and the Shadow of Nazism*, Hastings Center Report, Special Supplement, August 1976.
10 Ibid., p. 4.
11 Ibid., p. 7.
12 Ibid., p. 9.
13 Ibid., p. 10.
14 See Frank Dikötter, 'Throw-away Babies. The Growth of Eugenic Policies and Practices in China', *Times Literary Supplement* 12 January 1996, pp. 4–5 for an excellent account. See also 'Euthanasia Fears for Old in China', *The Sunday Times* 21 April 1996, p. 20.

15 *Biomedical Ethics*, p. 13.
16 Ibid., p. 16.
17 Ibid., p. 18.
18 *The Nazi Analogy in Bioethics*, Hastings Center Report, August/September 1988, pp. 29–33.
19 Ibid., p. 30.
20 Ibid., p. 33.
21 On the Cruzan case see Ronald Dworkin, *Life's Dominion. An Argument about Abortion and Euthanasia* (London 1993), pp. 180ff.
22 Arthur L. Caplan, 'The Doctors' Trial and Analogies to the Holocaust in Contemporary Bioethical Debates', in George Annas and Michael Grodin (eds.), *The Nazi Doctors and the Nuremberg Code* (New York 1992), pp. 258ff.
23 Arthur Caplan, 'The Relevance of the Holocaust to Bioethics Today', in John Michalzyk (ed.), *Medicine, Ethics and the Third Reich. Historical and Contemporary Issues* (Kansas 1994), p. 4.
24 Michael Burleigh, *Death and Deliverance. 'Euthanasia' in Germany c. 1900–1945* (Cambridge 1994).

8. A 'POLITICAL ECONOMY OF THE FINAL SOLUTION'? REFLECTIONS ON MODERNITY, HISTORIANS AND THE HOLOCAUST

1 On the 'Historikerstreit' see Piper Verlag (ed.), *'Historikerstreit': die Dokumentation der Kontroverse um die Einzigartigkeit der nationalsozialistischen Judenvernichtung* (Munich 1987); the debate regarding the 'historicisation' of National Socialism can be followed in Peter Baldwin (ed.), *Reworking the Past. Hitler, the Holocaust and the Historians' Debate* (Boston, Mass. 1990); for a sampling of 'postmodern' approaches to the Holocaust see Saul Friedlander (ed.), *Probing the Limits of Representation. Nazism and the 'Final Solution'* (Cambridge, Mass. 1993), or Dominick La Capra, *Representing the Holocaust. History, Theory, Trauma* (New York 1994). For a powerful critique of postmodernism and the Holocaust see Steven Aschheim, *Culture and Catastrophe* (London 1996), pp. 12ff.
2 The work of Christopher Browning is especially symptomatic in this respect; see his edited collection *The Path to Genocide: Essays on Launching the Final Solution* (Cambridge 1992).
3 Ian Kershaw, *The Nazi Dictatorship* (London 1993), pp. 80ff. Apart from films, novels and plays, see the different approaches discussed in Michael Burleigh, 'Writing the Holocaust', *Times Literary Supplement* 3 March 1995, pp. 12–13, a modified version of which appears as chapter 9 below.
4 Götz Aly, Jochen August, Peter Chroust, Klaus Dorner, Matthias Hamann, Hans-Dieter Heilmann, Susanne Heim, Franz Koch, Christian Pross, Ulrich Schultz and Christian Teller (eds.), *Beiträge zur nationalsozialistischen Gesundheits- und Sozialpolitik* (Berlin 1987–), 12 volumes. See also Michael Burleigh, 'Nazi Social Policies', *Polin. A Journal of Polish-Jewish Studies*, 4 (Oxford 1989), pp. 462–6 for an appreciation of the first six volumes.

5 Norbert Frei, 'Wie modern war der Nationalsozialismus', *Geschichte und Gesellschaft*, 19 (1993), p. 369.
6 Götz Aly, 'Wider das Bewältigungs-Kleinklein', in Hanno Loewy (ed.), *Holocaust: die Grenzen des Verstehens* (Hamburg 1992), p. 48.
7 Ernst Köhler, 'Das Morden theoretisch eingeebnet', in Wolfgang Schneider (ed.), *'Vernichtungspolitik'. Eine debatte über den Zusammenhang von Sozialpolitik und Genozid im nationalsozialistischen Deutschland* (Hamburg 1991), p. 89.
8 Susanne Heim and Götz Aly, *Ein Berater der Macht. Helmut Meinhold oder der Zusammenhang zwischen Sozialpolitik und Judenvernichtung* (Hamburg 1986).
9 Ibid., p. 31.
10 Ibid., p. 45.
11 Ibid., p. 50.
12 Ibid., p. 55.
13 Susanne Heim and Götz Aly, 'Die Ökonomie der Endlösung?', *Beiträge zur nationalsozialistischen Gesundhetis- und Sozialpolitik*, 5 (Berlin 1987), p. 8. The ensuing 1989 conference which debated these questions has been made more widely available in Schneider (ed.), *'Vernichtungspolitk'. Eine Debatte über den Zusammenhang von Sozialpolitik und Genozid im nationalsozialistischen Deutschland.*
14 Michael Burleigh, *Germany Turns Eastwards: a Study of 'Ostforschung' in the Third Reich* (Cambridge 1988). Angelika Ebbinghaus and Karl-Heinz Roth, 'Vorläufer des "Generalplans Ost". Eine Dokumentation über Theodor Scheiders Polendenkschrift vom 7. Oktober 1939', *1999. Zeitschrift für Sozialgeschichte des 20. und 21. Jahrhunderts*, 7 (1992), pp. 62–94, makes no mention of this author's discovery and discussion of these documents, an oversight corrected in a subsequent issue.
15 Heim and Aly, 'Die Ökonomie der Endlösung?', p. 14.
16 Götz Aly and Susanne Heim, *Vordenker der Vernichtung. Auschwitz und die deutschen Pläne für eine neue europäische Ordnung* (Hamburg 1991).
17 Susanne Heim and Götz Aly, 'The Holocaust and Population Policy: Remarks on the Decision on the "Final Solution"', *Yad Vashem Studies*, 24 (1994), p. 46; see also Götz Aly and Susanne Heim, 'The Economics of the Final Solution: a Case Study from the General Government', *Simon Wiesenthal Center Annual*, 5 (1988), pp. 3–48; and Götz Aly, 'The Planning Intelligentsia and the Final Solution', in Michael Burleigh (ed.), *Confronting the Nazi Past. New Debates on Modern German History* (London 1996), pp. 140–53.
18 Aly, 'Wider das Bewältigungs-Kleinklein', p. 51.
19 Christopher R. Browning, 'German Technocrats, Jewish Labor, and the Final Solution: a Reply to Götz Aly and Susanne Heim', in Browning (ed.), *The Path to Genocide*, pp. 59ff.
20 Hermann Graml, 'Irregeleitet und in die Irre führend', *Jahrbuch fur Antisemitismusforschung*, 1 (1992), p. 291.
21 On Reche see Michael Burleigh, 'Die Stunde der Experten', in M. Rössler and S. Schleiermacher (eds.), *Der 'Generalplanost'. Hauptlinien der national-*

sozialistischen Planungs- und Vernichtungspolitik (Berlin 1993), pp. 346ff., and *Germany Turns Eastwards*, pp. 126–8, 166–76, 224–6, 241–4, 246–7.

22 Heim and Aly, *Vordenker*, pp. 23ff., 49ff., 68.

23 Jeremy Noakes and G. Pridham, *Nazism 1919–1945*, III (Exeter 1988), pp. 1103–5.

24 Ulrich Herbert, 'Racism and Rational Calculation: the Role of "Utilitarian" Strategies of Legitimation in the National Socialist Weltanschauung', *Yad Vashem Studies*, 24 (1994), p. 133.

25 Ulrich Herbert, 'Arbeit und Vernichtung: Ökonomisches Interesse und Primat der "Weltanschauung" im Nationalsozialismus', in Dan Diner (ed.), *Ist der Nationalsozialismus Geschichte?* (Frankfurt am Main 1987), pp. 198ff.

26 Heim and Aly, 'Die Ökonomie der Endlösung?', p. 14, where this first question is posed but not answered.

27 On the targeting of all Jewish psychiatric patients see Henry Friedländer, *The Origins of Nazi Genocide* (Chapel Hill 1995), p. 282; on the 'euthanasia' programme see also Michael Burleigh, *Death and Deliverance: 'Euthanasia' in Germany 1900–1945* (Cambridge 1994).

28 Martin Housden, 'Population, Economics and Genocide: Aly and Heim versus All-Comers in the Interpretation of the Holocaust', *The Historical Journal*, 38 (1995), p. 485.

29 Dan Diner, 'Rationalization and Method', *Yad Vashem Studies*, 24 (1994), p. 87.

30 Dan Diner, 'Rationalisierung und Methode', *Vierteljahrshefte für Zeitgeschichte*, 40 (1992), p. 368; see also Aly, 'Erwiderung auf Dan Diner', *Vierteljahrshefte für Zeitgeschichte*, 41 (1993), pp. 621ff.

31 Cited in Matthew Cooper, *The Phantom War* (London 1979), p. 57.

32 Diner, 'Rationalization', p. 87.

33 Heim and Aly, *Ein Berater der Macht*, p. 4.

34 On this see Alain Finkielkraut, *Remembering in Vain. The Klaus Barbie Trial and Crimes against Humanity* (New York 1992), pp. 59–60.

35 Herbert, 'Racism and Rational Calculation', p. 135.

36 Michael Burleigh and Wolfgang Wippermann, *The Racial State: Germany 1933–1945* (Cambridge 1991).

37 Axel Schmidt, 'NS-Regime, Modernisierung und Moderne. Anmerkungen zur Hochkonjunktur einer andauernden Diskussion', *Tel Aviver Jahrbuch für deutsche Geschichte*, 23 (1994), pp. 4–5.

38 Mark Roseman, 'National Socialism and Modernisation', in Richard Bessel (ed.), *Fascist Italy and Nazi Germany. Comparisons and Contrasts* (Cambridge 1996), pp. 197ff. Roseman's otherwise cogent piece neglects the earlier forms of modernisation theory discussed by Schmidt. The introduction to this volume implies on pp. 4–5 that Wolfgang Wippermann and I tried in *The Racial State* to delegitimise historical comparisons by stressing the unique racial character of the Nazi regime. This is tilting at windmills in a book which apparently does not regard Nazi or Italian Fascist racism as worthy of separate consideration, an omission so redolent of its dedicatee, the late Timothy Mason. Apart from the fact that Wippermann has

published very extensively on comparative theories of Fascism, and indeed on Italian Fascist racism (for example, 'War der italienischen Faschismus rassistisch?' in Werner Röhr (ed.), *Faschismus und Rassismus* (Berlin 1992), pp. 108ff.), on p. 20 of the *Racial State* we explicitly state the need for more comparative studies.

39 Frei, 'Wie modern', p. 367; Maria Quine's long-awaited brief textbook on population policy, *Population Politics in Twentieth Century Europe* (London 1996), p. 130, refers to our discussion of 'defunct debates' about modernisation. Since her discussion of Nazi Germany functions without reference to any German-language literature she can be forgiven for overlooking the vast body of material discussed in this chapter produced in Germany in the last ten years and which can therefore hardly be described as 'defunct'. The neglect of arguments based on alleged overpopulation is especially unfortunate in a book on 'Population Politics'!

40 Roseman, 'National Socialism and Modernisation', p. 198, shrewdly points out that we are not even sure if 'modernisation' and 'modernity' exist.

41 Rainer Zitelmann, *Hitler. Selbstverständnis eines Revolutionärs* (Stuttgart 1990); Michael Prinz and Rainer Zitelmann (eds.), *Nationalsozialismus und Modernisierung* (Darmstadt 1991). Here I find myself in broad agreement with Hans Mommsen's 'Nationalsozialismus als vorgetäuschte Modernisierung', in Dan Diner (ed.), *Der historische Ort des Nationalsozialismus* (Frankfurt am Main 1990), pp. 31ff.

42 Detlev Peukert, 'The Genesis of the "Final Solution" from the Spirit of Science', in David Crew (ed.), *Nazism and German Society 1933–1945* (London 1994), pp. 274ff.

43 Ian Kershaw, 'Totalitarianism Revisited: Nazism and Stalinism in Comparative Perspective', *Tel Aviver Jahrbuch fur deutsche Geschichte*, 23 (1994), p. 34, for this rather charitable interpretation; and Richard Rubenstein, 'Modernization and the Politics of Extermination', in Michael Berenbaum (ed.), *A Mosaic of Victims. Non-Jews Persecuted and Murdered by the Nazis* (London 1990), pp. 20ff.

44 Jonathan Steinberg, 'The Holocaust, Society and Ourselves', *The Jewish Quarterly*, 153 (1994), p. 50.

45 Zygmunt Baumann, *Modernity and the Holocaust* (Cambridge 1991).

46 See James Miller, *The Passion of Michel Foucault* (London 1993), p. 309, for Foucault's enthusiastic description of the Iranian revolution as 'the first great insurrection against the planetary system, the most mad and most modern form of revolt', a perception that in respect of the ensuing madness, i.e. murder and torture, perpetrated in Iran and abroad by this terroristic state has proved all too true; see also Finkielkraut, *Remembering in Vain* (New York 1992).

9. THE REALM OF SHADOWS: RECENT WRITING ON THE HOLOCAUST

1 Jack O'Sullivan, 'Irving and Sereny go to War', *The Independent* 6 June 1996, section two, pp. 2–3.

2 Tony Kushner, *The Holocaust and the Liberal Imagination* (Oxford 1994).
3 E. Thomas Wood and Stanislaw M. Jankowski, *Karski. How One Man Tried to Stop the Holocaust* (New York 1994).
4 Yehuda Bauer, *Jews for Sale? Nazi–Jewish Negotiations, 1933–1945* (New Haven 1994).
5 Raul Hilberg, *Unerbetene Erinnerung: der Weg eines Holocaust-Forschers* (Frankfurt am Main 1994).
6 Michael André Bernstein, *Foregone Conclusions* (Berkeley 1994).
7 Steven T. Katz, *The Holocaust in Historical Context: the Holocaust and Mass Death Before the Modern Age* (New York and Oxford 1994).
8 Roger Boyes, 'Kinkel Urges Nation to Dispel Holocaust Guilt', *The Times* 9 May 1996, p. 13.
9 Christopher R. Browning, *Paths to Genocide* (Cambridge 1995), is very typical.
10 Philippe Burrin, *Hitler and the Jews: the Genesis of the Holocaust* (London 1994).
11 Daniel Jonah Goldhagen, *Hitler's Willing Executioners. Ordinary Germans and the Holocaust* (New York and London 1996). For an intelligent survey of the affair, see Volker Ulrich, 'Goldhagen und die Deutschen', *Die Zeit* Nr. 38, 13 September 1996, p. 2.
12 See chapter 8 below. Here there are signs that Goldhagen simply does not understand the arguments he is criticising.
13 Hans Safrian and Hans Witek (eds.), *Und keiner war dabei. Dokumente des alltaglichen Antisemitismus in Wien* (Vienna 1988).
14 Hans Safrian, *Eichmann und seine Gehilfen* (Frankfurt am Main 1995).
15 Dieter Pohl, *Von der 'Judepolitik' zum Judenmord. Der Distrikt Lublin des Generalgouvernement 1939–1944* (Frankfurt am Main 1993).
16 Gordon J. Horwitz, *In the Shadow of Death. Living outside the Gates of Mauthausen* (London 1991).
17 Calel Perechodnik, *Am I a Murderer? Testament of a Jewish Ghetto Policeman* (Boulder 1996).
18 David A. Hackett (ed.) *The Buchenwald Report* (Boulder 1995).
19 Hermann Langbein, *Against All Hope. Resistance in the Nazi Concentration Camps 1938–1945* (London 1994).
20 Yisrael Gutman and Michael Berenbaum (eds.), *Anatomy of the Auschwitz Death Camp* (Bloomington 1994).
21 Steven E. Aschheim, *Culture and Catastrophe. German and Jewish Confrontations with National Socialism and Other Crises* (London 1996).
22 Omer Bartov, *Murder in Our Midst. The Holocaust, Industrial Killing, and Representation* (New York 1996).

Index

Alexander, Leo 147
Allen, Jim 189
Aly, Götz 170ff
Amichai, Yehuda 195
Amsterdam 176
anti-partisan warfare 100ff., 177
anti-Semitism 155, 158–9, 160, 168, 172, 176, 179, 184, 190, 197–8, 201–4, 220–1
Antonescu, Ion 58
Arafat, Yasser 222
Applefield, Aharon 194
Arendt, Hannah 193, 221–2
Arnim, Hans-Jürgen von 69–70
Arrow Cross 192
Artamanen League 19–20
Aschheim, Steven 220ff.
Astel, Karl 164
asylums 14, 116–29, 130–41, 160–1
Aubin, Hermann 27, 28, 33, 36, 173
Auschwitz 71, 127, 167, 176, 183–4, 217–19, 233
Austria 204, 205, 210–12

Bach-Zelewski, Erich von dem 70, 104ff., 107–8, 177
Backe, Herbert 62, 89, 90, 94
Bandera, Stepan 81, 102
Bankier, David 156, 220
Barkai, Avraham 198
Bartov, Omer 220, 222ff.
Bauer, Erich 127
Bauer, Yehuda 142–3, 189ff., 220
Becker, Otto 26
Begin, Menachem 222
Belsen 185
Belzec 127, 167, 187, 206, 207, 209, 210
Beria, Lavrenty 38–9, 51
Bernotat, Fritz 117
Bernstein, Leonard 188
Bernstein, Michael André 143, 193
Bertram, Adolf Cardinal 140
Binding, Karl 3, 114–15, 121, 133
Bismarck, Otto von 10
Bland, Anthony 145, 151
Boeckh, Rudolph 125, 133–4
Boeters, Heinrich 133
Bormann, Martin 79, 140
Bornewasser, Franz Rudolf 41
Boswell, John 196
Botz, Gerhard 204
Bouhler, Philipp 122, 127
Borkenau, Franz 179
Bosnia 224
Brack, Viktor 126, 141
Brackmann, Albert 2, 10, 25ff
Brand, Joel 191
Brandt, Karl 122, 165
Braune, Gerhard 137, 138
Brauschitsch, Walther von 66
Brest-Litovsk 37, 39–40
British Union of Fascists 185
Broszat, Martin 180, 208
Browning, Christopher 175, 199, 201, 202
Brüning, Heinrich 163
Burger, Anton, 207
Burrin, Philippe 187ff., 223

CNN 181, 224
Callahan, Dan 149, 150
Cambodia 189, 224
Caucasus 80, 82, 84

Caplan, Arthur 150
Caritas Association 132, 133
Chamberlain, Houston Stewart 158
Chancellery of the Führer 122, 123, 124, 134, 165
Chechens 3, 79
China, Communist 5, 148, 149, 152, 180
Chuikov, Vasily Ivanovich 53
Class, Heinrich 15
Cohen, Cynthia 150
Conze, Werner 2, 173
Copenhagen 176
Coppola, Francis Ford 224
Cossacks 3, 42, 79, 84–5
Cracow 32, 33, 172, 207, 208
Crick, Francis 146
Crinis, Maximian de 124
Crossmann, Richard 216
Cruzan, Nancy 150–1
Czerniakow, Adam 193

Dachau 71, 166, 211, 217, 220
Darwin, Charles 156
Davenport, Charles 158
Davies, Norman 3
Dawidowicz, Lucy 146, 148, 193
Deininger, Franziskus 132
Dekanozov, Vladimir 37–8
Diner, Dan 173, 176–7, 178
Dirlewanger, Oskar 102, 209
Drancy 183
'Drang nach Osten' 27, 31
Dresden 183
Drögereit, Richard 27
Düsseldorf 167
Dwinger, Erwin 42

Eastern Marches Association 16, 26
Ebbinghaus, Angelica 170
Ehrenburg, Ilya 73–4
Eichberg 118, 127
Eichendorff, Joseph Freiherr von 9
Eichmann, Adolf 143, 190, 191, 204, 205, 206
Eicke, Theodor 71
Eimann, Kurt 123
Eisenstein, Sergei 9
Emmerich, Walter 171
euthanasia, contemporary debates 142ff.
'euthanasia' Nazi programme 3–5, 113ff., 122ff., 165, 167, 170
  churches and: 125, 126, 130ff.
  relationship to sterilisation: 161
  Weimar debates 114–15, 116–17, 130–3, 151

Faulhaber, Cardinal Michael 139
Fleischmann, Gizi 190
Finland 40–1, 42, 45, 53, 80, 96
Flossenbürg 71, 162
Foucault, Michel 181
Frank, Hans 32, 207, 208
Frank, Walter 26, 31
Frankfurt Parliament 14
Frankfurter, Felix 188
Franz, Kurt 127
Frederick the Great, 10, 12, 16, 32
Frei, Norbert 179
Freytag, Gustav 9, 10
Frick, Constantin 138
Frick, Wilhelm 26, 34, 165

Galen, Klemens August Graf von 41, 126, 139, 164–165
Gehlen, Reinhard 84
Gellately, Robert 3, 156
Generalgouvernement 94, 172, 176, 207, 209
Generalplan Ost 174
German Democratic Republic (DDR) 9–10
Gersdorff, Rudolf Christoph Freiherr von 82
Globke, Hans 160
Globocnik, Odilo 127, 141, 206, 208, 209, 210
Gobineau, Joseph Arthur Comte de 156, 223
Goebbels, Joseph 210
Goeth, Amon 183
Goldhagen, Daniel Jonah 196ff., 207
Göring, Hermann 26, 79, 104–5, 125, 175, 176, 200, 217
Gottberg, Curt von 106
Grafeneck 135, 137, 138
Graml, Hermann 175, 198
Grass, Günter 9
Grawitz, Robert 165
Greiser, Artur 206
Grossmann, Vasily 51
Gross Rosen 71, 162
Grotjahn, Alfred 157
gulags (Soviet) 49, 52
Gutman Yisrael 220
Gütt, Artur 165

Hackenholt, Lorenz 127
Hackett, David 216
Haecklel, Ernst 157
Haina 118
Halder, Franz 43, 52, 64, 67, 95
Hanseatic League 9
Harmsen, Hans 130

Hartl, Albert 138
Hastings Center for Bioethics 146
Hefelmann, Hans 139
Heim, Susanne 170ff
Heinrich I, 31
Hemlock Society 4
Hentoff, Natt 149
Hentschel, Willibald 19
Hephata 131, 136
Herbert, Ulrich 176, 178
Herder, Johann Gottfried 11–12, 13, 23, 156
Hereditary Health Courts 118, 161, 163
Heyde, Werner 123, 124
Heydrich, Reinhard 66, 92, 143, 166, 175, 176, 199, 200, 205, 206
Hilberg, Raul 6, 192ff.
Hillgruber, Andreas 170, 180
Himmelfarb, Milton 146, 147, 149
Himmler, Heinrich 20, 22–4, 31, 83, 88, 92–3, 94, 104, 126, 163, 165–6, 170, 175, 191, 196, 199, 200, 203, 206, 208–9, 218
Hindenburg, Paul 10, 20
Historikerstreit 169
Hitler, Adolf 10, 20, 26, 27, 31, 32, 35, 38, 40, 41, 42, 44, 47, 50, 52, 54, 57, 58, 59, 61, 64, 65, 66, 72, 77ff., 82, 88, 89, 90, 95, 105, 107, 113, 121, 122, 123, 138, 140, 141, 145, 146, 156, 158, 161, 165, 170, 173, 175, 180, 182, 190, 191, 196, 197, 198, 199, 200, 203, 204, 207, 210, 217, 221, 223
Hoche, Alfred 3, 114–15, 121, 133
Hoepner, Erich 68–9
Hoess, Rudolf 20, 127, 219
Hölzel, Friedrich 123
homophobia 162
Hoth, Hermann 55, 59, 69

Idstein 118
Imperial War Museum 185
India 78
Ingush 3
Inner Mission 182, 220, 222
Institut für deutsche Ostarbeit 32ff.
Israel 182, 220, 222

Jäckel, Eberhard 170
Jakobson, Sergei 26
Jaspers, Karl 211
Jaspersen, Karsten 125, 126, 135, 136, 139–40
Jews 3, 30, 34, 68–9, 75, 80, 93, 94, 108, 109, 110, 121, 125–7, 141, 155, 158–9, 160, 166, 168, 170, 172, 173, 174, 175, 176, 177, 179, 182, 183ff
Jodl, Alfred 42, 65
Johst, Hanns 218
Jones, Steve 144
Jordan, Wilhelm 14

Kalmyks 84, 85
Kaminski, Bronislav 102
Karski, Jan 184, 185ff.
Kasiske, Karl 29
Katherinenhof 133
Katz, Steven 195
Kaufbeuren 119, 127
Kehr, Eckart 28
Keitel, Wilhelm 65, 67, 79, 105
Keyser, Erich 10, 36
Kharkov 57, 97
Kiev 44, 53, 79, 81, 97, 99, 100
Kinkel, Klaus 196
Kirov, Sergei 95
Klee, Ernst 170
Kneissler, Pauline 127
Kobe 183
Koch, Erich 79, 82, 83, 90
Kogon, Eugen 216
Köhler, Ernst 171
Kolb, Gustav 115
Kolbe, Karl Wilhelm 9
kolkhozy 89ff.
Kononov, Ivan 85
Kotzde, Wilhelm 19
Kranz, Heinrich-Wilhelm 164
Kreis, Wilhelm 78
Krosigk, Lutz Graf Schwerin von 91
Ku-Klux-Klan 204
Kuchmeister, Michael 21–2
Kuhn, Walter 2, 33–4, 36
Kulka, Otto Dov 220
Kulmhof 127, 167, 218
Künsberg, Freiherr Eberhard von 33
Kursk 57
Kushner, Tony 184–5

Lammers, Hans Heinrich 79, 140
Langbein, Hermann 217
Lange, Herbert 123, 127, 206
Lanzmann, Claude 6, 183, 189, 197, 218, 220
Laughlin, Harry 158
Law against Dangerous Habitual Criminals 161
Law for the Consolidation of the Health System 165
Law for the Prevention of Hereditary

Diseased Progeny 118–20, 160–1, 164, 165
Law for the Reduction of Unemployment 163
see also Nuremberg Laws
Leeb, Wilhelm Ritter von 43
Lenin, Vladimir Ilych 40, 42, 50, 197
Leningrad 40, 44, 52, 50, 197
Ley, Robert 20–1, 165
Liebenau 135
Lobetal 137
Łódź 33, 175, 186, 210
London School of Economics and Political Science 157
Lorenz, Werner 35
Lublin 187, 199, 206, 208, 209, 210, 213
Ludendorff, Erich 18

Madagascar 190, 205
Madajczyk, Czeslaw 208
Magill, Franz 109–10
Malaparte, Curzio 63
Manstein, Erich 43, 48, 55, 58, 69
Mariaberg 136–7
Marienthal 140
Maschke, Erich 18, 29–31
Mauthausen 71, 162, 210–12, 217
Mayer, Joseph 132, 138, 139
Meinecke, Friedrich 179
Meinhold, Helmut 171–2, 175, 177, 178
Meisinger, Josef 166
Mennecke, Friedrich 127
Mel'nyk, Andrii 81
Meltzer, Ewald 121–2, 133
Meyer, Konrad 92, 93, 94
Mikoyan, Anastas 38
Minsk 39, 206
Model, Walther 57
Molotov, Vyacheslav Mikhailovich 37, 40, 45
Mombert, Paul 173
Mommsen, Hans 170, 171, 173, 197
Mommsen, Theodor 14
Morré, Fritz 29
Mortensen, Hans 28
Gertrud 28
Muckermann, Hermann 132
Musil, Robert 194

Nell, Adolf 136
Nevsky, Alexander 10
Neuengamme 71
Neumann, Franz 192
Nietzsche, Friedrich 221
Nitsche, Paul 123, 128
Nolte, Ernst 170, 174, 180, 182, 197, 221, 223
North East German Research Community (NODFG) 28–35
Nuremburg Laws 159, 160, 164

Oberhauser, Josef 127
Oberländer, Theodor 175, 177
Odessa 176
Oncken, Hermann 27
Ordensburgen 20–1
Orsenigo, Cesare 138
Ostforschung 2, 18, 25ff., 42, 92, 165, 173
Otto III 31
Otwock 212–13, 215–16

Pancke, Günther 35
Pannwitz, Helmuth von 85ff.
Paulus, Friderich von 52–3, 55, 57
People's Commissariat for Internal Affairs (NKVD) 37, 39, 40, 46, 50, 51, 81, 84, 101, 102, 105, 186
Perechodnik, Calel 212ff.
Peukert, Detlev 180
Pfaffenhausen 132
Pfannmüller, Hermann 119, 120, 123
Pilsudski, Josef 27
Pius XII, Pope 139, 183
Plauen, Heinrich von 15
Ploetz, Alfred 157
Pol Pot 181, 224
Poland, 43, 45
Ponomarenko, Panteleymon 101
prisoners of war 60ff., 155, 209
psychiatry
criticisms of 114–15
reform of, 115, 120, 124, 128–9

Rademacher, Franz 206
Radzinsky, Edvard 40
Reche, Otto 34–6, 175
Redl-Zipf 211
Reemtsma, Jan Philipp 170
Reichenau, Walter von 63, 69
Reichskristallnacht 168
Reimann, Bruno 25
Reinecke, Hermann 64, 65, 68
Reitermeier, Johann Friedrich 13
Ribbentrop, Joachim von 26, 38
Ritter, Gerhard 135
Ritter, Robert 164, 166
Rode, Ernst 104
Röhm, Ernst 162, 165
Roenne, Alexis von 84
Rokossovsky, Konstantin Konstantinovich 46

Romania 40–1, 81
Rome 176
Roosevelt, Franklin Delano 188, 192
Rosenberg, Alfred 21–2, 33, 79, 80, 82, 93, 101
Rosenberg, Hans 192
Roth, Karl-Heinz 170
Roth, Philip 194
Rubenstein, Richard 181
Runstedt, Gerd von 43

Sarrbrücken 167
Sachsenhausen 71
Safrian, Hans 6, 204ff.
Salza, Hermann von 21
Sappok, Gerhard 32–3
Sauckel, Fritz 79, 83, 97, 99, 101
Schellenberg, Walter 191
Scheuern 125
Schindler, Oskar 189, 192
Schlabrenndorff, Fabian von 82
Schieder, Theodor 2, 173
Schirmacher, Käthe 18–19
Schlaich, Ludwig 136
Schmidt, Axel 179
Schneider, Carl, 119, 124, 128, 131
Schorsch, Gerhard 136
Schreck, Josef 124
Schubert, Wilhelm 81
Schulenburg, Friedrich Werner Graf von der 38
Schultze, Walter 'Bubi' 117, 123–4
Schwäbisch-Hall 131
Scultetus, Bruno 107
Seraphim, Peter-Heinz 177
Shostakovich, Dimitri 97
Sienkiewicz, Hendryk 9, 10, 17
Simon, Hermann 115
Singer, Peter 144–5
Sinti and Roma ('Gypsies') 155, 159, 160, 161, 166, 167–8, 170, 197
Six, Franz Albert 32
Sobibor, 127, 167, 207, 218
Solzhenitsyn, Aleksander 52
Sorbonne 181
Sorbs, 29, 35
Sorge, Richard 49
Speer, Albert 83, 97, 210
Sporrenburg, Jakob 210
Sprauer, Ludwig 124
Stalin, Joseph 37, 38, 39, 40, 45, 47, 48–9, 50, 51, 54, 57, 58, 61, 95, 101, 145, 181, 188
Stalingrad 52ff., 75ff.
Stalinism, academic 144
Stangl, Franz 127
Steinberg, Jonathan 181
Steiner, George 220
Steinfels, Peter 146
sterilisation 130–2, 160–1
Stetten 131, 136
Strik-Strickfeldt, Wilfried 84, 87
Stuckart, Wilhelm 160, 163
Stühlpfarrer, Karl 204–5
Styron, William 194
Syberberg, Hans-Jürgen 224

Tal, Uriel 220
Tannenberg 10, 15, 18, 20
Tanzmann, Bruno 19
Tatars 3, 84
Taylor, Telford 146
Teutonic (German) Order 9, 81
Thatcher, Margaret 146
therapies 115–16, 120
Tirpitz, Alfred 15
Toeppen, Max 17
Trawniki 209
Treblinka 127, 167, 207, 210, 213, 214, 218
Treitschke, Heinrich von 10, 14, 17, 18, 19, 23
Treschkow, Henning von 82

Ukrainians 3, 79, 80–1, 83, 84, 85, 87, 90, 97, 98, 99, 100, 109, 197
University College, London 157

Veatch, Robert 147
Vergès, Jacques 182
Vienna 204, 205, 206, 208
Vinnitsa 87
Vlasov, Andrei Andreyevich 86ff.
Voigt, Johannes 13
Volga Germans 3, 46, 47
Volkogonov, Dmitri 40
Volkov, Shulamit 220
Voroshilov, Kliment Yefremovich 48
Voss 165

Wagner, Eduard 62, 66
Warlimont, Walter 42
Warsaw 27, 32, 175, 187, 210, 212, 215, 216
Webb, Beatrice 157
Sydney 157
Weimar Republic 3, 18–20, 25ff., 114ff., 117, 130–1, 132–3, 157
Weinberg, Gerhard 3
Weissmandel, Michael 190
Wells, H.G. 184
Wetzel, Erhard 93

Weiszl, Josef 207
Wienken, bishop Heinrich 126, 138–9
Wiesel, Elie 201
Wilhelm II, Kaiser 17
Wippermann, Wolfgang 5
Wirth, Christian 127
Wirth, Paul 29
Wisliceny, Dieter 190, 191
Wurm, Theophil 137
Würzburg 167

Zeitzler, Kurt 86
Zhukov, Georgi 39, 53, 54, 58
Zitelmann, Rainer 180